, as drawn by W.H. Jackson July 25, 1866.

TOLD AT THE EXPLORERS CLUB

Roy Chapman Andrews
President of The Explorers Club

Told at The Explorers Club

True Tales of Modern Exploration

Edited by
Frederick A. Blossom
*Librarian of the
Explorers Club*

ALBERT & CHARLES BONI, INC.
NEW YORK
1931

Printed in the United States of America by
J. J. LITTLE AND IVES COMPANY, NEW YORK

FOREWORD

After having been for several centuries the object of investigation by travelers from other continents, the "New" World, now no longer a novelty, is turning the spyglass around and searching the eastern hemisphere, as well as the hidden nooks and crannies of its own land. A renaissance of exploration is here, recalling the golden days of the sixteenth and seventeenth centuries in western Europe. Surplus energy and wealth are seeking out the far corners of the globe, either as pioneers of industrial development or in behalf of disinterested scientific research.

Despite this revival, a modern Hakluyt or Purchas would be a superfluity. On all sides there are publishers and film producers eager to record and distribute the home-coming traveler's tale. His book is on the stalls and his picture on the screen almost before his luggage is at the hotel. The pace of the age is too swift for ponderous tomes of "pilgrimes" and their pilgrimages.

For a collection of brief accounts of contemporaneous pioneer travel and research, however, this whirling world may find time and place. The present volume is an essay in this direction. In accord with its topic, it pretends to neither unity nor uniformity, but does endeavor to give a cross-sectional picture of modern exploration. By presenting a group of actual experiences, it may in a small measure offset the distortional effects of the current newspaper ballyhoo and motion-picture sensationalism.

The material benefits of this publication are to inure to the profit of the library of exploration maintained by The Explorers Club for the use of explorers and scientists in search of information about the less known regions of the earth or the experiences and discoveries of earlier travelers. The thirty-three authors, all of them members of The Explorers Club, who have contributed the material have received no other return than the pleasure of co-operating in the undertaking, and the grateful acknowledgment of their generosity which the Library Committee of the club here desires publicly to record.

Thanks are due also to certain publishers and holders of copyright for gracious permission to incorporate in this volume the following material which had seen print elsewhere: *Asia* magazine, "Bouncing Fish-balls and Other Tales"; *Forest and Stream,* "At Close Quarters with a Polar Bear"; *New York Herald Tribune,* "Walrus Hunting with the Eskimos"; *Outing* magazine, "The Cruise of the *Lone Star*"; Dodd, Mead & Company, portions of "In the Land of the Yaquis."

And lastly, all concerned, including the contented readers— if happily such there be—are under obligation to the publisher, who, through interest in the ultimate practical purpose of the publication, generously volunteered to launch the volume on its hazardous voyage and himself to risk all the perils of the adventure—save such as are inherent in the task of serving as editor to some two-score migratory authors scattered to the four winds of exploration.

F. A. B.

CONTENTS

vii

ILLUSTRATIONS

THROUGH THE WILDERNESS OF NORTHERN KOREA TO THE LONG WHITE MOUNTAIN

Roy Chapman Andrews

The title that Roy Chapman Andrews gave to his recently published autobiography, *Ends of the Earth,* was peculiarly appropriate. At middle life he has already traveled over nearly every important body of land and water on the surface of the globe. "I wanted to go everywhere," he once explained, in commenting on his ready acceptance of an assignment to make an expedition to Borneo.

Graduating from Beloit College in his native town in Wisconsin, he went to New York and insisted that the Museum of Natural History employ him in any capacity. He has been connected with that institution ever since and is now its vice-director.

From 1908 to 1914 he made extensive studies of whales, seals and fishes, covering a wide territory from Alaska to Celebes and building up a remarkable cetacean collection for the Museum.

Then turning to very dry land, he elaborated a plan for the thorough scientific exploration of the Gobi Desert, as the possible place of origin of northern mammalian life. The field work begun in 1916 has continued, with interruptions, to the present year and has yielded, in addition to the far-famed dinosaur eggs, a rich harvest of fossil remains, geological data and geographical, botanical and zoological information concerning that hitherto unexplored territory.

For his scientific achievements Dr. Andrews was awarded the Hubbard Gold Medal of the National Geographic Society and, by Brown University, an honorary degree of Doctor of Science. He is President of The Explorers Club.

In addition to many scientific treatises, he has published *Whale Hunting with Gun and Camera; Camps and Trails in China; Across Mongolian Plains; On the Trail of Ancient Man; Ends of the Earth.*

THROUGH THE WILDERNESS OF NORTHERN KOREA TO THE LONG WHITE MOUNTAIN

By Roy Chapman Andrews

I AM AVERSE TO WRITING ABOUT ADVENTURES, FOR I DIS-
like them. They are a nuisance. They interfere with work
and disrupt carefully laid plans. Still, even the best prepared explorer cannot always avoid what may be called adventures. It is impossible to foresee everything. I suppose
that I have had many adventures during twenty-three years
of wandering into the strange corners of the world, but in
retrospect I cannot say which single experience was the
most exciting. At the time it was happening, each one
seemed more interesting than any other.

It might be of some interest to tell of an exploration I
made of the wilderness of northern Korea in 1912—not
that it was particularly exciting, but things happened which
might easily have had unpleasant results. It was my first
prolonged land expedition, although I had worked along
little-known seacoasts for four years, with short trips into
the interior. My object was to explore the forests of the
Korean-Manchurian border lying south of the Paik-tu-san,
or Long White Mountain. No one knew what that wilderness contained, for until the Russo-Japanese War Korea had
remained a hermit kingdom.

I went up the east coast on a tiny freight vessel, accompanied only by a Japanese interpreter who spoke Korean.
As my knowledge of Japanese was passable, our conversa-

3

tion was conducted in that language. From the little village of Seshin, we went inland to the ancient walled town of Musan. There I engaged eight diminutive Korean ponies and four men for the trip into the border wilderness. The Koreans did not want to go. They never had been there and were frightened. It would have been impossible to obtain a caravan without the assistance of the Japanese gendarmes. They ordered the men to go. The ponies carried our camp equipment and food; all of us walked.

It was only fifty or sixty miles to the edge of the forests. There I camped for a few days, trying to get information, but it was useless. None of the natives had been more than a few miles into the wilderness. My Koreans were sad-looking men when we started northward. Every few miles, they stopped to build tiny shrines of birch bark, leave little offerings of food and pray to their own particular gods for protection from the unknown terrors which awaited them. I took compass directions, laying a course straight for the Long White Mountain.

The first day's march was fairly easy, up a broad valley through a thin larch forest. The second was not so good. By the middle of the third afternoon, we were fairly in the wilderness and making slow progress. The forest was dense, the ground littered with moss-grown logs and spongy from underground water. At the end of the fourth march, I camped two days, for the men were very tired and much depressed. I thought a rest and fresh meat, if I could find game, would revive their spirits. Luck was with me and I killed a bear. That bear haunts me yet, for I did not give the poor brute a chance. It was almost murder. He came ambling along while I was resting on a fallen tree. Totally unconscious of my presence, he walked to within thirty feet of me. The bullet caught him squarely in the heart. My one consolation is that he never knew what had happened.

Pack Train Going through Forest

Chinese Raft on the Yalu River

The bear meat did much to improve the morale of my men. Bear's paws are a great delicacy and the Koreans feasted like children, forgetting for a time that they were far from home and mother.

For days we did not see another sign of life. The forest became denser at every mile, with more swamps and surface water. Time after time, our ponies were mired and had to be lifted out of the mud. Lush ferns and rank grass made walking dangerous. The trees were interlaced with great festoons of gray "Spanish moss," which formed a thick canopy overhead. Down where we were, there was only a gloomy half-light, occasionally shot through with patches of thin sun. No sounds broke the stillness except the calls of the men. No birds or animals, not even a squirrel. To make matters worse, it began to rain—not a hard, refreshing rain, but a dull drizzle which continued for a week.

The men were completely disheartened, frightened at the gloomy stillness of the forest and exhausted by strenuous work. They began to talk furtively among themselves and, when we camped, were ominously silent if I passed their fire. The interpreter told me they were planning to desert that night with the ponies and food, leaving us to die or get back as best we could. He had overheard their talk the previous evening. It would have been fairly serious to be left without the caravan. I could find my way out easily enough but no game meant possible starvation.

We were only two days' march from the base of the Paik-tu-san and I had determined to complete my traverse against all odds. To leave it in mid-air meant that all our efforts were wasted. I told the men that we must reach the mountain; that I would give them double wages; further, that I should watch at night and, if anyone touched a pony, he would be shot without mercy.

They did not like it much. My ultimatum was received

in silence. The interpreter and I watched by turns through the night. Now and then, one of the men got up to replenish the fire, but they made no move to leave the camp. The next night was a repetition of the first. Both the Japanese and myself were utterly exhausted from lack of sleep and hard work. We wondered if we could stick it out another twenty-four hours.

In the late afternoon, we emerged into a great burned tract and the mountain rose majestically right in front of us. Banked to the top with snow, it looked like a great white cloud that had settled to earth for a moment's rest.

The open sky and the mountain acted like magic on my men. They began to talk and sing and call to each other in laughing voices. I knew then that the strain was over; they would not desert me. That night we camped in the shadow of the mountain, well out in the burned area, beside a pond of snow water. I slept for fifteen hours, utterly exhausted.

In the later afternoon, I shot a roe deer, and that completed the contentment of our party. One cannot wonder at the fears of the men. They knew that our objective was the Long White Mountain, but it seemed hopeless that we could get there. They had never seen a compass. To them, we were merely wandering aimlessly through the forest. When we actually arrived, and all by means of that little disk with the turning needle, their admiration knew no bounds. Of course, they did not understand how it worked, but it had brought us to the Paik-tu-san and that was good enough for them. Now they would follow anywhere I wished to go; they had complete confidence that I would not leave them to starve in a gloomy wilderness.

Four days at the Long White Mountain were sufficient. It was futile to attempt its ascent, for the snow was piled in great drifts from base to crown. But in any case, there would have been little to be gained, for James and Younghusband had reached the crater from the Manchurian side. My object had been to find what lay within that Korean wilderness over which they had looked thirty-three years before. I had a compass line straight through the forest to the base and a rough map of the surrounding country.

I determined not to return by the way we had come but to strike through the forest to the headwaters of the Yalu River, which could not be far to the west. It was a difficult trip, just about like what we had experienced on the way to the mountain. Dense forests, swamps and drizzling rain. But the men pushed on with light hearts, laughing at difficulties and hard work, supremely confident that my little compass knew the way.

We discovered a beautiful lake, set like a jewel amid the green larch forest, its shores a gray line of volcanic ash. Near by were two large ponds, swarming with mallard ducks. I shot three roe deer and a wild boar and trapped many small mammals. Birds were everywhere; flowers made a brilliant carpet in the park-like openings of the forest.

A day before we reached the Yalu, while hunting roe deer, I stumbled into the camp of eight Manchurian bandits—tall, brown, hard-bitten fellows, armed with long flintlock rifles. I suspected immediately what they were, but they saw me as quickly as I saw them. My rifle did not help any. They had me covered from several directions. There was nothing to do but bluff it out. Fortunately I knew a little Chinese. I said I was a friend, laid down my rifle and advanced.

After a little, they resumed eating and offered me tea and millet. Then they went to my camp. They looked over all our stuff, but there was absolutely nothing they could use except my rifle. I told the cook to get busy as he never had before and prepare a dinner of roe-deer meat. The bandits were pleased and accepted the invitation to eat with alacrity. My interpreter spoke bad Chinese but enough to tell them all about us.

After dinner the brigands became most friendly. They admitted that they were part of a band which held this region near the Yalu. All merchants sending goods between villages must pay them taxes. As we were not merchants and had been so hospitable, they would charge us nothing. Moreover, they told us how to avoid others of the band who might not be as friendly.

The next day, we camped on the bank of the great river, which at that spot was less than thirty yards across. Following down the stream for two days, we came to a Korean settlement. There was great rejoicing among my men, for they were heroes. Had they not been to the Long White Mountain and faced the terrors of the unknown wilderness, and all with the aid of a tiny compass? If I had given it to them, they would certainly have placed it in a shrine to worship as a god. Every villager came to see it. Reverently they passed it about, the old men wagging their heads and saying little, the younger explaining volubly how it worked.

Further down the river, we came to the first logging operations conducted by the Japanese. Here I dismissed my caravan and arranged to float down the Yalu on a log raft. It was very comfortable on the raft. The men made me a little house of bark and I had a huge deck for a play-ground. Sometimes at night we tied up to a bank, but usually the raft floated on, guided by two men with huge sweeps. I shot ducks and geese for specimens, retrieving them in a small boat towed behind the raft.

I watched the Yalu grow with every mile, for we passed dozens of small streams, each of which contributed its share to swell the giant river. The trip was very restful after the strenuous days of continued travel. With plenty of birds and fish, I lived like a king.

But I was a sorry sight in the way of garments when we reached Antung at the mouth of the river. My shoes and trousers were completely gone. I was dressed in Korean clothes, except for coat and hat. In this garb I reached Seoul and registered at the Sontag Hotel.

A cable to the Museum elicited a delighted reply. For nearly five months, I had dropped out of the world and the usual reports of death in the Korean wilderness had been cabled far and wide. I have "died" so frequently since that I am quite accustomed to it; it seems to be the best little thing I do.

The Museum was pleased with the results. I had explored and mapped a considerable area of unknown country and brought out a large collection of mammals and birds, many of them new to science.

MEN WHO CAN'T COME BACK

W. E. Aughinbaugh

Physician, lawyer, university professor, editor, author and worldwide traveler, Dr. Aughinbaugh has had a life of rich and varied human contacts. Important academic and journalistic positions in New York City have alternated in his active career with more than a score of years spent in medical research and practice among primitive surroundings on the far-flung frontiers of civilization.

He has seen service on the Bubonic Plague Commission in India, Burma, Arabia, Afghanistan and the Shan States, also in the investigation of the pneumonic plague in China. He has been in charge of leprosy hospitals in Latin America and has battled verrugas in Peru, trachoma in Egypt, Arabia and The Levant and the hay-fever problem in Labrador!

He has published *Selling Latin America* and *Advertising in Latin America* and is soon to bring out three volumes based on his experiences, of which the following story is a foretaste.

MEN WHO CAN'T COME BACK

By W. E. Aughinbaugh

T HE OUT-OF-THE-WAY PLACES OF THE WORLD ARE FILLED with the men who can't come back. I have seen them all over the earth and, due to the fact that I have attended many of them professionally in their last illness, have learned from their own lips the reasons for their exile—the secrets that they were hiding from their fellow men.

They have crossed my path in the most remote localities. In the Khyber Pass, that hostile thoroughfare between Northern India and Afghanistan, I met one serving under the British flag. At Oran, in Algiers, the headquarters of the famous French Foreign Legion, I ran into a lawyer from home who had killed two men—and disappeared. Others I have met in Persia, in Arabia, in Somaliland and in Jerusalem. Two years ago I encountered at the Assuan Dam in Egypt an old schoolmate in charge of a group of laborers. The reward for his return to the States had reached five figures. Hongkong, Shanghai, Port Said, Korea and the Mediterranean littoral harbor these social outcasts, scattered about in profusion; the islands that dot the dreamy Pacific conceal many from inquisitive eyes. But, of all countries, those of Latin America, owing to their nearness to the States, seem to offer the quickest haven to the frightened offender. Each of these republics has far more than its quota of men who are endeavoring to hide themselves and forget!

Many are trying to drown their remorse in drink and,

13

in their efforts to accomplish this purpose, have sunk lower
in the scale of civilization than beasts. I knew an ex-bank
president from this country, a defaulter, who by some
means had attached himself to a tribe of Carib Indians.
Ignored by the men of the clan, he carried water for the
women and did their chores. His feet had not seen shoes
for years and his matted beard and disheveled hair reached
the waist-line of his ragged undershirt, which with his
trousers formed his only raiment.

At the sea wall of a Central American port, gazing eastward with inquiring mien from dawn to dusk, stands
"Napoleon." When he came there or how, no one knows.
Even his name has been lost in the years that have passed
since his arrival, for he is now over seventy. But a faded
soldier's uniform, his precise mannerisms, a hat such as the
famous military genius affected, the wisp of hair on his
forehead, the fingers of one hand concealed beneath the
front of his coat make him a startling reproduction of the
Little Corporal and give him the name by which he is
locally known. He speaks to none, but stiffly salutes all
passers-by. Mild and inoffensive, the police let him sleep in
the balmy tropic air of the little park; the local tailors patch
his tattered uniform; the charitable hand him food or
money, and each morning for more than twenty years he
has been the first customer of the local barber, whose tonsorial attention he repays with a gracious elevation of his
hand to the brim of his *chapeau*. Rumor has it that he was
a West Point graduate who in a fit of passion killed his
fiancée and escaped. Fate has been kind to him, for time
has blotted from his mind all recollection of the tragedy.
Yet each sunrise sees him at his post and each sunset finds
him on guard, wistfully, sadly looking out to sea.

In nearly every instance that I recall, a woman has
played a leading rôle in the drama which has left its princi-

pal actor stranded on these foreign shores. I know that I could fill a book with the pathetic stories told me by these world-weary ones in their faltering journey to meet mine host of the inn at the end of the road.

. . . . . .

Of all that I knew in my twenty years' practice of medicine, the one that surges to the front when I think of these men is White—at least, that is what we called him, but we knew it was not his right name. In the outposts of civilization it does not behoove one to be unduly inquisitive. I knew him as "White" for nine years and learned his real name only two hours before his tired spirit entered the next country.

I was the surgeon of a railway in a Latin American country, which out of respect to the memory of White shall be nameless. The road ran from a typical coast town on the Caribbean Sea, with its pastel-shaded adobe houses, up through coffee *haciendas*, perched high on the side of verdant mountains, and on into the rich hinterland. Its termini were the capital, in a valley of the interior, and the port I have just spoken of, which is today, as it was then, a hotbed for beri-beri, bubonic plague and yellow fever epidemics. The hospital of which I was in charge was situated half-way up the mountain, so as to be readily accessible to both ends of the line and in order that the patients might benefit by the salubrious air.

The station-master at the port end had just died of yellow fever when White walked into the office of the general manager and applied for the vacancy. He spoke Spanish perfectly, was well built, deeply tanned and heavily bearded. His clothes were torn and travel-worn. He told the road official that he had walked over the mountain into the city. A few questions elicited that he was an experienced railroad man, and, despite the fact that he was without testimonials or references, he was employed, for men were hard to get who would stay in the heated inferno of the port.

The new station-master made no friends. The English-speaking engineers, conductors and others could not fathom him. He was polite, but distant, and had no confidant among them. He knew his business—kept the docks free of cargo and ran the trains on time—and that was all that was expected of him.

His palm-thatched adobe hut was in a coconut grove, so close to the beach that during the equinoctial storms it was often splashed by the spray from the restless, troubled sea. Its furniture was meagre. An old hag of an Indian woman cooked his scanty meals and spread the news around that each night, after the cares of the day were over, the *señor* drank rum until he became maudlin drunk and then, alternately talking and crying, went to sleep. He was always the first to be up and around the railway yard in the morning, however, and none the worse for his debauch.

He never received any mail. He never borrowed books or asked for papers from the States, the one thing that outcast men crave. Once each month he would give the chief engineer of a ship that came from New York a letter to post. What he did with his money, no one knew. What he thought, no one cared. Thus he lived for the nine years he was with the company.

In the sixth year of his service, he sprained his ankle by jumping from a shifting-engine in the yards. I attended him, but he refused to go to the hospital, preferring to remain in his hut by the sea. During the first few days of his illness, I came down the mountain to treat him and was conscious that my ministrations were being appreciated. Although he was decidedly taciturn, it was apparent that he had had a thorough education. I recall him quoting Omar

Khayyam, another time Thanatopsis, once Virgil, and also
Confucius.

Twice a week after his recovery, he would send me a
live fish in the water tank of the engine, for we had no ice,
and once in a while a large lobster. These were the nearest
approaches to friendship which he made toward anyone.
My repeated efforts to get him to spend Sunday or the
week-end with me were politely declined. To the consul,
the only other American in the town, he was distant and
cold.

One day a case of plague, that dreaded tropical disease,
was reported at the port. Before the week ended, there were
three hundred new victims and the "Angel of the Darker
Drink" was gathering a rich harvest. The town was suffering from its usual epidemic, which this year was attacking
Europeans and Americans and was of a particularly violent
type.

The engineer of one of the "up-trains" sent me a note
saying that White's old Indian servant had hobbled to the
cab door to tell him that her *señor* was complaining, and
she asked that I be notified. I had the operator telegraph
White, asking how he felt, and received an assuring reply.
The evening train brought up a large lobster, as proof of
his ability to be around. The next day he did not report
for duty. I telegraphed again and was informed that he felt
all right. About midnight the watchman came to the hospital with orders from the general manager for me to meet
the light engine which would arrive shortly and accompany
it to the port, where I was to attend White, who was reported in a precarious condition from the disease then so
prevalent.

I can never forget that night ride down the moonlit
mountainside, with the sea at its base. Two o'clock in the
morning found me at White's bedside. His was a typical

case of plague and it was apparent that medicine could do nothing to aid him. I told him of the seriousness of his condition and stated that dissolution was usually preceded by a period of coma, from which one passed into the great beyond. "Have you any message to send? Do you wish to make a will? You can trust me," I urged.

Telling me where to get paper, ink and pen, he dictated his last testament, leaving his money to a daughter, whom he named and whose address he supplied. After signing the document, he turned to me and said:

"Doc, my name is not White. It is, as you see, ————. I was the manager of the (here he named a famous Latin American road). I graduated from Cornell, married a beautiful girl from my home town and took her with me to live in a bungalow facing the sea. Our happiness was ideal. A girl was born, to whom I have left everything.

"My assistant was a Jamaican—a half-caste with sufficient Negro blood to make him positively handsome. He was as lithe as a deer and strummed a guitar as he sang romantic songs of Spain. It was the old story. The spell of the tropics came over my wife. If a woman is to go wrong and a hundred men are to know it, her husband's number is one hundred and one. I came home one day and the mother of my baby was gone. So was the Jamaican. When I expressed surprise, everyone intimated that they had expected such a thing for a year or more.

"I took our baby home and left it with my sister, who has devoted her life to raising and educating her. Then I came back to locate the woman who had seared my soul and the man who had wooed her from me. I knew I'd find them with some railway in these dago lands, and so I wandered for four years from road to road seeking them.

"At last, in the mountains of Peru, I found them. In the dead of night, with the winds howling a requiem and the snowflakes to soften my approach, I entered their home. Sleep was heavy on their eyes as they lay together, and, by God, I cut their throats!"

I can never erase from my mind the dramatic fervor of the man—his tense emotion, as tremblingly he raised himself from the bed and, with glaring eyes and shaking hand and rasping breath, drew an imaginary dagger across their throats. The moan of the wind through the palm trees, the lisping, sobbing waters as they lapped the shore, and the shimmering light of the tropical moon, all added a nocturnal accompaniment that intensified the scene.

Then, after a pause, he resumed.

"I closed their books forever and gloated over my work that night. With the coming of day, I made my escape from the scene and walked and walked, a haunted man, through the backwoods of Peru, Bolivia, Ecuador, Colombia for nearly six years, until I found myself here and secured the position I now hold. Every month I send a draft to the little daughter that I carried home in my arms. She has now grown to early womanhood. I have never seen her and don't want to, for she is a replica, I am told, of the mother in beauty and mannerisms. She does not know that I live. That is why I have kept from my fellow men and from you. That is why each night I sought forgetfulness and solace in drink. I have but one favor to ask—promise never to tell my family name to anyone."

When the sun rose, its rays filtered through the window blinds and rested on the quiet form of White—peaceful in the majesty of death. And I, his only friend, the only one to whom he had confided his life's secret, fulfilled his every wish and buried him and kept my promise.

WITH THE ABORIGINES IN AUSTRALIA

Edward P. Bailey

Australia was Colonel Bailey's birthplace and has remained his dominant geographical interest; he has been called "the unofficial ambassador of Australia to the United States."

As the son of a pioneer railroad builder, he early became familiar with some of the wilder sections of that interesting continent while still in their virginal state.

After a period of work in the hardware trade, interspersed with breaks back into "the bush" again, he took up the study and practice of medicine and in 1907 migrated to southern California, where he has since resided, practising medicine, lecturing and traveling extensively.

WITH THE ABORIGINES IN AUSTRALIA

By Edward P. Bailey

BORN AND BRED IN THE AUSTRALIAN BUSH, THE SON OF A pioneer railroad builder—which in those early days meant real trail blazing and adventuring and took us constantly into new country—I commenced my explorations at an early age. What today would be thrilling experiences were merely episodes in our daily life. As we penetrated areas of unsettled country, we were encroaching on the hunting-grounds of the aborigines. Our most lively experiences naturally came from that source.

This was particularly so when some of us young fellows, more venturesome than the rest, would wander far afield from the railway camp to hunt the bounding kangaroo or the fleet emu and then encounter some members of these nomadic tribes similarly engaged. Several times, in the denser bush, our first intimation of their presence was the whirring of spears over our heads, a fair warning to depart, as the natives could easily have winged us had they desired. At other times we instinctively knew we were being followed, but not a trace of the black fellows could we detect, so skilful were they in moving quickly and quietly, and yet keeping out of sight.

Amongst our railway men there were many old bushmen. From them we learned much of the characteristics of the aborigines and were warned never to be the aggressors, never to interfere with their camps or belongings, espe-

23

cially their sacred ceremonial grounds or burial places, nor to touch weapons or things in the vicinity of these areas. There were times, though, when we had to resort to a show of force and burn a little powder to drive them from the vicinity of our camp or put a stop to their spearing our stock.

Coming in close contact with the Australian native as we did, I was much impressed with the way he fitted in with the natural scheme of things in the bush, where he certainly was king of all he surveyed. Out on the ranges, beyond the touch of civilization, he is alert, erect, his carriage is dignified, his skin firm and shining with health, his eye piercing and clear. In many cases the aborigines show great courage; they can be good friends but very bad enemies. In their tribal life they are true comrades; a strict moral code is maintained in their domestic relations; they are very fond of their children, proper in their behavior, unassuming, generous and grateful, fond of their own jokes and cheerful under the various privations they have to endure in extreme seasons or in accord with their ceremonials.

.   .   .   .   .

In course of time I found myself more interested in studying the life and customs of the black fellows than in hunting animals. The spirit of exploration grew on me; I preferred to go into the ranges searching for caves or up the sides of the cliffs, which bore many evidences of ancient aboriginal life, depicted in crude drawings on the rough rock with ochres or chipped in with flints as crude chisels. These drawings existed in a thousand and one places on rocks and caves, not only in the bush but also on the plains, where almost every rock bore a myriad of cryptic designs, reptilian forms and representations of animal, bird and human life. Some of the huge circular designs covered areas

Australian Aboriginal Rock Carvings

Australian Native with Shield and Spears

close to a hundred square feet, with a symmetry of curves and complicated tracings and a marshalling of lines that proved the black man was an artist.

The more I studied this art the greater the fascination. In the earlier days I would journey alone into the depths of the jungle or wander over the hills and gullies, seeking new scenes in that land of an old geological period, or into its deserts, which have a charm all their own. This brought me into frequent contact with the wandering tribes. Many times I would travel long distances or spend many days thus exploring without seeing a sign of human beings, perhaps because the natives wished to observe me without being observed, but most likely because they were else-where, as they were constantly on the move to new fields, their numbers being small compared with the great area of unsettled bush country.

While the blacks never stay long in one place, their wanderings are limited to their own tribal territory, which is mutually understood as within certain defined bounda-ries according to the topography of the region, but cover-ing large areas. In this, as in their moral relations, inter-tribal etiquette is punctilious to a degree. I found, how-ever, that, when my activities were understood, I had noth-ing to fear from the natives; they were honest and loyal and, if treated fairly, they were all right. I am referring, of course, to the aborigines away from the civilized fron-tiers, in their native haunts. Where, however, they touched civilization they were too prone to take on all the white man's vices without the compensating value of his virtues. I never had any serious misunderstanding with them. I learned to mind my own business and to show no fear, no matter how the goose-flesh might creep over me—and the cold shivers did run up and down my spine many times.

My most thrilling experience in connection with these explorations and the one most indelibly fixed in my memory occurred in the earlier days, before I had become accustomed to the tactics of the natives.

I had gone off on one of my expeditions into the bush in the Gippsland Lakes district in eastern Victoria, to explore certain ranges and incidentally to hunt for large quandongs, a fruit growing on large wide-spreading shrubs which the emus are very fond of and which was plentiful in that section. The stone of this peculiar fruit is large, round and strangely ridged and indented, as if carved with fine tracings. It was used by the railway men for making into tie rings, to pass away their spare time.

It was always my custom to carry a compass on these trips, but more generally, to retrace my journey, I relied on remembering the characteristics of the trail I had made. I was in strange territory and crossed many gullies and elevations, into a maze of wooded country. The trees were teeming with bird life of many varieties. Brilliantly plumaged parrots flew about in restless activity; cockatoos cawed and screeched. That wonderful mimic, the lyre bird, now almost extinct, the shyest of all avian creatures, frequenting only the secret places of the wild bush, could be seen in numbers. The beautiful bower birds with their dancing and courtship mounds were there. The bell birds were also holding high carnival with their ringing bell-like notes.

It was a glorious day. The eucalyptus trees and fragrant boronias were in bloom. Wild bees were gathering honey, and their buzzing in the air was like the drone of a distant machine. Kangaroos and wallabys were numerous, feeding on the hillsides. With the exhilaration of nature in all its beauty, I lost track of time, direction and place, until the sun was well over the meridian. I had been successful in my mission, had had a glorious time and had seen several species of snakes that were new to me, so I decided to call it a day.

I started on my return trip, as I thought, but after nearly two hours' tramping I recognized that, by some trick of the maze, I was still near to where I had started to return. I speedily realized that I was a long way from the camp and temporarily lost. As it would be folly to wander around in the bush after dark, the only thing to do was to camp for the night and make a fresh start with early daylight.

As I always went prepared to camp out if necessary, this was no hardship. There are no man-eating or otherwise dangerous mammals in Australia; reptiles are the only real menace in the bush. As it was mating season, it of course made a difference where and how one camped, that is all. I knew that at seven o'clock in the morning the ballast-wagon locomotive at the camp would give the usual three piercing blasts on the steam whistle to call out the men, and it was possible that I should be able to hear it and orient myself, and then travel by compass.

Locating my night camp high up on a hill, away from the creeks and gullies, I put the billy on to boil to make some tea and settled down to write up my notes of the many interesting things I had seen that day, including a cave I had found with its walls covered with aboriginal ochre drawings, with all the indications that it had been at some time in the distant past an important native rendezvous.

During the day I had not seen, or found trace of, any human beings, nor heard their *coo-ee* in the distance. I was busy with my notes and absorbed in the thoughts of the day's experiences as the silence of the bush with approaching sundown began. I had heard no sound but the laughter of the companionable kookaburra in the trees. What attracted my attention I could not say—it may have been a moving shadow or a chance glance about me—but I became suddenly aware that there was a group of ten or twelve aborigines not ten paces away, silently watching me, with their weapons poised as if they were portraying a tableau of an attack. It was as startling as it was unexpected.

I want to say right here and now that the man who says he has never experienced fear has never been in a really dangerous position—or does not tell the truth. I know that for the moment I thought I was paralyzed. However, I controlled my feelings and regained my poise. I mechanically waved a salutation and, lighting a cigarette and extending the package, got up and walked toward the natives, grinning like a clown.

This broke the tension and in a few minutes we were all laughing hilariously as I used up my cigarettes and matches, teaching them the baneful habit of smoking and thus probably starting them in the practice of pestering the settlers who later followed our steel trail with requests for "just a little baccy."

BRINGING THE CRIPPLED *Roosevelt* HOME

Robert A. Bartlett

Born in Newfoundland of sea-faring stock, brought up in the seal fisheries and placed in charge of a ship while still in his 'teens, "Bob" Bartlett stands out with unique distinctness as a modern Viking. Few men can approach his record of arctic voyages, fourteen of his cruises ending in shipwreck and seven of his ships sinking under him.

At the age of twenty-two he turned from fishing and seal hunting to exploration, and this has been his principal occupation ever since. Going north with Peary first in 1897, he was the polar explorer's trusted captain in 1905 and again on his final try for the Pole in 1909. It is the heroic life-and-death struggle to save the ship and crew of the 1905-1906 expedition which he here relates.

In 1914, as commander of the ill-fated *Karluk,* of the Canadian Arctic Expedition, Captain Bartlett led his party to Wrangel Island and then set out for the mainland of Siberia to organize their rescue.

Undaunted by his hardships and adventures in northern seas, he has returned to those perilous waters almost every year. For his service to arctic exploration, he was made an Honorary Member of The Explorers Club and has received many other honors, among them the Charles P. Daly Medal of the American Geographical Society, the Back Grant of the Royal Geographical Society of England and the Hubbard Gold Medal of the National Geographic Society.

He has published *The Last Voyage of the "Karluk"* and *The Log of "Bob" Bartlett.*

BRINGING THE CRIPPLED *ROOSEVELT* HOME

By Robert A. Bartlett

ON SEPTEMBER 6, 1905, THE *Roosevelt* REACHED CAPE Sheridan, Grant Land, about fifty days from New York. When we left New York, it was hoped that we would winter at Porter Bay, on the southwest side of the Fielden Peninsula, Grant Land. This would have been an ideal spot for winter quarters, but we succeeded in getting only to Cape Sheridan, and the low fore-shore on the southwest side was filled with grounded bergs, so that we could not get shelter there, but had to lay on the outside of the bergs in the hinge of the ice-foot.

During our stay from fall to spring, nothing short of a miracle kept the heavy arctic ice from grinding us to pieces. When the warm June days came, melting the snow and ice and making large fresh-water rivers, there remained no longer any shelter for us, so I endeavored to get into Lincoln Bay for shelter and wait for Peary to return to us. It was July fourth; not until the day before Christmas did we reach New York.

We were almost over the worst part of our trip, which was getting around Cape Union; this we negotiated successfully. Only a short run to Lincoln Bay and we were safe. But a big floe at the end of the flood-tide struck us on the quarter and, sliding along aft, dug its point into our skeg. The ship began to climb up the ice-foot and I was in hopes that, as she came up, the point of the floe astern of us would take the strain; it did for awhile but the strain being too great, it broke. This caused the floe again to move and, as it did, it lifted her almost clean on the ice-foot, but not before it had broken the rudder-post, the rudder and the skeg where it joined the main part of the keel under the propeller-well, also carrying away two blades of the propeller. Fortunately it carried away the two blades in line, that is the upper and lower blades, leaving us with two blades. No wood put together with iron bolts could withstand this terrific strain, for this great floe, miles in circumference, drawing several fathoms of water and moving at the rate of one to two miles an hour, was irresistible.

Before the skeg broke, it opened up the upper part, where it ran through the overhang, at least an inch. Whilst the ship was flung onto the ice-foot, I drove oakum and strips of blankets into the seam and used pitch and American tar with lime to cover the seam. This I hoped to a certain extent would stop the big flow of water from coming into the ship. When the ice moved off, she slipped back into the water and, with the two deck pumps going constantly and three in the engine-room as well, we managed to keep her dry.

At the first opportunity, we tried the engine, but it refused to move. The chief thought the broken skeg had jammed the blades, so we cleared away the ice and found one of the broken blades had been wedged in between the skeg and the boss. When the ice moved off, we sailed and warped her to the river delta and, behind the grounded bergs, put her on shore. The rise and fall of the water is only a foot or two, so it was very difficult to saw the broken skeg and get it clear of the ship, as it was now broken and twisted. It was a detriment and in such a position that we couldn't hang the rudder, as it was canted forty-five degrees

"The ship began to climb the ice-foot."

2. The Jury Rudder

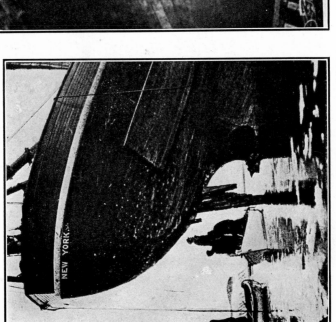

1. Stern of the *Roosevelt*, the Rudder Blown Away with Dynamite

to starboard. With this bent and twisted mass of heavy 16" x 16" oak timber, the ship could not be maneuvered. I thought that again I would fall back on my old friend Dupont—seventy-five per cent dynamite. By putting long wooden handles in our augers, we bored holes in the broken skeg and in these holes I put small pieces of dynamite and a cap and in time blew the whole thing clear. I had great difficulty in saving the gudgeons and braces, but by fastening a rope to them, I managed at length to recover all that were any good to us.

The next thing was to make a rudder, so I went to the hold and got out one of the main-deck beams, 11" x 14", and used this for a rudder-stock and used the diagonal braces in the hold for the back. By the time it was finished, Peary came back from his western trip to the ship over mountains and bare rocks and through icy rivers of water swollen to a size where very often in wading he was up to his armpits. His footgear was so saturated with water that it had long ceased to be of any use. He had on his feet pemmican tins and the inside ones were even reduced to the size of a Canadian nickel. Can you imagine a man with all his toes gone doing this? But he did.

. . . . . .

It was marvelous the way Peary took the accident to the *Roosevelt*. He didn't turn a hair. It was this attitude in the face of privations and dangers that made us love and respect him. When the first opportunity came, we shoved off, but the ice was not in a receptive mood and our trip southward was tedious, to say the least.

Getting caught in the ice, we were driven into Lady Franklin Bay and here we spent many days. We had little or no winds to change the ice and our grub was beginning to get short, as we had left a full year's supplies at Cape Victoria, Kane Basin, in the event of our retreat. It was decided that I should go on a hunting expedition and I prepared to leave the ship, but a southwest wind, although moderate, set us out of this pocket into Kennedy Channel and, the ice opening, we reached open water and loose ice, which carried us down Kennedy Channel to the middle of Kane Basin. Here we had calms, with no movement of the ice southward. It looked as if we were going to spend the winter in the pack, but a strong south wind loosened up the ice and we at length reached Etah.

It was well along in September when we were here, and the young ice was making rapidly in the fjords. Strong winds were blowing and short days told us plainly winter was upon us. The first thing we did was to pick up our anchor and chain, about a hundred and twenty fathoms in length, the anchor weighing three thousand pounds. Going north we had left it, eliminating weight, for we wanted all spare buoyancy for coal. I then moved her up the fjord and, putting her stern on shore as far as I could get her, we began caulking her stern, also tightening up the nuts on the studs which fastened the blades to the propeller boss, and drove pine wedges around the nuts.

Owing to the slight rise and fall of the water and the long shelf running out from the shore, it was difficult to dry her out, so that we could make a good job of the propeller blades. But the caulking we could make a good job of.

We secured about fifty tons of rock ballast and then moved down to the point, where about sixty tons of coal in bags had been left by us and some from the auxiliary ship *Eric* the previous summer. Again I had to call on my old friend seventy-five per cent Dupont to loosen up the bags which were frozen from the melting of the snow in the summer warmth. The young ice was making rapidly in the fjord and moving in big sheets with tide and wind, so that it took all our gear to hold her alongside the rocks.

At length the coaling was finished and we left to spend a couple of days walrus hunting. We had on board very little food. But up at Victoria Head, Bache Peninsula, Kane Basin, we had a full stock for sixty people for twelve months, besides two brand-new whale boats and two new dories. This had been left by us on our way north in the event of our having to retreat but, owing to ice conditions on our way south, we couldn't reach it.

I suppose, had we left the Eskimos at Etah and gone direct for home, they would have managed somehow to exist until Smith Sound would freeze for them to get to the cache at Victoria Head, and, with the hunting, they could have managed all right. But Peary had promised them that, before leaving them, he would get enough fresh walrus meat. He had also promised to land them with the meat at any place they wanted, either with their friends or at some village that they chose. Some of them were homesick. They hadn't seen their families for over a year, so they were brought to the place where their relatives lived. We had lots of good reasons for not doing this. We were short of coal and food and in a crippled condition, with winter upon us and a long stormy route to follow. Peary knew this better than anyone on board. But "Pearyokshwa" had given his word and he never broke it, so the thing must be done. It is no wonder these people loved and respected Peary. No other man in the past or future can or will get these people to do what he did. He "though dead, yet liveth" in the hearts and minds of the Cape York Eskimo.

At Kookan, an Eskimo village, the ice drove us on shore. The night was dark and the anchor wouldn't hold, so ashore we went. I did not feel any too good over this, but it was a blessing in disguise. The water was deep right up to the shore. Her stern caught on a narrow shelf and, with the deep water from the main rigging forward, she tipped so that the boss of the propeller came out of water. The chief engineer made some pine wedges and jammed the nuts so securely that we had no trouble with the blades right into New York. Had we not obtained this chance, there is no doubt but we would have lost the blades. This gave us a good opportunity to do further work on the battered stern and we had a better chance of driving in some more oakum.

Finally we reached Cape York and our last Eskimo family went on shore. A strong southeast gale was on, with heavy swell and snow squalls. Whilst waiting for the wind to moderate and the weather to clear, we made the ship ready for her trip south. The wind moderating, with a long southeast swell prevailing, we cast off from the land ice and proceeded south.

Night soon came upon us and with it snow. We reduced speed but, as far as seeing anything, one might as well be below. The next afternoon we ran into a gale of southeast wind. The ship was light and rolled terribly. To make matters worse, the pumps got choked and this put out the fires. With the pumps working in the engine-room and the two deck pumps driven by a chain messenger to the steam winch, we could manage to keep the water out of her. But now, with the fires out, we could get no help from the engine-room.

The bulkhead between the fire-room and the hold was of double hard-pine planks, one layer vertical and the other horizontal, the whole fastened together with nuts and bolts headed up on one side. There was nothing in the hold but about fifty tons of ballast; fortunately this was away forward, but at one time a couple of hundred dogs and many families of Eskimo lived in this hold. We didn't have time to clean up things, so, when the water got in there and she rolling, it was a dirty place. The bulkhead was almost water-tight, but at the skin were two limber holes, which soon got choked up. A sailor and myself with chisels, hammer and saw after a time had the water running out of the stoke hold into the main hold, by rigging up a Spanish Burton and attaching pork barrels to it. In this manner we managed to get the water under control and clear the boiler-room, so that the chief soon had the fires going and the pumps in the engine-room working.

I had a great crew of Newfoundlanders, handy men all of them, and they certainly did accomplish a herculean task. When Percy Barnes and myself were boring the holes through the engine-room bulkheads, we had on oil clothes, with the sleeves and legs tied tightly. There would be times when the water would go clear over us. I have been swimming in much cleaner and warmer water than we had then.

Mr. Wardwell, our chief engineer, was a great man, always jolly and never a bit disconcerted about anything. His troubles were legion in the engine-room, but he always seemed to overcome every obstacle.

· · · · · ·

During the time we were hove to, the ship behaved splendidly, riding under the double-reef foresail as easily as a sea gull. At midnight of September thirtieth we rounded the ice of the middle pack. This was indeed comforting. The next day another gale from the southeast, carrying away our fore topmast. The broken topmast came down alongside in the water, so we secured it and the crow-nest as well.

The next day we made the land at Cape Dyer, going through loose strings of ice which made the water smooth. Passing Cape Walsingham and Mercy soon opened out the mouth of Cumberland Gulf. The weather clearing, with the wind hauling more to the north, this gave us smooth water crossing Cumberland Gulf. I was in hopes that the good weather would continue into the next afternoon and carry us into some harbor on the Labrador where we could get some coal, water and food. And, knowing the inside route along the Labrador coast, this would give us smooth water all the way south.

Coming on daylight, I went to my room to get a smoke standing up. Dozing off, I heard the engine stop; I was soon on deck. The rudder had broken at the neck. Thank heaven, dawning was beginning to show in the sky, the wind had freshened and began hauling back to the eastward. As long as the wind was forward of the beam, she steered well and no undue strain was brought on the rudder, but, with the change of wind abaft the beam, it called for more weather helm, bringing, as I say, undue strain on the rudder.

We were only a few miles off shore, and the wind hauling around would make it a lee shore. The back of the rudder had floated up under the injured part of the stern and would soon, with the rough sea making, tear away the temporary fittings I had around the stern. It was held in place by a $7/8''$ steel wire rove through the back and both ends of the wire brought forward through the bow chocks. This was for the purpose of giving a fore-and-aft support to the rudder. This we soon got rid of.

Having lowered the mizzen, I tried to wear her, but she would not pay off. Then I tried the engine going astern, with fore staysail and jib sheets to windward. Nothing doing! I then lowered all head sails and hoisted the mizzen, steaming ahead and hauling in the sheet as she came to. After a half-hour I managed to get her so that the wind canted her and she paid off on the other tack.

By this time we had the double-reef foresail all ready and, hoisting it, stopped the engine and she rode out the breeze like a Gloucester Banker. I then took the mizzen-boom, which was about sixty-five feet long, to make a sweep. Taking a small kedge and lashing it to the jaws of the boom, I filled in the space with rope, bits of wood and iron. This made a good blade. Then I rigged up sheer legs in such a way that the crotch would be right amidships and over the taffrail. Having secured the sheer legs, in the crotch I placed a walrus skin, with the fat still hanging on to it. This, wrapped around the spar or sweep, gave it plenty of lubricating.

From the starboard quarter we ran a spar which had a block lashed at the end and large enough to carry a four-inch line with the line rove through the block; it was fastened to the boom and the end in board around the steam capstan aft. Then at the waist on the port side we had the same thing rigged up, with the inboard end running to the steam winch. These were our tiller ropes.

When the wind and sea moderated I put it out and steered along on her course at the rate of four knots per hour. I then began building another rudder, taking another 11″ x 14″ beam out of the hold, all hands working. There wasn't much loafing or yarning these days.

Just before dark the wind veered around southeast, with snow. It came so fast we had to cut our sweep adrift. We hove to under double-reef foresail.

The next day, we kept working on the rudder and, by the time the gale blew out, had the rudder built. After a few hours, the sea moderated a little, so we began rigging up the sheer legs. This required a lot of rope for tackles and guys, for, with the rolling of the ship, it required plenty of gear to secure the sheer legs, also to secure the rudder as it was hoisted in space.

For sheer legs we used gaff and spare fore-boom, but we were woefully short of rope to make tackles and lashings.

By unreeving other gear and taking the boat-falls, sub-stituting stoppers in their place, we finally set up the sheer legs. The rudder post had a big rake forward, so we had to rig the sheer legs up to meet the rake. With the rolling of the ship and having to place them right aft with no means of support, this had to be done by rigging booms and pre-venter backstays, where ordinarily a little rope would have done.

The length of the rudder was such that, when hoisted high enough for the heel to clear the rudder-post, which ran several feet above the deck, it admitted but little drift and resulted in the tackles going two blocks. I knew this beforehand, but I grabbed the heel with my two arms and canted it so that it just grazed the aft end of the post and yelled "Lower away!" It was a great relief to me to see the rudder rapidly disappearing down the rudder well.

• • • • •

When secured, the ship was put on her course and at dawning the next morning we made land. There was no wind but snow was falling. We could see perhaps a quarter of a mile. After a while, I recognized the land. We were now amongst the Pot Rocks, some of which showed up above the water, but it was the worst piece of coastline on the Labrador coast. One thing we had in our favor—the beginning of the day—and with luck we would get through before dark. The wind freshened a little to the northeast, with snow. I went aloft so that I could see the bottom and the breakers better. In this way we managed to get through.

Dark found us clear of all danger. We were short of coal, water and food, but I knew, if we could reach the Moravian settlements of Ramah or Hebron, we could get food, water and perhaps enough coal to bring us from one settlement to another down the coast, where we would

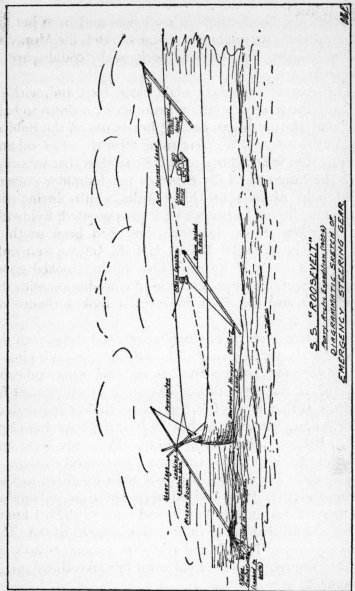

S.S. "ROOSEVELT"
Peary Arctic Expedition (1905-6)
DIAGRAMMATIC SKETCH of
EMERGENCY STEERING GEAR

Drawing by Alexander MacPhedran

run across the Newfoundland mail boat and from her get coal. And again we might be in time to catch the Moravian Mission steamer *Harmony* and perhaps she could spare us some coal.

The weather during the night cleared up, and, with no wind and the water smooth, we were now cut down to half-speed and already began cutting beams out of the hold to burn in the furnace. We were using all spare wood, oil and anything that would burn, with the coal dust that we swept up in the bunkers. I fully expected the Labrador current would help us at least thirty miles south during the twenty-four hours. In this we were disappointed. Evidently the prevailing winds along the coast had been south. I expected to be off Saglek Bay by daylight, but we were only a few miles south of Ramah. The weather looked good, the water smooth and no wind. So in consultation with the commander and the chief engineer, I took a chance on Hebron.

It was long after night when we reached there, with the engine barely turning over. The missionaries, thinking it was the *Harmony*, set up bonfires and had boats at the entrance of the harbor with lanterns, so it was easy to get in. With the anchor down, I pulled off my clothes and slept as I hadn't done for many nights. In fact, since leaving Cape York, I had not taken off my clothes except my boots and stockings and most of the time was spent in oil clothes.

The next day was Sunday, so I went on shore to visit the missionaries. They had all been one time or another at Turnavik, visiting my father, and some of them I knew, so they did all that lay in their power to help us out. The *Harmony* was still north and they could spare us no coal, but they thought, if we waited until her arrival, we might get some.

In going around, I saw some coal lying under a store

and, asking the missionaries if I could have it, they said "Certainly." It had lain there for many years. So I got the crew to gather it all up and bring it on board. I stayed there myself and picked up every lump. We secured from them three lighter-loads of spruce wood, whale and seal oil, also some blubber.

After getting a supply of fuel which we thought would bring us to Nain, we left Hebron. I might say that there are no charts of the inside passage of the coast, except a small General British Admiralty one and this had been burnt up in a fire in my room. However, both the mate and myself knew the coast, he much better than I.

That night we reached Black Island. I had never been up the inside passage back of Black Island. At Hebron an Eskimo asked me for a passage to Nain, so I took him along. I asked him if he had ever been through the inside passage in a steamer as big as the *Roosevelt*. He told me that he had been up through it in the *Harmony*, so he made a chart for me. He said one place was narrow, and a shoal lay right in the middle of the narrowest part. I told him to lie down on the floor in my room and get some sleep, and when I got up there, he would be called.

The night was clear and star-lit, with the *aurora* lighting up the northern heavens from west to east. I went to my room to have a look at the Eskimo chart. On the floor the Eskimo was asleep, lying on a piece of musk-ox skin that I had loaned him. I was there for only a few moments and had just started up the ladder to the bridge, when I heard a yell. I went back and found the Eskimo trying to put out a fire. What had happened was that, in going out, I stepped on a parlor match, which had set the long hairs of the musk-ox skin on fire. That settled his sleep for the night. Afterwards he came on the bridge alongside me and every once in a while he would chuckle to himself. He thought it a pretty good joke.

The sky became overcast and it was very close, especially now that we were steaming along through channels which had high mountains on either side. So I anchored. At daylight we got under weigh, with a fresh breeze from the northwest. Our engines were barely turning over and, with a headwind and tide, we were making a poor hand of it, but along toward noon the wind dropped and for a while we made better way.

In going through one of the many narrow passages, the tide caught us on the starboard bow and, before we could anchor, we were aground. By running out a kedge, in an hour or two we were afloat. Getting through the passage, we had the tide with us and reached Nain without further incident. Here we obtained more wood, whale and seal oil, also blubber.

From here to Hopedale we hadn't an ounce of coal, doing this run of one hundred miles or more with wood. True, we were in the inside passage, but the way was narrow in many places, full of hidden shoals and strong currents. Just as long as we could keep her end on to the wind and in line with the axis of the current, we were all right, but, should the wind get on our quarter or the current on either bow, then the rudder ceased to be of any service in guiding the ship. The only thing to do was to let go the anchor and straighten her up. In some cases I let her go stern first, snubbing her with the anchor.

There were times when the steam went so low that we had to anchor and wait for it to come up again; at times we had to anchor and wait for the tide to turn, or anchor and get a full head of steam and run her as long as the steam held. Luckily, I knew the road and now was accustomed to such occurrences. Really it's marvelous how one can adjust himself to conditions; it got so that I didn't mind it one bit in the world and would wait until the right time offered and go to it. Fortunately, we had good weather, almost like spring, and very little wind. However, I knew from experience, when the weather changed, it would be strong westerlies and snow, so I kept hammering away, trying to get along.

. . . . .

After a couple of days, we reached Hopedale, another Moravian mission settlement. Here it was like home; only twenty-four miles to the south lay Turnavik, a fishing station of my father's, where for years I spent the summer seasons. The missionaries at Hopedale knew father well, as did also the Eskimos. They were more than kind to us, but could not give us any coal, as they usually burnt wood.

I still had the *Harmony* astern of me. So, if it came to a showdown, I could wait for her and get coal. The reason I was so anxious to get to Hopedale was to catch the Newfoundland mail boat. Her route was as far north as Nain during the fishing season. But the Newfoundland fishing schooners had all gone south, so her Nain trips were finished. I was afraid that we would be too late to catch her at Hopedale, as this would be her last trip to that point.

Just as soon as the anchor was down, I went ashore to inquire and found that they expected the mail boat any day and this would be her last trip. Getting some more wood, blubber and oil, I thought we might risk trying Turnavik. Father always came to this fishing station with a steamer and used a steam launch to supply bait to the fishermen. He, of course, had gone home, but his man would be there who had charge of the station during the winter months. The coal was stored near the wharf, so I thought I would risk it.

But, in getting out of the harbor, the wind was strong

from the N.N.W. and, getting the wind on the quarter and with very little steam, it was impossible to do anything with her. So we anchored and, when the wind moderated, steamed back to the anchorage and the next morning put her stern on shore.

We now began building a new rudder. The 11″ x 14″ beam we used was taken from the hold. What we really should have had was one that, when rounded, would be 16″, which was the size of the brace. That was the size of the original oak rudder-stock. We overcame the difficulty by using several lengths of two-inch piping, which carried our steel wheel ropes along the deck. These pipes were ripped up and placed up and down the rudder-stock and secured in place by steel wire and chain lashings.

I now wanted to build a fore-and-aft brace to take care of the fore-and-aft strain on the rudder, also the side strain as well. Hitherto I had been using wire pennants. I went to the commander and asked him to put the plan on paper.

This brace was about 24 feet long and made of heavy plank, shaped when finished very much like a cigar, only the middle was hollow instead of solid. The ends were solid, being filled with wooden ends; the middle, of course, had bracing fore and aft and 'thwart-ships as well. One end of this was secured in the propeller-well. A solid plank platform was built at the bottom of the propeller-well; this was just high enough to keep clear of the ends of the pro-peller blades.

A lot of this work was done under water. Many bolts were thus driven under water. One end of the brace lay secured on top of the platform forward. The after end, which was solid and filled in with wooden ends and steel wire seizings, had a davit socket secured in the end. This went aft far enough to be plumb under the heel of the rud-der-stock, which had a 2½″ steel bolt driven up it. This sat

in the socket at the end of the brace. To take the strain off
the brace and neck of the rudder, two 2″ steel pennants
were fastened to an end of this brace and were suspended
from each counter by two turnbuckles, which would take
in or ease up any undue strain.

From the first, we had no trouble, but, by everlastingly
watching, it carried us to New York harbor without any
more trouble. It was fortunate we did all this work at Hopedale, for, besides making a good job, we secured enough
coal from the mail boat to bring us to Hawke Harbor, a
whaling factory, and, getting five tons of coal from Ryan's
agent there, the next morning I left for Battle Harbor.

It was late at night when I came up to the harbor, man-
aging to get by the Ribs and other shoals. The night was so
dark that you could feel it—not a star shining, the water
like molten metal cooling off, and as level as a floor. I was
in hopes someone would see our lights and come off to us.
Getting closer, I determined to go in. The entrance is
about three hundred feet wide, with a rock right in the
middle of the channel. Coming up to the entrance, one has
to make a sharp turn and straighten up the harbor. One
thing, on the starboard side you will hit above water rather
than below. Taking the head close aboard, I went right on
without hitting anything and off the wharf dropped my
anchor. There is not room enough to swing at anchor, but
I had a boat already down and ran the line on shore to the
wharf. By this time a few people on shore began to stir
about and from them I found out that the buoys on the
mooring chains were still out, so, after a little while, we
found them and had her moored head and stern.

Here is the funny thing. When we came in to report the
discovery of the Pole at the wireless station in 1909, I had
a pilot on board. It was broad daylight, no wind and the

ship in perfect condition, yet I struck the rock on entering and stayed aground on it for four hours.

. . . . .

Just as soon as I could get the agent the next morning, I pulled in alongside the wharf and took on fifty tons of coal. The wind had risen from the S.E. and blew strong as the day advanced, with rain and fog. I held on, thinking the wind would veer to the N.W. but it kept S.E. with a heavy sea, so that we couldn't get out and had to stay there for nine days. We broke our best bower anchor, and all the heavy moorings in the harbor that are used to moor the large fish steamers at one time or another parted. At times, I thought she would never come out of it. The western tickle astern of us would run dry with the big undertow heaving in. At length it moderated and we got away in a thick snowstorm.

From here I steamed up to Azzizze's Harbor, as the weather was thick and threatening and a big sea still running outside. However, the next morning the wind moderated and it stopped snowing, but, still overcast with a rough sea, we put out and steamed on through the Straits of Belle Isle.

As the day wore on, the wind hauled to the N.E., so we came on. Coming down the west coast of Newfoundland, the wind gradually worked around western, making the Newfoundland coast a lee shore. This slowed us down and, worse still, took a lot of our coal. I was in hopes that I could reach Port-aux-Basques, the terminus of the New-foundland Railway, where coal was plenty, as the mail boats make a daily run between there and North Sydney, Cape Breton.

When between Red Island and Cape George, the wind headed us so that we couldn't lay our course. I put her on a wind and we had to make many tacks before we could weather around Cape George. At length, with the Cape close aboard and passed, we gave her the long fore-sheet and ran up to the bottom of Bay Saint George. Here we anchored off a little village called Sands Point. Going ashore, I inquired if one could obtain coal. There was none to be had, so, in conversation with some of the residents, I told them how we were situated and, if we could get enough to bring us to Port-aux-Basques, that would do. I told them that five tons would do, so we obtained a horse and cart and went around from house to house until I got the five tons. From here, we steamed to Port-aux-Basques, where we obtained fifty tons, which brought us to Sydney, Cape Breton.

Getting 200 tons of coal at Sydney, I left and, going through the Bras d'Or Lakes, I had a funny experience. It occurred just before we entered St. Peter Lock. Having to make a sharp turn, the helm was hove over hard. The tide was taking us on the port bow. The *Roosevelt* went on as if nothing like a rudder was attached to her and up she went on to the bank. Right under her jib boom, a girl, sitting on a stool, was milking a cow. When the jib boom began to get too close, the cow, with her tail over her back, started up the incline, leaving the girl, stool and milk pail scattered all over the lot.

We lowered a boat and ran a line to a tree on the opposite side of the bank and hove her off. We had very little room to spare in the locks; it was only a matter of inches. Going through the channel leading to the open sea, she became contrary, getting one of those crazy fits which by this time we were accustomed to, and ran aground. The tide was falling, so, when it rose, we pulled her off with a kedge and started on our way.

We had strong winds down the Nova Scotian coast, which gave us lots of trouble, and our boiler, becoming salted, necessitated our going into Shelburne. Here the chief fixed her up again and we started across the Bay of Fundy. The wind was a little abaft the beam and she kept always carrying a weather helm. On the way, she headed up about three points to windward of her course. One would think it would be Thatcher's Island we would make. But, luckily for us, just before dark one evening we made the highlands of Cape Cod and, later, Pollock Rip Lightship.

The wind began to haul around to the S.E. and looked very greasy. So I kept on through the slue. The night was very close and dark and the ebb-tide running full force. In trying to round the Gas Buoy, she took a sheer and, before the anchor was dropped, she was aground. Perhaps she was there for fifteen minutes—it seemed much longer. But we kept the engines going full speed astern and, with the strong ebb-tide running, she freed herself, and about that time along came a long tow, bound to the eastward. How we cleared that tow I never could understand. It didn't look any too good.

The wind kept breezing up from the N.E. and that was no place for us at that time of the year, so I tried the slue again. God, wasn't it dark! The strong ebb-tide rendered our passage through difficult and dangerous. Often she could not stem the tide; then she would sheer and, in the twinkling of an eye, she was across the channel and in shallow water, so I would let go the anchor, and, when she brought up, heave away again on the anchor and go on. Again and again we had to anchor and, at length, by tacking back and forth, I finally got to the lightship at the inside of the bend. Heaven knows what would have happened had there been a tow coming in or out.

The next afternoon, I anchored in Vineyard Haven and, in talking to Captain Cleghorn, one of the old Vineyard and Sound pilots, he said he would come with me to

New York. I didn't tell him our condition and, when he came on board, I kept him close to me, so that he wouldn't talk with the crew. We stayed all night in the Vineyard and the next day it was calm but foggy, but we went over to Tarpaulin Cove and anchored. When the fog cleared, we hove up anchor and came on.

Everything was fine until we got in the Sound and there the wind came out of the W.N.W., with snow squalls and frost. She began her old capers of doing what she liked. She kept on her own way, regardless of her rudder. The pilot was not at all complimentary in his remarks about the *Roosevelt*—or me, in bringing him aboard of a vessel in such an unseaworthy condition. So I said, "You go below and I will handle her."

So, when she would get over to the Long Island shore, I would anchor and let her come into the wind, watch her sheer, heave away the anchor, casting her toward the Connecticut shore, and so on. At length, around noon of the day before Christmas, we anchored at City Island and I telegraphed Mr. Herbert Bridgman, secretary and treasurer of the Peary Arctic Club and editor of *The Brooklyn Standard Union*, to send me a tug.

When it came, we left for New York, the tug going ahead with the line. That didn't work, as I told the tug captain, and he came alongside and all went well with us until the Wall Street ferry came down on our jib-boom. It didn't do anything to us, but we had a lot of the upper structure of the Wall Street ferry on our jib-boom and topgallant forecastle.

An hour or two after dark, Christmas Eve, 1906, we anchored at the foot of Seventieth Street, North River, one hundred and seventy-three days from Cape Sheridan, Grant Land, Lat. 82.30 N.

The following day was Christmas. With Mr. Bridgman

I called on Morris K. Jesup. He had been to church and the fine old face of him lightened up, as briefly I told him the story of the trip. On leaving he gave me a $20 gold piece. I have it yet and hope to be able to keep it as long as I live.

I don't believe that trip could be duplicated again and we get away with it as we did.

THE CRUISE OF THE *Lone Star*

Warwick S. Carpenter

Outdoor life has always held a fascination for Warwick S. Carpenter. On graduation from Columbia University in 1904, he took up newspaper and magazine writing and became editor successively of *The Journal of the Outdoor Life* and *The Conservationist* and, later, secretary of the New York State Conservation Commission.

He is the author of many books and articles on outdoor life, travel and the conservation of forests and wild life. He is at present Pacific Coast representative for a group of leading magazines.

THE CRUISE OF THE *LONE STAR*

By Warwick S. Carpenter

T HE *Lone Star* RODE SNUGLY IN HER SHELTERED harbor. Outside, the west wind across Kasakokwog kicked up a vexing sea.

We had come down the Dawson route in western Ontario, Pink and his wife and I, from Windigoostigwan to Sturgeon. Then, swinging north through Batchewaung Lake and McAlpine to Kasakokwog, within reach again of our jumping-off place, the others had gone out, leaving me to venture alone the long trail to Rainy Lake.

One trims a canoe for the work in hand. The blow was hard, but not dangerous, so the *Lone Star* rounded into the open lake, swung into the west with a twist of the paddle and bore steadily into the teeth of the wind for the outlet and portage to Quetico.

All the aspects of the wilderness are heightened when one travels alone. In a country that is unfamiliar, little traveled and still partly unmapped, there is even some of the tang of exploration. "Rise free from care beyond the dawn," said Thoreau, "and seek adventures. Let the noon find thee by other lakes and the night overtake thee everywhere at home. There are no larger fields than these, no worthier games than may here be played." In this buoyant spirit the *Lone Star* coquetted with each beckoning point and kept her forefoot on the unfolding trail.

For a whole day on Quetico she was wind-bound. I had

camped where rangers had been building a log cabin, on the large island which commands the two main arms of the lake. It was a wonderful day, with brilliant sunshine, fleecy, scudding clouds, and waves dashing on the shore below the camp. The day passed with many pipes, the reading of Thoreau, a delightful companion on a wilderness voyage, and solicitous tending of the bean kettle over the rangers' stone fireplace.

Followed a day of erratic zigzagging down the long south arm of the lake from point to point, each vantage disclosing a different charm. Gradually the light failed and loons serenaded the westering sun, with Jean Lake still two portages away.

The first portage was easy in the long Ontario gloaming. It ran beside a tumbling brook, scarce a hundred and fifty yards, to a little muddy lake on the side of a divide. It was nearly dark under the trees and a wise time to camp. But the mud-hole was dismal and mosquito-infested, while over the divide was Jean, whose charms had been foretold by rangers.

The canoe went first, while yet some faint suggestion of a trail persisted in the deepening gloom. At the end was a narrow inlet, its black surface relieved by the skeleton arms of a fallen tree. On either side the tall, black ranks of the forest shut in like a canyon. In the dusk between twilight and dark, the detail of the trees was lost, though their feeling remained, like the impressionism of a pictorialist. The last trip went stumblingly, with uncertain feet sensing the different impact of the trail through the soft soles of the moccasins. Impressionism was gone. Floors and walls of the canyon were blended alike in a black, impenetrable void, over the center of which ran the narrow, gray half-tone of the sky, shot across with tremulous flashes of far distant lightning.

Under the narrow gray band, the *Lone Star* stole cautiously, following the turns at quarter-speed. The band widened gradually. At intervals it was luminous with pulsating light. The impending, invisible walls drew back and a feeling of space ensued, as when one passes into a larger room. The air blew fresher and with it came sharper flashes, disclosing a little bay, at whose far side a jutting point gave promise of camp.

Outside the point the waves slapped saucily in the stiffening breeze. On its hither side the *Lone Star* tied up and made reconnaissance. Lightning flashes and the flare of a match showed small hospitality. There was scarce room to sit among the jagged rocks, let alone pitch a tent and sleep. The now vivid flashes disclosed a farther shore, alluring at a distance and surely no worse. The lightning and the low, dull rumbling of thunder promised an even race with the approaching storm, so the *Lone Star* turned quickly into the coming waves and made a run for it.

With each succeeding flash the shore line bulked higher. Then it rose close at hand. In its shelter the restless water smoothed out and the canoe ran in beside a shelving rock, behind which spread a level forest floor, bedded with thick, dry moss, which gave under the feet like a feather bed. It was the work of a moment to string the tent between two trees, guy the ropes to one fallen behind and anchor the sod cloth with broken limbs. Then came the duffle, piled along the wall, with the blanket laid on the moss beside. As the canoe came up the sloping rock, the promise of wind was fulfilled in the tree-tops. The next second it struck the walls of the tent with a bang and whipped them straight out from their light restraint. But still no rain. While the tent flapped in the wind, I groped hurriedly on the shore for rocks and weighted it down past all mischance.

The vistas of the lightning gave place to a picture by

candle-light—the snug, closed walls of the tent; a pile of dunnage; the warm, inviting blanket; a pail of water from the lake; some cold boiled rice—no need of Omar's wine. And among all these changing scenes an aural memory persists—the sweeping rush of wind through pines, shattered with crash on crash of thunder; a smaller note of water dashing constantly upon stones. Constantly, too, falls the sound of rain on taut-stretched silk.

. . . . .

On Burntsides Lake the map ran out. It showed no outlet. The way was a blank. So the *Lone Star* cruised anxiously around the shore line and nosed expectantly into every reedy bay and sluggish inlet. Night shut down with the search unfinished. The abandoned poles of an Indian's teepee and splinters where he had built a canoe made camp and supper easy. In the morning the outlet was found, completely hidden behind a point. It was still and wide, like an arm of the lake, and led through many turns to a falls, with a portage. From here a slender river, the Clearwater Over Sands, ran down. Long grasses lined its shores, and gray tamaracks, and it twisted and wound bewitchingly.

Throughout all the winding course from Burntsides only dead reckoning had indicated that we might come out at the lower end of Sturgeon, across from Maligne Portage, where the miscalled and generally peaceful river of the same name makes a bold start. Dead reckoning was right and the *Lone Star* tied up in the fading twilight beside a camp-site under dwarfed oaks at the head of the rapids. Came a day of exploration around the foot of the lake, of quiet fishing, or loafing in a little bay that held all of the elusive spell of the wild north country, and then a start down the river and an adventure of moment.

If one thinks that it is not adventurous to meet a strange craft with two men in the wilderness, let him cruise for a

Tenting beneath the Pines

The Consort Picked up on Lac La Croix

week alone. She was spoken at the beginning of the second portage on the Maligne. Duluth she hailed from, with McLaren and Deighton, her owners, aboard. We hauled out and boiled the tea pail, warmed beans and baked biscuits, then sat on a rock and talked it all over, with a thread on the shutter of the camera. Launching their craft, they waved farewell and paddled away in the distance.

They had scarcely gone when another outfit came over the portage. It was borne by two rangers for the Ontario government, Johnson and Gibson. We pitched together at the end of the portage and turned in at a disgraceful woodland hour. They had been exploring the Quetico Preserve, discovering its unmapped lakes and tracing its streams, and time passed quickly with stories of unfished lakes teeming with bass and of the highways and byways of the country. They told also of an Indian village below, on Lac La Croix, where some silent, smoky denizens might join with the freebooting *Lone Star*.

Next morning they tracked up the rapids and for two days the *Lone Star* loitered down the Maligne, before she ran into a stiff west wind on Lac La Croix. All the late afternoon she bucked it and gained the farther shore when dusk brought cessation of the blow. Somewhere among those deceitful points was the village. It might be miles. It might be around the next point. Already behind the western tree line the last red glow had faded. Far away in the dim half-light, against the dark side of a hill, rose an evening mist. It hung sluggishly in the still air. But no sign of a village appeared.

The *Lone Star* went on uncertainly, scouting for a favorable landing. Gradually the mist faded in the gathering dark. It was a peculiar mist and spread like smoke from a fire. The paddle dipped quietly in the water. A rhythmical pulsation was in the air. It gained in volume until it became the beat of a drum. The bark of a dog punctuated it. Rising and falling in primitive and human cadence came the sound of a song.

The lagging pace of the *Lone Star* quickened until the tiny ripples at her bow became wavelets, which spread out into the gathering dusk of Lac La Croix. She lifted slightly at the bow with each thrust of the paddle. Astern she acquired a wake, in which little bubbles danced away over the receding trail. Though still far off, the song swelled louder and the measured beat of the drum came clear and distinct. It was rude and uncultured, but across the bows of the *Lone Star* it carried the thrill of a port and the promise of companions. Then the drum and the song ceased and the speed unconsciously slackened. It had been a hard day's paddle and the distance to go seemed long.

I looked back over the little bubbles in the wake. They floated unsteadily and led into a vista of wide water and up a river. They blended strangely with the hard, dry ground of portages and ran unaccountably around far points where one should not have been able to see. Here and there the red light of a fire glowed beside them and reflected softly from white walls. In this dim and alluring vision the little bubbles bobbed lightly and beckoned backward as they went.

At the call of the drum the *Lone Star* picked up her speed again and bore down on the village. Here a consort would be found and, with two stars on the standard, I could drop rapidly down the unfamiliar current of the Namakan, out to Rainy Lake and Fort Frances, and so away from the Abandoned Highway and homeward.

AN AWKWARD PREDICAMENT
George K. Cherrie

A modest and genial man of the world, George K. Cherrie has an impressive record of nearly forty years' work as a scientific explorer, devoid of bluff, bluster or ballyhoo.

He has collected mammals, reptiles, insects and always and especially birds in Costa Rica, French and British Guiana, Trinidad, the Orinoco valley, Santo Domingo, Colombia, Ecuador, Brazil—and Chinese Turkestan.

He has served as taxidermist, curator or field collector for the U. S. National Museum, the American Museum of Natural History, the National Museum of Costa Rica, the Field Museum of Chicago, the Tring Museum in French Guiana and the Brooklyn Museum.

He accompanied Theodore Roosevelt on his River of Doubt expedition and, in 1925-1926, the late president's sons Kermit and Theodore into Central Asia.

Some of the experiences and observations of this active life he has told engagingly in *Dark Trails*.

AN AWKWARD PREDICAMENT

By George K. Cherrie

I HAVE WRITTEN ELSEWHERE THAT, AMONG THE BEST AND staunchest friends I ever had, were numbered some native South and Central Americans. At the present moment I have in mind the family of a poor but independent owner of a small coffee plantation not far distant from the city of San José, capital of Costa Rica. I had taken refuge in their humble little home to escape the fury of an oncoming thunderstorm. Their genuine hospitality was so pleasing that I kept up the acquaintance and, whenever my work took me in the neighborhood of their straw-thatched cottage, I would drop in for a short visit.

Juan Sandoval was not a Spanish *hidalgo*. He was only an Indian (with perhaps a little Spanish blood) but he had a shrewd outlook on life and an appreciation of the advantage of "schooling." Pacífica, the oldest daughter, aspired to become a teacher.

Juan Sandoval died from the bite of a rattlesnake and poverty descended upon the family. But they clung together and managed to eke out an existence from working the little plantation, while Pacífica continued at school.

I interested myself in the family and at intervals would stop at the house for an hour's chat with the mother of Pacífica. The chance acquaintance ripened into a genuine friendship.

Once a solid acquaintanceship has been built up with

63

a family of rural South Americans, one may be called on to participate in all sorts of duties—and there are few limits to what these duties may be. My acquaintance and friendship with the family of Juan Sandoval was to bear much fruit.

One day toward the end of the rainy season in the early '90s—it was an afternoon in November—while working in my laboratory, I received a telegram from the little village of Curridabat, which lies ten or twelve miles beyond the city limits of San José. "Come, mother dying, bring candles," it read. Within an hour a second message reached me. Its laconic words were, "Bring shoes for mother." Both messages were signed "Pacífica."

Even had I not known the family intimately, I should have read into the second telegram a pathetic story. It is the pride and the tradition of the Central American native, with a strain of Castilian blood, that members of the family be buried in their best clothes—if possible, in better raiment than they had ever worn in life. Poverty, no doubt, had prevented the mother from possessing shoes—indeed it is questionable if she had ever worn them. But the grieving children were determined to do their duty and see that their mother went to her grave in the proper costume; and no costume would be complete without shoes.

I immediately made preparations for the journey to render what aid and sympathy I might. I took with me a friend, a recent arrival in the tropics, who had evinced a sympathetic interest in the natives and their customs. It was night when we started, through a drizzling rainstorm, on the ten-mile ride to the native *rancho*. The long, cheerless ride, with thoughts of meeting a gloomy, saddened household, had hardly prepared us for the reception that awaited us.

As we rode into the stable-yard, gay strains of music

met our ears. The wake was in full swing. The house was aglow with the light of many candles, which threw their rays through the chinks of the wattled walls into the damp darkness without, while from the near-by kitchen came savory odors that sharpened the appetites we had built up on the long ride. The cheerful sounds from within the house and the seductive odors made it hard to realize that we had journeyed to a funeral.

We were met at the door, where I delivered my packages, and conducted into the crowded living-room of the house, in the center of which lay the body, surrounded by the family and friends—the former obviously content in its temporary notoriety. Many were standing, a few rested on low chairs or benches and others sat on the bare earthen floor. The family's hospitality was generous; rounds of drinks came one after another in swift succession, followed by plates piled high with roast meats and fowl. A master of ceremonies broke through the conversation and music intermittently, as in a fine baritone voice he intoned a rosary for the dead, telling off his beads one by one as he did it. Warmed by the hospitality, to say nothing of the wine, the guests joined vigorously in the chanting.

Our presence seemed to call for a new round of drinks and more food, but presently I was called aside by the daughter of the house. She thanked me for bringing candles and was greatly pleased that I had brought the shoes. Further to show her appreciation, she accorded to my friend and me the honor of fitting the shoes. Rarely have I experienced such embarrassment. Even in private the task would have been little to my liking, while to carry it out under the curious eyes of the dead woman's friends and neighbors was disconcerting. We hesitated and drew back, but the daughter was insistent. Despite the warmth of good cheer about us and the encouragement of the wine that we had drunk, we yet shrank somewhat from the work.

In the purchase of the shoes I had made some allowance for the fact that the mother had led an outdoor agricultural life, reasoning that her bare feet would have spread under such conditions, but unfortunately I did not realize that her feet had been so large in the beginning. The shoes I had brought, big as they were, were not large enough.

We struggled vainly, no doubt the subject of much veiled criticism by those about us. Self-consciousness added to our discomfort. Perspiration dripped from our faces, but, work as we would, the shoes would not go on.

"No use, Cherrie," said my friend.

But I knew better than to fail. Friendly as they were, our hosts were possessed of the captiousness common to their race; the stridency of the festivity was a measure of the wrath that would surely descend upon us if we admitted that, due to my lack of imagination, we had been the cause of the mother going to her grave in the same barefoot condition as that in which she had attended to her daily chores.

We were at our wits' end—incidentally growing more heated every moment—but something must be done and done quickly. Our working so long over the woman's feet had begun to attract attention. Our actions were receiving unfavorable comment. The rounds of drinks were being neglected and plates of roast meats remained untouched, while all eyes were directed toward us. Unconsciously the master of ceremonies came to our relief by calling upon all present to join in a chant or requiem for the soul of the dead. My companion had an inspiration. During the respite, while eyes were turned from us, he deftly slit the backs of the shoes. We were then able to draw them on and lace them in front. No one was the wiser and family and friends were alike content.

Early the following morning, without ceremony of any sort, the poor, tired body of an Indian woman was carried to its eternal resting-place, the grave was filled by a twelve-year-old son and a rude cross without inscription was placed at its head.

Pacífica mothered the household for a time, but one after another found homes elsewhere and I lost touch with them.

Months later, after a long, hard expedition, I returned to San José in a weakened condition. I fell a victim to pneumonia. One night, when life was hanging in the balance, I awakened from a fitful, troubled slumber to find Pacífica Sandoval bending over my bed. That night was the crisis. Three or four of "the boys" had learned from the doctor that Cherrie would not last through the night. Just why they came, I have never been quite able to understand. Was there some sort of fascination in the idea that a soul was straining to be free? That night is one I shall never forget, although it was long ago. As I lay, probably in a semi-comatose condition, I had no power to speak, no desire to speak, but was conscious of all about me and of a freedom from pain, although the body must have given evidence of a struggle, for I could hear the awed whispers of those who sat and waited, "He is going!"

Then followed a period of profound coma, in which I had almost reached the point where "both worlds at once they view that stand upon the threshold of the new." My body seemed no longer to rest upon the bed but to float in space. There were no rainbow-tinted clouds enveloping nor storm clouds rent by the zigzag lightning's glare. There was perfect peace and quiet, broken only by the faint whisperings, "Is he gone?" But no. Pacífica was bending over me, holding me back—she would not let me go.

With the dawning of a new day, the struggle was over, the crisis past. I slept and Pacífica watched over me.

"With careful nursing he will live," said the doctor.

Weeks later, when I would have rewarded the girl for her services and faithful, loving care, she shook her head and said, "You brought the shoes for mother." And an Indian girl went out of my life forever.

ONE NIGHT IN THE GRAND CANYON

Frederick S. Dellenbaugh

Frederick S. Dellenbaugh, one of the founders of The Explorers Club and today one of its oldest and best loved members, is also one of the few surviving pioneers of western exploration.

When a lad of eighteen, he embarked as artist and topographer on the hazardous journey down the Colorado River of which he here tells one of the many dramatic episodes. A second trip to the Grand Canyon was followed by several years of travel and the study of art in Europe, and repeated sojourns in the Southwest to sketch and paint scenes of Indian life.

In 1899 he was the artist of the Harriman Expedition to Alaska and Siberia. The years since then have been well filled with painting and sketching trips to Iceland, Spitsbergen, Europe, the West Indies, Venezuela and always the Southwest, and with writing and lecturing and radiating the warmth of his lovable personality.

Among his many writings are *The North Americans of Yesterday; The Romance of the Colorado River; Breaking the Wilderness; A Canyon Voyage; Frémont and '49; Life of Gen. George A. Custer.* He also edited the *Seven Log Books of William Scoresby, Sr.,* published in a limited edition by The Explorers Club for distribution among the leading libraries and scientific institutions of the world.

ONE NIGHT IN THE GRAND CANYON

By Frederick S. Dellenbaugh

Before DESCRIBING THE NIGHT IN THE GRAND CANYON TO which I refer particularly in this article, it may be desirable to review briefly the conditions which led up to our being there.

The Grand Canyon of the Colorado River of the West (so named by the first white man to descend through it with a party of explorers, Major John Wesley Powell) lies entirely in the State of Arizona. Including its upper portion, Marble Gorge, sixty-five miles long, it is two hundred and eighty-three miles in length as the river runs. Its depth reaches more than a mile—the most marvelous example of erosion in the world.

The Spanish explorer, Coronado, entered our Southwest in 1540. That same year one of his scouting parties under command of Don García López de Cardenas discovered the great chasm, but give it no name. As stated above, it was named by its first navigator, Major Powell. This was in 1869, three hundred and twenty-nine years after Cardenas had looked into the gorge.

Major Powell, recently out of service in the Union army of the Civil War, desiring to investigate the geology of the canyons of Green River and the Colorado River of the West, passed through them all from Wyoming to the mouth of the Virgin River in rowboats with a party of nine men. Or rather, he started with nine; one left at the mouth of the Duchesne, three deserted below Diamond Creek near the end of the Grand Canyon. So the entire trip was accomplished by only six.

Because of various difficulties and disasters, Powell had failed to get what he wanted in the way of scientific data. Consequently, although he was a one-armed man, his right arm having been shot off at the battle of Shiloh, he immediately planned a second descent. This was the first U. S. Government expedition. The year 1870 Powell spent in finding ways to send in rations for this second trip.

On May 22, 1871, he pulled out again from the Union Pacific Railway with three boats and eleven men. I had the good luck to be accepted as one of this party and was two years in this service. One of the men left us after two or three weeks. The rest held together for six months, till we came to the mouth of the Paria River, where we temporarily left the river to carry on geodetic and other scientific work during the winter. Three men left at this time, two because the constant wetting disabled them; and no substitutes were available.

The result was that, when we were ready in 1872 to enter the Marble-Grand Canyon, we had only six men besides Major Powell himself. We were, therefore, obliged to abandon one of our boats. All three had been cached for the winter and they were thoroughly dried out in that desert air. The one we left, the *Nellie Powell,* was the boat with which the notorious John D. Lee, leader of the Mountain Meadow Massacre, who had come in the spring of this year to hide in this secluded place, started "Lee's Ferry," later so well known. Major Powell gave him the boat.

The other boats, the *Cañonita* and the *Emma Dean,* which had been badly battered by the previous year's work and had also suffered much from the drying-out mentioned, we patched up as well as we could, let them soak submerged for days to bring the planks nearer together, caulked them and painted them, till, so far as appearance went, they were all right for the rough passage of the Grand Canyon. They were destined to get some far worse knocks in that gorge than ever before.

The Colorado River was phenomenally high in that summer of 1872. High water makes navigation of the rapids easier, but it also prevents portages at bad places and sometimes makes control of the boats impossible. In one distance of about four miles we had no control whatever. Luckily the river was only swift, with numerous whirlpools about twenty feet in diameter, which turned our boats round and round but were no special menace.

.   .   .   .   .

It was the thirteenth of August, 1872, before we were fully ready to cut loose from "Lonely Dell," as Lee called the valley at the mouth of the Paria River. Everybody in the region thought we were taking desperate chances. Perhaps we were. It seemed so on several occasions, one being the night I am going to describe.

The season was rainy. The skies frequently treated us to a deluge accompanied by thunder which seemed to shatter the mighty cliffs. People who think it does not rain in the Grand Canyon region should go down in the Canyon some rainy summer. Especially at night does it seem to be wrecking the entire chasm and knocking it into chaos. Sometimes one is rather surprised in the morning to find the walls just the same as the day before.

As we dashed down through Marble Gorge, the river doubtless was rising, but we did not stop anywhere long enough to find out—in fact, we did not think much about a rising river till the night in question. A swiftly rising river has its peculiar dangers.

The day before our bad night was particularly difficult.

The skies—what we could see of them—were dark and emptied themselves upon us with an abandon that was magnificent, while the crashing thunder added to the dramatic character of the situation. Of course there are always rapids and big ones in this canyon. We had our time with them. We arrived at an unusually difficult descent. As it would have been next to impossible to climb out and we could not go back, there was always only one course—to go on, smash or no smash, day after day.

In order to guard against a smash, we had to be extra cautious and made portages where perhaps we might have run through successfully. In this particular case, had we been bolder, much hard labor would have been saved; yet these lines might never have been written.

At this time we were working through the first Granite Gorge. There are three of these granite gorges. The second follows the first closely; the third is below Diamond Creek. In these gorges the walls are well-nigh vertical and extremely rough, with projecting buttresses forming alcoves occasionally. Around these buttresses the rushing river beats and swirls with wild energy.

We had worked our way with difficulty down on the right toward one of these alcoves, in order to avoid running the rapid, which had a heavy fall and was full of great rocks. One boat was lowered as far as its hundred-foot line would permit. From that boat the second was lowered till it stuck in between two enormous boulders at the very head of the rapid. The first was then pulled back to the men who were holding the rope from some rocks at the foot of the wall. They got on board. Then, by clinging with our hands to projections in the granite wall, we managed to slip down to the position of the second boat. From that vantage point we were able to work the two boats across the broken riverside to the alcove mentioned. There we passed the night.

It was the next night that forms the main subject of this story.

In the morning there was rain, as there had been most of the day before, but there was also daylight. We could now see the real situation, which was that we were hardly past the very head of the violent fall. We could not pull out into it from so disadvantageous a starting-point. That would have been far worse than running it from above.

We discovered another alcove about three hundred yards below our camp on our side of the river. As soon as we could get started, we began the task of working the boats cautiously down to this place, intending there to shoot the boats out into the lower part of the rapid and sail on to new conquests.

The river was narrow here; the rapid by daylight was even fiercer in its impetuous descent than was apparent at night. Nevertheless the water along the immediate wall between our position and the alcove where we hoped to arrive was not turbulent, though it was flowing faster than the traditional mill-race. The main difficulty was the absence of any footing along the base of the canyon wall. This was remedied by the discovery of a narrow ledge, about one hundred and fifty feet above the river, along which several of the men could clamber, holding taut the lines of both boats, tied together to make one two-hundred-foot line, while I remained in the bow of the boat with an oar. As the boat descended with the swift current, my duty was to keep her head in toward the wall by working the oar on the outer, or starboard, bow like a paddle, against the gunwale. Of course, if the current had pressed too strongly on the inside, or port bow, the boat would have taken the diagonal of forces and would either have pulled the men into the river or compelled them to let go, giving me the opportunity of swinging the boat about and running the end of the rapid by myself. This did not happen, however, but I was well aware of the chance. We did it a second time, with the other boat. And there we were in the alcove of our desire, from which we intended to pull out and run the remainder of the rapid.

Rain was falling most of the time and the sky above was dark and thunderous. But we felt that we were free now to launch out and put this troublesome fall behind us in short order. It was high noon by this time. As soon as we could get away and reach a landing-place below, we would have dinner.

In Grand Canyon navigation, nothing can with certainty be foretold. This was emphasized just now by finding that both boats were leaking badly. To stop for the necessary repairs was imperative. We halted and examined the alcove. It was approximately the shape of a letter U, with the sides unscalable. At the rear was the talus of broken stones on which we had landed, lying against the wall at that point.

On these stones the boats were hauled out. Their cargoes were placed at the upper end, as far as possible above the water, which rolled and dashed into the alcove from the rushing rapid—a wild side-wash of the plunging river. As the day was only half gone, we could repair the boats before dark and go on to a favorable camping-ground. The alcove offered no facilities whatever for a camp. This particular patch of jagged rocks was about as uninviting as can be imagined and was barely thirty by forty feet.

The repair work on the boats consumed more time than expected. While we were at the job, we kept getting more and more into the water, till finally someone exclaimed, "The damned river is rising," and put a marker to find out. In the next hour the water rose four feet and was continu-

ing. It seemed that the patch of rocks might soon be submerged. Night was now coming on. We were in a trap. The
boats would be pounded to pieces if the river covered the
rocks they were lying on. In that case we would be in an
uncomfortable situation. It was six thousand feet to the top
of the wall above us, to the edge of the canyon. Without the
boats we certainly could not go down the river; even with
them it would not be possible to go back up the river.

                .   .   .   .   .

It is only now, 1931, looking back after these many
years, that I comprehend the full measure of our isolation
on that tempestuous night. At that time we took it all as
something "in the day's work." We looked around to find a
way of preserving the boats and their cargoes, no less important, also to discover some comparatively level spot for
a camp.

At the rear of the alcove, about fifteen feet above the
top of the talus on which the boats were lying, we found a
narrow ledge, five or six feet wide, which we could reach by
means of crevices for foot and hand holds. To this ledge we
passed up the cargoes, rations, instruments, photographic
outfit, etc. They would be quite safe there, we judged, as
the river hardly would reach the shelf—yet, in climbing
around above to study the situation, we had found driftwood one hundred feet above the present level of the river.

The next thing was the boats. Darkness was upon us,
with more rain, before we had finished repairing them. At
last, by means of lines let down from the ledge and much
hard lifting, for the boats were half waterlogged and therefore very heavy, we succeeded in raising them against the
back cliff till their keels were four or five feet above the
topmost rocks of our footing and perhaps ten feet above the
raging river. This was the best we could do at the moment,
and we felt rather confident that the river would not rise to

them. However, we intended to keep watch through the night.

While this boat-lifting was going on—or a bit earlier, before it was really dark—Powell discovered an adjoining alcove, where, about thirty feet above the river, there was a considerable area of broken rocks on which we could camp. To reach the place, we were forced to walk very carefully along a narrow shelf on the down side of our alcove, turn the point about twenty feet above the surging waters, roaring below with a speed of not less than twenty miles an hour, and by another narrow ledge, or shelf, gain the camping-place. Distinctly I remember climbing around that point, the way so narrow that one had to flatten himself against the wall to avoid slipping off. We did it frequently in the dark.

Although we carried all the cooking outfit and our blankets around that risky place, we did not think much about the danger at the time, yet, if one had dropped, he would never have been seen again.

With some driftwood and dead mesquite, Andy managed to cook supper. The coffee, as usual under such conditions, was a real godsend; it is superior to anything else as a stimulant, as there is no reaction. Alcohol, of course, must be avoided. We had none with us, except a small quantity in the photographic outfit.

We slept as well as we could on the rocks. There were no level spots. My own bed was with my knees over one rock and my back against another.

Dawn straggled down from on high. It was a gloomy morning. The black granite was wet with the falling rain and was more dismal than ever before. The clouds hung low like a roof to the gorge. The great rapid roared louder. It surely was a trap we were in. How to get out was the question. Andy succeeded in getting some breakfast, which we ate quickly. Then everything was portaged around the point to the friendly shelf where our goods were reposing safely. The boats were hanging against the cliff. The river had remained about the same as when darkness fell. There was a patch of rocks above water. The backwash dashed in against them furiously. The river shot past the mouth of the alcove even more tempestuously, twenty to twenty-five miles an hour.

The boats were carefully lowered and put in the water. They bounced around like wild bronchos, although one man strained his utmost on each to hold it off the rocks. The goods were passed down from the shelf and we prepared to load the *Emma Dean* quickly and pull out. Then we discovered that a stream of water was shooting into the middle cabin. The hole had either been overlooked or was a fresh one. To stop to repair her now might mean another night in the trap—or worse. Rain was falling, which meant higher water.

The Major hesitated a moment; then, with quick judgment, he said, "By God! we'll start—load up!" Rapidly the goods were thrown into the compartments with a sack of flour jammed against the leak, supported by other sacks; the hatches were fastened in place, rifles thrown into the bottom of the cockpits, which already had sand and water in them, and we jumped to our oars, Hillers at the stroke, I at the bow, Jones with a useless, long steering oar and the Major in his chair on the middle cabin-deck. At the lower side of the alcove, projecting out into the current of the rapid, was an enormous rock, against the end of which the river beat with determined fury.

Would we be swept against this rock and smashed, was the question. To help us avoid this and gauge his own action, Thompson, in command of the second boat, with his crew held our boat till our bow swung out into the river, when they gave us the signal prearranged. Hillers and I pulled with all our power. The rock was about fifty feet below, but we cleared it sufficiently and dashed out into the main current. Down we shot with great speed, the gunwale of our boat being barely an inch out of the water. I feared she would sink under us. As soon as we discovered a landing place on the right, a narrow talus, we ran in and pulled the boat out.

The other boat was delayed by the necessity of cutting down a large spare oar to rowing size, one oar having been lost. When the oar was ready, two held the boat from pounding, while the third bailed out. Thompson then climbed in at the stern. At that moment Andy, the other man on the rocks, was pulled off his feet but managed to climb aboard while the *Cañonita* swept down to the big rock.

On the Colorado one never can be sure of what will happen next. By all the rules of navigation on any other river, the boat should have hit the great rock. It did nothing of the kind, but, like a wild broncho, charged up the river some twenty-five feet. The crew quickly turned the bow into the main stream and, with a couple of swift strokes, cleared the menacing rock, bounding down to us over the long waves like a hunted deer.

We unloaded the *Emma Dean* and pulled her up on the rocks to complete the repairs.

One night in the Grand Canyon was behind us.

THIN ICE

W. Elmer Ekblaw

Now professor of geography in the graduate school of Clark University, editor of *The Home Geographic Monthly* and assistant editor of *Economic Geography*, Dr. Ekblaw won his spurs by four years of arduous work in the field (1913-1917) as geologist and botanist of the Crocker Land Arctic Expedition, under the leadership of Donald B. MacMillan. During that time he lived among the polar Eskimo of Thule, the incident here recounted being one of the many that befell him in that inhospitable region.

He has written many scientific books and articles, but this stirring story is his first venture in the narrative field. It should not be his last.

THIN ICE

By W. Elmer Ekblaw

N O USE. THE ICE IS TOO YOUNG AND THIN. WE CAN'T make it." And to prove his point, Mene dropped the head of his killing-iron ever so gently on the dark, frost-free ice and it broke through.

"But it's our only chance. We can't possibly get to the shore on either side and the storm is coming fast. The snow drifts higher and higher, the wind blows harder and harder. We have to try it; we have no other way. We can only hope that the lead isn't wide and the ice will hold." Even as he spoke, Sechmann drew his dogs back from the lead to give them a running start.

I had taken no part in the terse argument. I was a novice at sledging; they, two veterans of the trail. Mene, an Eskimo boy, reared and educated in the States, had lived the life of an Eskimo hunter ever since Peary had brought him back to Thule years before. Sechmann, a South Greenland half-breed in the employ of Knud Rasmussen's trading station, had driven dogs over the treacherous ice of Disko Fjord since boyhood. Both were skilled dog drivers, wise in the ways of the arctic trail and survivors of many a perilous adventure. Whatever my own feeling, I must follow their judgment, accept their decision.

We faced our finish. Before us lay a stretch of dark, young, thin ice, of which we could not judge the width; behind us, where we had been hunting, a southwest storm was breaking up the winter's ice and tossing it out to sea. The shore lay fifteen or twenty miles away on either side. Our chances were slim in any direction. Every minute was precious, whatever the decision. The moment Sechmann made the choice, Mene fell in with it and, without a further word among us, we all three moved to our positions.

. . . . .

The ice rarely lies long about the outermost promontories of Thule, as the Danes have designated that part of Northwest Greenland which is the home of the Polar Eskimo. Only once or twice in a generation, perhaps, does ice freeze in the tide-swept currents along Cape Alexander and permit sledging about the point. At Cape Parry, farther south at the mouth of Inglefield Gulf, it forms more frequently, but rarely lies long and is always treacherous. At Cape Atholl, along the southern shore of Wolstenholme Sound, it persists more tenaciously but is always undercut by the tides and currents between the mainland and Wolstenholme Island.

When the spring tides surge along the coast, the ice breaks out rapidly around these rocky promontories and open water forces the traveling Eskimo to the ice-foot along the cliffs or over the glaciers across the rugged plateau back of the promontories. The inner fjords and bays lie calm and solidly frozen long after the open seas thunder on the rocky headlands. In the early open water about the headlands, abundant game first appears for the spring hunting. Then the Eskimo hunters comb the treacherous edge of the ice for seal, or walrus, or narwhal, in the hope of making a kill to replenish their depleted larders.

Spring had come to Thule. The daily temperatures still sank below freezing, but the daily sunlight approached the twenty-four hour maximum. In the sunlit niches among the rocks, the snow was fast evaporating. Every day the open

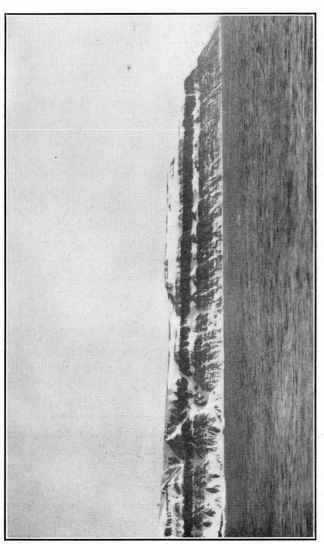

"The ice rarely lies long about the outermost promontories of Thule."

"When the spring tides surge along the coast, the ice
breaks out rapidly."

water was breaking in toward the land. The spring hunting was on. At the first opportunity, Mene, Sechmann and I had set out from North Star Bay for a hunting trip at Cape Parry.

When we arrived, we found other hunters already rendezvoused there, comfortably quartered in snow houses along the shore and well stocked with walrus and seal that they had killed. We stayed with them three days and then started back toward North Star Bay, hunting along the edge of the ice as we sledged southward toward Saunders Island in the mouth of Wolstenholme Sound.

Halfway between Beechwood Point and the northern point of Saunders Island, but well out to sea, we came upon a deep re-entrant of the open water, where a large herd of walrus were disporting themselves along the edge of a patch of hummocky old ice—an irresistible lure for Mene and Sechmann, who would not go on without a try at this game. By a stroke of good fortune all too infrequent in an Eskimo hunter's experience, Mene sank his harpoon at the first cast deep into the flank of a big cow walrus that swam up to the low berg behind which he had stalked the herd.

In due time we "landed" the huge carcass, cut it up on the ice and, after feeding the dogs all they could eat, set up our tent and made ready to turn in for a sleep, while the dogs settled the meal they had eaten. It was well after midnight. The sun had hardly set. In the soft night light, the pale moon swung high in the sky, almost invisible. Flocks of fulmars, guillemots and eiders, but lately returned to the north, winged their ways still farther northward. The sky was well-nigh cloudless, the water rippled calm and dark before our tent and the ice toward the land gleamed solid and white as far as we could see.

Yet Sechmann shook his head and seemed uneasy—the sky in the south did not please him. Mene and I could detect nothing dubious and made light of his fears. Tired as he was, Sechmann got into his sleeping-bag reluctantly and, while Mene and I made the most of the chance to rest, he kept restless vigil.

.   .   .   .   .

Early forenoon came. The sun had risen well into the sky when Sechmann called us urgently. We turned out at once. A gray glare hung in the sky over the open water seaward and gusts of eddying winds swirled the loose snow about. The dogs were stirring uneasily. Not a bird was in sight on the water or in the air.

But it was none of these signs that had alarmed Sechmann enough to call us; he directed our attention to a long, wraith-like horizontal pennant of cloud flung out like a weather-vane from the tip of a lone monadnock rising high above the plateau back of North Star Bay. To the Polar Eskimo, this pennant of cloud is a dread warning of the approach of a violent southerly gale and storm that will carry the ice out to sea. The moment Mene, who knew full well its grave import, saw this, he excitedly yelled to us to waste not a single moment in getting away.

We untied our dogs and hitched them to the sledges in less time than it takes to tell. We left our tent, our sleeping-bags, our heap of walrus meat and, with our whips snapping in angry staccato, raced away as fast as our well fed dogs could carry us. We headed straight for North Star Bay, dodging the patches of rough ice as best we could, straining our eyes for the smoothest going ahead, running behind our sledges to lighten the loads for the dogs. The dogs sensed the alarm we felt. As the wind strengthened and the snow sifting before it rose higher and struck harder, they increased their speed rather than slowed down.

For an hour or more we raced along, hardly calling a word to one another—Mene, with the biggest and best dogs, in the lead; Sechmann, with poorer dogs but a better driver, close behind Mene's sledge; and I close behind Sechmann, merely because my dogs would not let the others get away.

And then came the crisis.

Spread black and threatening before us, a dark lead of new, thin ice stretched across the whole sound. How wide it was, we could not see in the haze of wind-driven snow. How thin it was, we could readily see, as our killing-irons broke through it of their own weight. How far it extended, we could only guess, but probably it reached from shore to shore.

During our absence the ice had parted under the urge of the ebbing spring tide and had drifted seaward. The water had frozen again over the lead, but only a thin film of ice had formed—so recently that no frost had yet whitened it. There it lay, barring our way, a dark, treacherous band that we had to cross. We could not tarry a moment, for not far behind us the storm was rolling in, a dark mass of tumbling cloud and wind-tossed snow.

As Sechmann drew his dogs back from the lead for a good running start, Mene moved along the lead a half hundred yards and drew back a little farther than Sechmann had done and I took my position still farther along the lead and still farther back; for, as Sechmann explained, we must not strike the ice at the same time or near together.

As Mene and I held our dogs back to give Sechmann a chance to get started, we waved to each other but neither spoke a word—our feelings were too tense. As Sechmann's dogs struck out across the thin ice, they spread wide apart in the line; low and swift, with feet wide-spread, they ran; astride and well back on his sledge, Sechmann cracked his whip fast and furiously, encouraging but not striking his dogs. It was easy to see that they realized as well as he the danger they faced. Beneath the runners of his sledge, the yielding ice bent down; it rose in a wave-like fold before and behind.

Almost before Sechmann's dogs had got well out on the thin ice, Mene's team was on its way toward the edge. As his sledge struck the dark band, I saw, as I had not seen with Sechmann's sledge, that, while the rounded front part of the runners was holding up on the ice as the dogs sped along, the sharp, square corners at the back were cutting through and little jets of water were spraying up on either side of the runner. The runners were actually cutting two narrow lanes through the ice.

My own dogs had already dashed forward and, as my sledge neared the black, thin ice, I dared hardly hope that it would hold me, for I weighed at least fifty pounds more than either Mene or Sechmann. But my runners were shod a quarter-inch wider and, though the ice bent deep under the sledge, this extra width carried my greater weight. My dogs were doing their best to keep pace with Mene's and Sechmann's, so I had no need of using my whip.

With my heart in my mouth, scarcely daring to breathe, I sat rigid, watching the water spraying out from the sides of both runners; at times half the runners were cutting through. If a dog had stumbled, or bumped into another, to slow the sledge a moment, we should have dropped through. But not a dog faltered; every one knew as well as I what would happen if he did. Never had my team made such speed. The first moments were the most perilous. The young ice was thin, but it was also smooth as glass and we gathered momentum as we raced on; yet, even so, the minutes seemed hours. The lead proved to be over half a mile wide and it seemed an age before we got across.

As he struck the solid ice, Sechmann gave a wild yell of relief; Mene gave another as he achieved it a moment later;

but, until I had taken a breath or two, I could not even whisper. To them, particularly to Sechmann, who came from the hazardous ice of the Disko region, it was an old, oft-repeated adventure; to me—well, I vowed it was my last hazard over such thin ice!

We could not take time to greet each other and congratulate ourselves on the safe outcome of our decision. The storm still raged and there might be other such leads ahead. We could lose no time. We drove relentlessly on through the gathering blizzard and finally made shore just within Cape Abernathy. There we built a snow shelter and stayed till the storm swept by.

AT CLOSE QUARTERS WITH A POLAR BEAR

Anthony Fiala

Before becoming the outfitter of explorers *par excellence,* Major Fiala saw much active service in widely separated fields: first as photographer of the Baldwin-Ziegler Polar Expedition, 1901-1902; then as leader of the Fiala-Ziegler Expedition, 1903-1905, which, although its ship was lost, explored and mapped a large area in the Franz Josef archipelago; later in Brazil with Theodore Roosevelt on his River of Doubt expedition, in charge of the equipment, and on independent exploration of the Papagaio, Juruena and Tapajoz rivers.

His books on exploration are *Fighting the Polar Ice* and *Scientific Results of the Ziegler Expedition.*

AT CLOSE QUARTERS WITH A POLAR BEAR

By Anthony Fiala

ON OUR EXPEDITION SHIP WE HAD A NUMBER OF OLD Henry rifles of a caliber .45/90. The bullets were copper-capped and paper-patched and the cartridges were made of very thin sheet brass, wound in diagonal strips and quite delicate to the touch. We also had some .45/70 Springfields and an assortment of Marlins and Winchesters in calibers .30/30, .303 and .45. For our sled party I had provided 8 mm. Mannlicher carbines; these, of course, were the most effective weapons of our equipment.

I had an experience with the 8 mm. which I would not care to have again. I had given instructions to the expedition that no bears were to be killed unless we needed them for food. On one occasion when we needed bear meat, I happened to be out walking about a thousand yards from our hut, watching the motion of the ice fields off the west coast of Crown Prince Rudolf Land, where we had lost our ship. Looking down into the bay, I noticed one of our men, Sergeant Long, taking a tide observation in the ice crack where the ice of the sea met the shore ice. A couple of hundred yards from where he was in the rough ice, I noticed an enormous polar bear approaching him. As I was unarmed, I did not waste any time, but ran into the hut, seized the 8 mm. Mannlicher and two clips of ammunition and ran as fast as I could toward Sergeant Long. When I reached him, I told him to go to the hut, as a bear was stalking him. He thanked me and moved off.

I looked for the bear, but could not see him, even when I searched for him from the highest point of ice. I knew then that he was sneaking along somewhere and it occurred to me that it would be unnecessary work to look for him and that, if I would find a big cake of ice and lie on that, he would undoubtedly come and try to get me. Besides, it would be very difficult to haul him in from the rough ice after he was shot, while on one of the large cakes of ice near shore, it would be a simple matter to haul the carcass to our hut.

I put myself down into the center of a cake of ice about two hundred feet square and made out that I was a seal by bobbing my head up and down, lying down as if asleep every once in a while and then kicking my feet to imitate the tail of a seal.

The temperature was at least forty-five degrees below zero and, lying on the ice cake in feigned sleep, I was becoming rather anxious for Mr. Bear to come. I flopped around every once in a while, as it would be rather embarrassing if he came from behind while I was looking out toward the sea.

Once, just as I put my head down again to simulate sleep—with my eyes open, of course—I saw to the left, where an enormous piece of ice went up toward the sky, the tip of a big, hairy paw. I kept very quiet and then the entire paw and a black nose and two black eyes came in sight. I remember they looked like the eyes of a fiend. I kept quiet in spite of the cold and then, with a spring, an enormous bear jumped with all four feet on the cake of ice.

I had loaded my rifle just before lying down on the ice and all I had to do was to jump up, raise it, aim at that big head and pull the trigger. The bear was only about seventy-five feet away from me and so I expected to have him drop in his tracks with the bullet through his brain. Instead of the crack of the gun, however, there was just a little sucking noise and, to my horror, the firing-pin simply struck the cartridge with a gentle tap.

Despite the below-zero temperature, the perspiration started to run down my face as I realized that my gun was useless. Some time before, I had instructed one of the sailors to clean the Mannlichers and remove all the oil from the firing-pins and locks, but he must have left some oil on the firing-pin of this gun.

I passed the gun to my left hand and drew my knife. I looked at the five-inch blade and then at that big beast coming toward me, and put the knife back in its sheath. I knew that, if I retreated an inch, it would be my end, so I advanced on the beast, called him all sorts of names as loud as I could and told him to move off the cake of ice. To my joy, he stood still in his tracks and observed me, hissing like an enormous snake. He was mad all the way through, but somehow or other lacked the courage to charge.

I took advantage of this and tried to make him feel that I was going to jump on him and bury my teeth in his neck.

It occurred to me that possibly I could get the gun to work by warming the bolt with friction. While talking to the bear and telling him what sort of a fool he was and what I was going to do with him, I rubbed the bolt back and forth, losing some cartridges that way, for I was so intent on watching the bear and talking to him that sometimes I pulled the bolt all the way back and, of course, flipped the cartridge out. It was a difficult thing to watch the bear and the gun at the same time and so, when my five cartridges were gone, I put in another clip, which was my last, and drove the first cartridge in that clip with all my might, as I was getting a little mad at that old bear.

In spite of my scathing remarks and threatenings, the big beast came slowly toward me and now we were only fifteen or eighteen feet apart. I had put the rifle to my shoulder a number of times with only that sickening misfire when I pulled the trigger. As I put the rifle up this time and pulled the trigger, there was a snapping explosion and, though I missed the bear, not having expected the rifle to go off, the powder undoubtedly filled his face, as he went head over heels backward.

When I saw him again, he was running like a jack-rabbit, fully two hundred and fifty yards away. I aimed at his nose and hit him in the hind-quarters and then worked my way slowly through the rough ice to where he was and ended his troubles with a bullet through his brain.

On coming back to the hut, I found that the sailor who had cleaned the rifles—a very thorough man, by the way—after cleaning all the guns from the barrel to the lock, as I had explained, thought it was absolutely necessary to put a thin rubbing of oil on the firing-pin, because it had always been required in the naval service of which he had been a member.

IN THE LAND OF THE YAQUIS

Harry L. Foster

A vagabond by nature and a writer by profession, Harry L. Foster has known where to go for unique adventure and how to write about it afterward in a successful series of travel books: *The Adventures of a Tropical Tramp; A Beachcomber in the Orient; A Gringo in Mañana-Land; A Tropical Tramp with the Tourists; A Vagabond in Fiji; The Caribbean Cruise; If You Go to South America; Combing the Caribbees; A Vagabond in Barbary.*

IN THE LAND OF THE YAQUIS

By Harry L. Foster

L UCK, ACCORDING TO TRADITION, IS APT TO FAVOR THE beginner at cards. Similarly, on occasion, it appears to bless the novice who sets out to roam the world in search of strange adventures.

Though, to confess the truth, when the experience which I am about to relate first started, I was scarcely seeking an adventure of my own. I was sitting on a hitching-post in front of an adobe hotel at La Colorada, in the Mexican state of Sonora, with another free-lance newspaper man. We were both in search of thrills, but we were availing ourselves of the newspaper man's prerogative to obtain them vicariously, by pumping someone else.

We were quizzing old John Luy, who earned his livelihood by driving a battered Ford truck across the desert to mining towns farther in the interior and who attributed his deafness to having listened to so many bandit volleys.

"How does it feel," asked Curtis, "to ride through this Yaqui Indian country on a truckload of dynamite?"

"Heh?"

"I said," and he raised his voice to a shout, "just what are your sensations when you're traveling through the brush, where somebody's likely at any minute to take a pot shot at you from the cactus?"

John puffed reflectively at his pipe. He glanced at the semi-circle of hard-boiled American mining men who had

99

gathered to listen—khaki-clad, flannel-shirted fellows who might recently have stepped from the pages of some tale of the old, wild, woolly West.

"Now just look here," he suddenly exclaimed. "In five minutes I'm pulling out on one of my trips. I'm running a nice big load of dynamite out to MacFarlane, whose diggings are right in the middle of the Yaqui country. If you're so anxious to know how it feels, why don't you come along?"

Now personally, Curtis and I considered ourselves fairly adventuresome in having penetrated even this far from the beaten track of the average traveler. La Colorada was forty miles from the nearest railway. And just at that time—it was in 1920, during the last days of the Carranza régime—anyone who wandered even that far from the federal-patrolled highways must rely on his own six-shooter for protection from the Indians.

The Yaquis, at the moment, were reputed to be on a rampage—and Yaquis, when unfriendly, were notoriously "bad *hombres*." From time to time in the past, groups of them had made their peace with certain leaders; they had fought in the armies of Villa or Obregon; some of them were serving at the time in the forces of Carranza. Yet most of them, up to 1920, had preferred to remain in their own mountain fastnesses, refusing, as their forefathers had refused since the days of the Spanish conquest, to acknowledge the authority of any Mexican government. They tolerated the American miners—usually upon payment of tribute. But just two days before our arrival, a party of local bandits, presumably Yaquis, had ambushed and shot an American truck-driver and his assistant, employees of a company which considered itself immune from their attacks. And this on the very outskirts of La Colorada itself.

Both Curtis and I, complete novices in the business of

Ready to Start

Yaqui Indian in Dance Costume

adventure, heard John Luy's suggestion without enthusiasm. But the knot of miners nodded their approval.

"You said it, John!" The speaker was a raw-boned youth, Kelly by name, who wore a revolver as large as a cannon and swaggered in unconscious imitation of Bill Hart. "These birds get my goat, sitting around here, asking other guys a lot of fool questions." He turned to us. "So how about it? Are you game, or ain't you?"

We had no alternative. The reputation of the journalistic profession was at stake.

"Sure," we answered in unison. And five minutes later we were on our way.

.   .   .   .   .

There were two trucks in the expedition. They were laden high with crates of provisions, machinery and blasting powder, and atop each load sat a squad of hired Mexican gunmen, each with several yards of cartridge belt draped around his waist and crisscrossed over his shoulders.

John drove one truck. MacFarlane, a tall and ruggedly built engineer, drove the other. He welcomed our company.

"Two extra guns always help," he explained. "This guard goes only half way with us. After that we change to mule-back, and we'll be entirely on our own."

The trail we followed across the desert was nothing more than the track of the automobiles which had made the journey before us. Sometimes we traversed an empty expanse of dull, brown sand; sometimes we ran through scrubby forests of thorn bush and cacti. When in the open, our gunmen laughed and talked; when we approached the thickets, they fell silent and gripped their rifles.

From time to time we passed a heap of stones surmounted by a crude wooden cross.

"This," explained Luy, "is where some poor devil got his."

Occasionally, too, we came to an abrupt *arroyo*, a groove in the desert cut by some river which had long ago vanished, leaving only a deposit of soft sand. In one such bed we finally stuck fast and, while the gunmen from the other car stood guard over us, our own Mexicans struggled to extricate us.

"It was in a place just like this that White and García were ambushed two days ago," explained our mentor. "They come around a bend and hit the waterhole and was plowing through it when a dozen Mausers blazed out of the mesquite. Three bullets got White squarely in the head. Maybe García got it on the first volley, too. But you couldn't be sure. When the fellows found him, the Yaquis had chopped him up and stuck sharp sticks into him until his own mother couldn't 've recognized him. Dig the sand away from that other wheel, will you?"

At rare intervals we passed a native village, a cluster of mud hovels surrounding an aged Spanish church, and our passing was an event. A host of mongrel dogs but slightly removed from the coyote stage hailed us with furious yelps. Children raced barefoot beside the trucks to get a better view of us. Half-naked Indian women, pounding clothes on the flat rocks beside a shallow brook, ceased their work to stare. Even the adult male population, reclining against the shady side of the low adobe hovels, sat up to look at us.

These natives showed little Spanish ancestry. Their features were purely Indian. A few, by their prominent cheekbones and dark complexion, suggested a trace of Yaqui blood, yet most of them were of other tribes, and all carried arms as precaution against Yaqui raids. In an open-air barber shop which we passed, the barber wore a

six-shooter and a machete as he shaved a patron who like-
wise had a rifle across his knees. Many of them greeted us
with the question, "Did you meet any Yaquis?"

The day passed without incident and nightfall brought
us to our first stopping-place, the village of Matape.

. . . . . .

In the morning, our numbers reduced to five, we continued the trip on mule-back by a trail which led through
narrow ravines, down sandy embankments where the animals bunched their feet together and literally slid, along
deep and shadowy cañons strewn with giant boulders, up
sharp inclines, along narrow ledges where a misstep meant
a plunge into eternity.

It was a desolate region, yet awesome in its ugly
grandeur. Mountains reared themselves aloft, their lower
slopes grown with huge candelabra cactus, their higher
peaks towering in battlements of naked rock. Just as a second night descended upon us, we emerged into the valley
of the Moctezuma, its broad, shallow river curling like a
silver ribbon among the purple shadows of the hills.

Here we found another mud village, Suaqui de Batuc,
a hamlet so picturesque that on the following morning I
sallied forth with my camera.

"Be careful," warned MacFarlane. "And ask permission
before you snap a native. These Indians still have a few
superstitions about photography. They think you're stealing their soul, or something, and that, if anything happens
to the picture, something may happen to them."

I took the precaution, but invariably, when asked to
pose, the local natives said "No." The more picturesque
they were, the more resolutely they said it. At length, well
out beyond the edge of town, I came upon a picture which
I could scarcely resist. It was an aged squaw, filling deerskin water sacks in the center of the river and loading them

upon the backs of a pair of diminutive burros. The moment I unslung my camera, however, she started wading cautiously upstream. To get the sun at my back I must overtake and pass her. But the faster I walked, the faster she did. When I broke into a trot, she broke into a gallop, gathering her skirts about her waist and sprinting like a terrified rabbit through the shallow water.

From the village behind me there suddenly arose a chorus of war-whoops. Glancing back, I beheld some forty or fifty natives in hot pursuit, brandishing an assortment of knives and firearms which might have delighted a curio-collector. And behind them, apparently bent on rescue, came Curtis and MacFarlane, waving their revolvers. I was presently surrounded by a gesticulating mob, with whom the mine boss was arguing in vociferous Spanish, apparently in my behalf.

"They seem to have misjudged your intentions," he finally explained. "But everything's O.K. now. You can even take her picture, if you want to. Her husband here—this old geezer with the whiskers—says he doesn't care what happens to her."

But the squaw had already gathered up her skirts again and was rapidly vanishing, still dragging the two burros behind her.

. . . . . .

It was but a few hours' ride from Suaqui to *El Progreso* mine, a group of gaping shafts beside a stone blockhouse, with a village of thatched quarters for the workmen close by.

In the past it had escaped molestation from the Yaquis, but at the moment of our arrival armed guards stood at each corner of the blockhouse, their eyes fixed on the circle of mountain peaks that hemmed in the bowl-shaped valley. From the half-dozen American bosses with whom we lunched, we learned that a party of Indians had just raided a mine in the vicinity.

"But the *Gavilan* buys protection, same as we do!" protested MacFarlane. "Are you sure about the news?"

"Yeh," grinned another engineer. "But it didn't keep the Yaquis from looting the place. They didn't hurt the white men, but they stripped 'em of everything except their coats. That's how we heard about it. Jones sent over to see if he couldn't borrow some trousers from us. Said he had fourteen coats and not a pair of pants."

"And it didn't keep the Yaquis from shooting up White and García," added a third miner. "Their outfit had an understanding with the Indians, too."

"There's something mighty funny about it," persisted MacFarlane. "I never knew a Yaqui to go back on his word before. But just the same, I'd better head back to Hermosillo tonight and get the *jefe político* to send out some federal troops."

"They won't be any good. Half the *federalistas* are quitting the government right now and turning bandits themselves."

Nevertheless, MacFarlane planned an immediate departure, and late afternoon found us again in the saddle, recrossing the mountain trail.

"It's going to mean a hard ride," he explained, "but it's usually safer in the dark. The Yaquis are superstitious about the crosses along the trail. The ghosts of the murdered are supposed to be out for revenge at night, so we're less apt to meet the living."

For an instant, as we passed Suaqui, the sunset painted the mountain peaks a magic crimson. Then the swift dusk of the desert was upon us and in the deep fastnesses of the cañon the air grew strangely chill.

Perhaps the mule could see the pass. I myself could see

nothing, except occasionally the shadowy outline of the rider ahead, looming abnormally large against the sky. Then he would disappear, as though he had entered a tunnel, and only the crunching of gravel under his animal's hoofs told whither he had vanished.

When at times a faint moonlight seeped down into the pass, it merely converted each cactus into the semblance of a crouching Yaqui. And despite MacFarlane's assertions regarding the safety of night travel, neither he nor the others were taking any chances. The howl of a coyote or the cooing of a dove brought every revolver from its holster, for even these noises, so common in the mountains, might be an Indian signal. Once, when something trailed us for half a mile through the brush, we all rode half-turned in the saddle. Quite possibly it was merely a mountain lion, following us from idle curiosity, yet we covered it whenever it betrayed its whereabouts by the crackling of the brush.

In the years which have passed since that ride, I have found myself in many strange places and occasionally in trying situations, yet I can recall nothing more trying than that journey through the black defiles of the Sonoran hills.

For hour after hour we rode in silence through an inky void. The nervous strain seemed to affect even the taciturn mules. When we paused at a mountain stream to water them, my own beast suddenly lashed at me with his heels and bolted, and I was obliged to pursue him up the ragged bed of the watercourse, stumbling blindly over slippery stones and splashing into pools, creating sufficient racket —or so it seemed to me—to awaken any Yaqui within a mile.

And then, within much less than a mile, we turned a bend and found ourselves in the very center of an encampment! A score of campfires, dwindled to smouldering red ashes, lined the trail and about each of them men were sleeping, spread out like the spokes of a wheel, with their feet toward the blaze, in the fashion of the Yaquis. Apparently they had posted no sentries, for we were among them even as we recognized their presence and my mule was actually stepping over their recumbent figures.

One of the men awoke, yawned and raised himself upon an elbow to stare at us.

"¿ Quién es?"

"Friends," responded MacFarlane. "Who are you?"

"Federal soldiers," the voice muttered, sleepily. And the man composed himself for another nap.

.   .   .   .   .

We rode into Matape at dawn, and John Luy's truck carried us back to La Colorada. John himself was chuckling.

"It's funny," he explained.

"What's funny?"

"How you rode straight through the Yaquis' own camp last night."

"But I thought they were Federal soldiers."

"They was. They was some of the Yaquis who had been *federalistas*. Only we been learning a few new things since you rode in to the mine. It seems these *federalistas*, when the government couldn't pay 'em, just quit and turned bandit, like a lot of others before them. It was that gang 't raided the *Gavilan* and the same bunch that shot White and García. It's lucky for you they were sleepy last night when your mules were stepping over them."

THE FIRE-DOG OF ASU

Lewis R. Freeman

Athlete, writer, explorer and correspondent in the Russo-Japanese War and the World War, Lewis R. Freeman has already at middle life had enough adventure to satisfy two ordinary mortals.

Running a scow down the White Horse Rapids, at the time of the Klondyke gold rush, aroused a special fondness for boating that has since led him to navigate the principal rivers of North America and many in foreign lands, visit the six continents and sail the seven seas.

Of the sixteen books that have come from his facile pen, ten deal with these extended wanderings: *In the Tracks of the Trades; Down the Columbia; Down the Yellowstone; The Colorado River—Yesterday, Today and Tomorrow; Down the Grand Canyon; On the Roof of the Rockies; By Water Ways to Gotham; Waterways of Westward Wandering; The Nearing North.*

THE FIRE-DOG OF ASU

By Lewis R. Freeman

As WE CAME OUT ON THE OPEN VERANDA FROM THE dinner table, the gold and orange banners of gorgeous sunset had flickered out in the west and the gray gauze of the tropical twilight was thickening into the soft velvet of night. The bay was piling full of purple shadows, through which the foam spurts and patches along the rocky windward wall glowed with increasing luminosity as the darkness deepened and the heavy swells of the Pacific, plunging against the cliffs, signalled their despair with ghostly rockets and bonfires of phosphorescence.

Overhead, save for a few squadrons of hurriedly marching trade clouds, the heavens were clear and, where the sky above the eastern valley wall was lightening before the rising moon, the transient silhouettes of flocks of flying-foxes, dark and spectral in their noiseless flights, flashed and disappeared. Inland, the throaty croak of the wood-pigeon boomed at intervals in the fathomless blackness; above, the lisp of the leaves of the coconut and banana blended to the rustling of crisp silk; seaward, awakening a mile of mellow music, the fingers of Neptune ran up and down the reef's ever responsive keys of coral.

We had come since morning—the Judge,* the Lieutenant and I—all the way from the naval station at Pago-

---

* Judge E. W. Gurr, for many years Robert Louis Stevenson's friend and lawyer in Apia, later Judge of the American naval station at Tutuila.

III

Pago, toiling up through the sweat-box of bush at the end
of the great bay to the lofty wind-fanned summit, dropping
again to sea level at Fauga-sa, and from there running down
with a fair wind to Mala-toa in the Judge's *malaga*. On the
way we had put in at the village of Asu, on Massacre Bay,
for a glimpse of the monument erected by the French in
commemoration of their countrymen who figured in the
event which gave the cove its sinister name. Singularly impressive it was, that plain little tablet of bronze set in a
base of hewn coral, and eloquent in their simple appeal
were the words graven thereon.

MORTS POUR LA SCIENCE
ET LA PATRIE
LE 11 DECEMBRE, 1787

Below were the names and the ranks of those who had
fallen—nothing else.

The Judge told us in brief outline the story, whilst we
sipped our coffee and watched the moon come up.

The *Boussole* and *Astrolabe,* fitted out by the French
government to search for the Northwest Passage, after failing in their original object and cruising for some months
on the eastern coast of Asia, extended their voyage of exploration to the South Pacific. In December of 1787 they
anchored off the leeward coast of Tutuila, one of the
Samoas, to be most kindly received by natives as friendly
and hospitable then as they are today. Dances and feasts
were arranged for the visitors whenever they landed, no
unpleasantness of any description occurring until just before the ships were ready to sail.

At that time a large party, headed by Vte. de Langle of
the *Astrolabe* and De Lamanon of the *Boussole,* head natu-
ralist of the expedition, landed at Asu with the intention

of inducing some of the natives to accompany them back to France. Failing to accomplish their object by persuasion, an attempt was made to carry off a half-dozen or more of the villagers by force, the ill-advised Frenchmen foolishly imagining that the easy-going, light-hearted Samoans would lack the courage to oppose their high-handed and inhuman plan.

The little bronze tablet tells most of the rest of the story. "For Science and for Country," De Langle and De Lamanon were killed, while the rest of the party saved their lives only by putting off in the boats and abandoning the bodies of their comrades. With the spread of the news to the surrounding villages, the natives gathered in such numbers that the warships were forced to sail without venturing another landing. After some further months of voyaging, both *Astrolabe* and *Boussole* were lost with all hands by being driven ashore in a hurricane on a small island to the north of the New Hebrides.

· · · · ·

That was about all the story, said the Judge, except that the natives told of a big dog that was with the landing party, which, after fighting desperately for the lives of its masters, made off into the hills, bleeding from many spear thrusts. Closely pressed, the great animal, after turning many times and scattering by savage charges the horde of warriors that pursued him, finally rushed to the brink of a lofty cliff and threw himself off into space. The natives heard the thud of his body striking the rocks below and fled back to Asu, holding their ears to shut out his dying roars.

Some time later a native, journeying by land from Asu to the next village, failed to return. His friends trailed his footprints to the heart of the deep valley at the foot of the cliff and, while endeavoring to account for their sud-

den disappearance, were confronted with an apparition
so terrible that, though they escaped it and reached Asu
alive, the blood in their veins turned to water from fright
and they were ever after as little children. Their babble
till they died was of a great blood-red dog, as big as a wild
bullock, which held the body of their friend crosswise in
its mouth, as a pelican holds a fish too big to gulp. The
valley immediately became *tabu,* none venturing there
even in times of famine, when its great groves of coconuts,
bananas and breadfruit and its beds of yam and taro, might
have prevented actual starvation.

The dog, or his ghost, grew larger and fiercer with the
years and his color changed—probably through some dis-
pensation of the devil, the natives thought—from red to
that of smouldering fire. He was never actually seen carrying off another man, but all disappearances from the village, and in time even sickness and failure of crops and
ill-luck in fishing came to be laid at his door. Throughout
the Samoas the expression "as bad as the Fire-Dog of Asu"
became the superlative of all that was terrifying and
dreadful.

The Judge set his coffee cup on the arm of his chair
and stepped to the end of the veranda, motioning us to
join him.

"You gentlemen see that black wall over there, with
the shadow from the moon creeping down it?" he asked,
pointing to a towering basaltic barrier that shut off half the
western heavens. "That's the cliff the Dog is supposed to
have jumped over and the farther side of that big grove
of *maupes* is where he landed. And that same dog—or at
least the impression the memory of him has left on the
minds of the natives—is what made it possible for me to buy
this whole valley of Mala-toa for five hundred dollars. He
is also responsible for the fact that I have expended five

times that sum on it without getting back a single cent, even for copra. He is responsible for my coming over here now, when I should be convening court at Pago-Pago, and before morning he (or the fear of him) will be responsible for us all being waked up to let that bunch of big boobies (indicating the Samoans, where they were grouped around their *kava* bowl in the twilight) inside for protection.

"Every time I get a gang well started at clearing and planting," he continued, as we resumed our seats, "the Dog shows himself and work is off for another year. I tried it first with gangs of natives alone, but after these had been frightened away a half-dozen times I was unable to get any to go without a white man. My first white foreman, a hard-bitten Australian whom I picked up in Apia, was getting things opened up in good shape when he was taken with the fever, upon which the natives, declaring that the Dog had set its mark on him, stopped work and left at once.

"The result of my last attempt to keep men here you will probably have heard about at the naval station. A young Virginian named Brent, whose time in the Navy was up and who was anxious to remain in Samoa, was in charge and, according to the weekly reports he was despatching me, doing very well indeed. Then, one morning last July, a half-crazy native was picked up on the beach and brought to Pago-Pago. From his delirious chatter we gathered that the Dog had appeared at Mala-toa and killed Brent and that the natives, fleeing in an overloaded *malaga*, had been upset in the heavy southwester that was blowing and, except himself, all drowned.

"Accompanied by the naval station doctor, I went around at once in the government launch. Brent was indeed dead. With a revolver full of unfired cartridges tightly clenched in his hand, he was lying across the veranda yonder, his face still rigid in the lines of terror that had distorted it when he died. Death was due to heart failure, the doctor said, and recalled that, some months previously, his stethoscope had shown that Brent had an enlarged valve. The immediate cause of the heart failure was violent nervous excitement.

"Of course, the sight of a huge fiery dog such as the natives described might have caused such excitement, but more likely a fight with his unruly gang of natives was at the bottom of it. This would account for the flight of the latter, thought the doctor; probably they were not drowned at all but only in hiding. This had become the generally accepted theory at Pago-Pago, especially since a pack of bloodhounds I brought over from Apia failed to run down anything more terrible than a lot of wild pigs. Still," the Judge concluded, rising to go inside, "no ordinary encounter with a gang of natives can entirely account in my mind for the look that was frozen on poor Brent's face when we found him."

.   .   .   .   .

The Samoans left their fire and brought their *kava* and sleeping-mats up on the veranda as soon as we had left it. After they had kept us awake for a couple of hours by setting up a nervous shuffling and chattering at every unwonted sound from the bush, the Judge, fearing they might take fright and make off with the *malaga,* got up and let them in to sleep on the floor.

The next morning the Judge put his men to work re-clearing for a new setting of cacao trees, while the Lieutenant and I made pigeon shooting an excuse for exploring the valley. It was not until some time after dark that we straggled back to the house, changed from khaki to duck and re-assembled at the dinner table. We had done full justice in turn to turtle soup, red snapper baked in *ti* leaves, and roast sucking pig dressed with the inimitable *miti hari* sauce and were just turning gloating eyes on dishes of that greatest of all delicacies, coconut-sprout salad, when an ear-splitting yell of terror rang out from the bush. An instant later there came the sound of running feet and, before we had risen from the table, the low west window shivered to fragments under the impact of a great brown body which was launched through it and fell, bruised and bleeding, inside the room. In the wake of the first, followed another brown body, while through the doors the rest of the Samoans came trooping, bellowing with fright.

For five minutes none of them was able to say much but *"Oka, Oka; him dogga come!"* When we finally got them quieted down, it was to learn with disgust that two of the boys, Toa and Luka, the ones who had come in through the window, had gone to the stream a hundred yards away for a can of water. While they were filling their can, the Fire-Dog rushed out of the bush and charged them so savagely that they had barely managed to save their lives by jumping through the window. When we found that Toa's and Luka's wounds were all from broken glass and that none of the other boys had seen the Dog in pursuit of them, our first impulse was to drive the whole lot outdoors and finish our dinner. On second consideration we decided the opportunity for investigation was too good to miss.

Accordingly, the Lieutenant and I with revolvers and the Judge with his shotgun, we set off down the water path after vainly endeavoring to force Toa and Luka to show us the way. The moon had not yet risen and the narrow trail, closely walled in with bananas and guava scrub and overarched with intertangling breadfruit-tree branches, lay in inky blackness, save where the darting fireflies laced the air with evanescent wires of gold. Presently, as we emerged from the bush into the clearing along the bank of the stream, we became aware of a spattered line of dull luminosity running at right angles to our line of advance, such a trail as one might leave by scattering broadcast handfuls of glow worms as he walked. I heard the heavy breathing of my companions and was conscious of something like a gasp from myself at the dawning recollection of how the Fire-Dog was always described as leaving behind him a wake of light.

Glancing nervously to right and left, we advanced to examine the spectral spoor. The glowing matter was cold and wet to the touch and emitted enough light for us to discern the indistinct marks of the feet of some animal on the tender grass. The tracks seemed heading inland and in that direction we followed them for a hundred yards or more, only to find that they ultimately looped around and headed back into the original trail just seaward of where we had first encountered it.

Before long a faint glow, such as might have been thrown from a smouldering campfire, was perceptible through the trees ahead and, as we neared the beach, between the sharp, slashing blows of the surf on the shingle, came the confused but unmistakable sounds of coughing, snorting and wallowing, such as a large animal makes when bathing.

Every symptom of complete and unmixed fear that I have ever heard described—dry lips, trembling hands, quaking knees, going hot and cold and turning to goose-flesh —I can distinctly recall experiencing in that last fifty yards to the beach and my companions have since admitted as much respecting their own sensations. The coughing and snorting increased in volume as we advanced and the ghostly light flashed on the cliff in quivering lines of green and blue. These, reflecting, struck faintly through the bush,

revealing to each of us the tense lines of puzzled appre-
hension in the faces of the others.

As we struck out upon a bar of pebbles near the mouth
of the stream and the hard round stones began rattling un-
derfoot, the noises from under the cliff suddenly ceased and
the fluttering waves of light grew dimmer and died low.
The deepening darkness descended and wrapped us like
a pall. In the ominous silence we waited, tense and ready
but undeniably shaken with the grim, unearthly mystery
of it all.

As the uncanny sounds broke forth anew, we pressed
forward again in the shivering light and reached a point
where only a dense clump of pandanus palm shut us off
from the foot of the cliff. Around this we were stealthily
picking our way when a sea shell cracked sharply under
someone's foot and the wallowing ceased again. This time
the heavy, sputtering respirations of a large animal were
distinctly audible.

It may have been only a few seconds that we waited
thus, or it may have been a minute, or two, or three, when
the Lieutenant's patience or his nerves—or both—gave way.
Without a word of warning, he dashed forward, rounded
the clump of pandanus and fired blindly in the direction
of the cliff. The next moment there burst forth a hoarse
snort of rage and the ghostly light flared up again, to show
the young officer, wide-eyed with terror and surprise, staring blankly ahead and discharging his revolver into the
coral clinkers at his feet. An instant later the Judge and I
had sprung out beside him, to recoil in turn before a fearsome and unearthly sight.

In an angle of the cliff, a dozen yards or so back from
the crest of the wave-piled shingle of the beach, was a
glowing pool of liquid fire, dimly luminous for the most
part but bursting forth in spurts and flashes of green and

blue flame where it was churned by the legs of a large animal that was ploughing through it to the bank.

For the beast itself, words fail me. Reeking with fire, snorting fire, scattering fire, it would have seemed terrible enough to an unimpassioned observer watching from a safe vantage at the top of the cliff; the effect of actually standing in the path of its advance, with nerves already racked to the point of giving way, must be left to the imagination.

With a rush and a roar the Thing of Terror gained the bank and charged straight down upon us. The Lieutenant's revolver exhausted itself into the broken coral. My own, unfired, hung loosely on nerveless fingers. But the Judge, who seemed suddenly to have pulled himself together, squared away and discharged both barrels in quick succession almost under the nose of that hurtling Bolt of Wrath. I heard the heavy buckshot grind home through flesh and bone, heard the snorts of anger change to shrill squeals of pain and saw the great gleaming form reel and stagger and tumble forward into a quivering heap at our feet.

For a few moments we peered down at the inert mass, still veined with trickling lines of fire, and stared incredulously at each other as comprehension burst upon us. The Judge was the first to speak.

"Gentlemen," he said, "we have killed a pig! And that pool of 'fire' over there is a 'skim-hole' of phosphorescence, quite the livest and brightest one I have ever seen. We'll see how it formed in the morning. For the present, let us return to our dinner."

The next day we found the "Fire-Dog" still lying where it had fallen. It was of enormous proportions, quite the largest wild boar of which there was any record in Samoa, but must have been almost harmless from the fact that its great tusks had grown back almost into a circle. In the

morning light the glowing pool of the night before presented a surface of dirty brown, but so charged was it with
phosphorescence that it showed faintly luminous streaks on
being stirred with a stick, even when the noon-day sun was
shining directly upon it.

Its existence was due to a hollow behind the pile of
shingle thrown up by the waves on the beach. The animal-
culae which are responsible for the phosphorescence in sea
water, dying at regular intervals and floating on the surface
of the bay in a brown scum, had been washed over into the
hollow at high tide. The lowest level of the hollow chanced
to lie at the foot of the cliff and to here the phosphorescence
had drained, to be left behind as the water drained away
through the porous coral.

Such fish as were occasionally washed over the beach
were also carried to this pool and it was these, no doubt,
which attracted the old boar there to wallow and feed. The
half-dozen sticks of dynamite which the Judge set off in
the cliff to fill up the obnoxious "skim-hole," brought down
a shower of basaltic blocks which piled themselves in a
rude mausoleum above the body of "The Fire-Dog of
Asu."

Robbed of its terror, there was no longer trouble in
keeping native labor at Mala-toa, which soon became a
lucrative copra and cacao plantation. When I last visited
Pago-Pago, in the course of the 1925 Australasian naval
cruise, the Judge had retired and was making his home
there.

WALRUS HUNTING WITH THE ESKIMOS

Robert Frothingham

As a tireless traveler, expert photographer and big-game hunter, Robert Frothingham has tramped and camped during the past twenty-five years all over the West and in Mexico, Alaska and the Canadian Rockies, gathering trophies with his gun and, with his notebook and camera, material for lectures, magazine articles and books.

Among the latter are *Around the World, Playgrounds of the West* and *The Pioneer,* besides several anthologies of outdoor verse.

The episode told in the following pages occurred during the 10,000-mile Alaskan cruise he made last year on the U. S. Coast Guard cutter *Northland.*

WALRUS HUNTING WITH THE ESKIMOS

By Robert Frothingham

A MILD SUMMER SEASON IN THE ARCTIC, WITH ITS LONG, balmy, windless days of nearly twenty-four hours of sunlight, is an inevitable forerunner of starvation conditions for the Eskimo and his dogs during the following winter. Plenty of walrus meat is an absolute necessity for the huskies and is the sole dependence of the native as well if, as sometimes occurs, there is a scarcity of his favorite dish, whale blubber, or *muktuk,* as it is termed in Eskimo lingo.

Walrus frequent the polar ice pack by the tens of thousands and it is there they must be hunted. When, however, the ice floes lie from fifteen to twenty-five miles offshore, the walrus can be hunted only at great risk by the Eskimo in his *umiak,* or skin boat. A change in wind or tide may imprison him in the ice pack or sweep his frail outfit so far from shore as to prevent his getting back.

In other words, successful walrus hunting is conditioned on the ice field swinging shoreward, within at least five or six miles of the land. Then the Eskimo can do his slaughtering leisurely, load the meat into his boat and bring it safely home, where it is divided, share and share alike, with each member of the tribe, in conformity with the community life characteristic of the Eskimo.

.   .   .   .   .   .

It was a mild summer season in 1930, when the U. S. Coast Guard cutter *Northland,* Captain E. D. Jones commanding, dropped her hook off the village of Wainwright on the twenty-seventh day of July, under the most ideal cruising conditions imaginable—a glassy sea, brilliant sunshine and cloudless skies, with the mercury at sixty-five degrees. It was the annual cruise of "the Angel of the Arctic," as the *Northland* is affectionately termed by both whites and natives, because she always arrives "with healing in her wings" and constitutes the one and only touch that some of those distant folk have with civilization during a twelve month.

Skipper Jones was in no way surprised when Jim Allen, ex-whaleman and trader for a score of years at Wainwright, came aboard and soberly stated that it looked like a real scarcity of walrus meat for the coming winter unless some way might be devised for transporting several native crews out to the ice field where it had been lying, twenty-five miles offshore, ever since the winter break-up. They had been hunting every time the ice approached the shore, but the summer thus far had yielded only sixteen animals— rather slim picking for over two hundred huskies for the winter, not to mention the natives themselves, as the whaling had been nothing to brag about.

Yes, they were all feeling a little blue. It was a gentle hint, and the captain was listening intently. "Did the skipper think that he might possibly take a bunch of native hunters with their boats out to the ice pack and give them a chance to do a bit of hunting from the cutter?" The skipper 'lowed that such a thing might be possible, especially as he had a passenger aboard who was keen to do a little hunting. Jim Allen 'lowed, in his turn, that he would be glad to give the skipper's friend the place of honor in the bow seat of the leading boat—which honor carried with it the first shot at a walrus, providing said passenger did not take too long to make up his mind when to shoot. And he went on to explain that natives who were hunting for winter's meat were not overly interested in the size or length of a pair of tusks and that it might be difficult to hold them back when they came within rifle shot of the game. All of which sounded quite reasonable.

The amenities having been duly observed and a score of jubilant 'Skimos having vigorously shaken the captain's hand in token of their appreciation, it was agreed that, on the return of the *Northland* from Point Barrow two days later, we would take Jim Allen and his native cohorts aboard, with their *umiaks,* and see what might be accomplished.

Notwithstanding there was no ice nearer than twenty-five miles off Wainwright, radio advices from Point Barrow, eighty miles farther north, were to the effect that the shore line was packed with ice and that there was little probability of the ship's launch making a landing. Therein lies the uncertainty of Arctic cruising, even under ideal weather conditions. The polar ice pack is always somewhere in the neighborhood. A southwest wind is apt to blow it ashore and a northeast wind will almost always blow it seaward. The fact that there was no wind at all at Wainwright and sufficient wind eighty miles north to block the Point Barrow coast line with ice was no assurance that conditions would not be reversed within a few hours. As Captain Jones put it, there was but one way to determine which wind would have the upper hand the next day, and that was to be there.

Keeping in mind the old adage that has held good with the whalemen on that far-flung coast for over half a century, "Get in Point Barrow and get out," we slipped away from Wainwright that night, arriving at Point Barrow early the next morning, to find the coast line clear and no ice nearer shore than five miles. The mercury stood at sixty-three degrees and the northeast wind was so zephyr-like as to cause those who went ashore to leave their sweaters behind.

Chased by a heavy fog which indicated a change in the wind and a return of the ice, the *Northland* sped down the coast that night and anchored off Wainwright once more, to find Jim Allen with three *umiaks* and fifteen natives, all ready for the offshore hunt. Strange hunting equipment that of the Eskimo—high-powered rifles and spears, the first for distance, the second for dispatching wounded animals that have not managed to work their way off the ice floe into the sea, also to moor to the floe by a long walrus-hide thong attached to the spear-head dead animals which otherwise would sink. The Eskimo is an indifferent rifle shot and feels much more at home with his spear, in the use of which he is most expert.

. . . . .

A quiet, introspective individual, the walrus. Though allied to the seal family, he resembles nothing so much as a gigantic bologna sausage, ten to twelve feet in length, with a corrugated hide from an inch to an inch and a half thick, covered with a sparse, reddish-brown growth of coarse hair. His favorite occupation is sleeping. Try to visualize 2,500 pounds of inert and supreme laziness, lying prone on its back, its repellent, misshapen head thrown back, mouth distended, snout decorated with a bunch of spiny, gray "whiskers," with a pair of formidable ivory tusks two to three feet long, two huge flippers partly crossed on a chest about four feet wide in an attitude absurdly suggestive of "the morning after the night before"—and you have a good picture of a perfect gentleman (or lady) walrus. Furthermore, if you will multiply him five to twenty times over, you will have a bird's-eye view of the average ice floe in the polar ice pack off Point Barrow or Wainwright, Alaska.

From all this one might thoughtlessly deduce that walrus hunting is a sure thing. Not so. It has its uncertainties, just as all big-game hunting has. While the walrus's eyesight is poor and he has no external ears, he has a very serviceable pair of nostrils and, even when half asleep, frequently lifts that ridiculous-looking head, minus neck, and twists about with a view to catching any vagrant odors that indicate the presence of his ancestral enemy, the polar bear, or that other animal, man.

When alarmed, he's wide-awake as an owl and slips off his icy roost into the sea, with a huge splash that can be seen several hundred yards away. He may come to the surface within a few yards of the floe, or he may put five hundred yards between it and himself before his curiosity gets the better of him. And there is no use in shooting him in the water because, whether wounded or killed, he quickly sinks out of sight and is lost. There is little or no buoyancy in a walrus carcass—not enough, at least, to keep it afloat. Hence, all killing must be done on the floe, with the hope that the carcass may not slip overboard before it can be secured.

There's another mighty good reason why the walrus must be "killed dead" on the ice. If he slips off his floe, wounded, he becomes forthwith a wicked customer, a very dangerous antagonist who, instead of trying to make his escape, stays on the job until he has sunk or overturned a boat. He has been known to grip the gunwales of an *umiak* in his mighty tusks and capsize it. He has also been known to turn on his back under a boat and rip the bottom out of it. Remarkable to relate, this sluggish mammoth, with nothing but a set of four flippers—one on either side at the shoulders and two lying closely joined, like a pair of wide-spread, immense hands, at his tail end—is as active as a cat when in the water. When frightened or wounded, he lets out a roar closely resembling the bellow of a bull, followed by a series of deep, resonant, raucous barks somewhat similar to the sea-lion's but, of much greater volume.

.   .   .   .   .

Nine o'clock found the cutter under way, bound for the ice pack, with a bunch of wildly excited and chattering Eskimo hunters swarming over the vessel, like so many curious children. They made a most picturesque sight as they climbed up the ship's ladder, every face wreathed in smiles, and arranged themselves with Jim Allen for a photograph on the quarter-deck. Proud was no name for them! Had they not been honored by selection from the whole tribe by Jim Allen for the most important event of the year? That they should be further distinguished by being permitted to take their *umiaks* aboard the *Northland* and be carried out to the ice pack, where their hunt would be an assured success, with a minimum of labor and risk, was more than they would have dreamed of. They were keyed up to the limit, but not one whit more so than the favored passenger, who was trying to imagine what a bow seat in an *umiak* felt like and whether he would manage to accomplish something in the way of photography, as well as bagging a trophy.

To one who has never seen the polar ice pack, there is a very real thrill in trying to cover it with a pair of binoculars. As far as the eye could see, to the very horizon itself, a limitless expanse of moving ice. And what were all those black specks we saw in every direction? "They are walrus," says Jim Allen. "But," I rejoined, "they can't all be walrus; why, there are thousands—yes, tens of thousands of them!"

And it was so. It staggered the imagination. Right and

left and dead ahead, every ice floe seemed to have been selected with a view to determining how many of these amazing brutes it would hold. Small floes with two or three
monsters crowding every available square foot; big floes,
the size of a city square, jammed with scores of animals,
lying so close together that it was difficult to see whether
there were any tusks at all on the particular brute that the
hunter might be compelled to take. In certain instances, it
seemed as if they were all lying with their heads under
cover, with nothing but their tails to be seen.

On another floe one huge fellow was observed sprawling
over the body of his next-door neighbor, sound asleep with
his tusks stretched out horizontally. Beyond all question,
it was the most bewildering display of sheer brute weight
and massiveness imaginable. It could not have been more
impressive if they had been so many elephants.

Every few moments one might note a huge, misshapen
head rise from the dead level of somnolent "sea-horses" and
twist around uneasily, as if trying to solve some troublesome dream that had arisen in a much-befuddled brain,
after which it would subside like a deflated balloon as the
monster resumed his slumber. Captain Jones stated that,
in all his twenty years off and on in the Arctic, he had never
seen such an aggregation of walrus in the ice pack. "This
remarkable summer weather probably has something to do
with it," he said. "Any hunter caught in the midst of that
tremendous acreage of walrus might find the tables turned
on him. It's a great day for the Eskimo and for you as
well," he continued. "The hunt will be soon over, as most
of them will disappear as soon as the shooting commences."

Meanwhile the *Northland* had come to a stop about a
mile from the edge of the ice pack and preparations were
being made for the launching of the *umiaks*. Jim Allen
asked for quiet. The air was absolutely still and the sea

gleamed like a polished mirror, with hardly a ripple disturbing its burnished surface. Never was Coleridge's famous line more appropriate:

"As idle as a painted ship
Upon a painted ocean."

In tense silence the three *umiaks* were lowered from the davits and the excited natives, quivering in every nerve, dropped down the ladder, each taking his place with paddle, rifle and spear, five men to each boat. Jim Allen beckoned me and we took our places in the first boat, I in the bow, Jim right behind. We were about to push off when Jim, noticing my camera, which I had placed between my feet, said, "What are you going to do with that?" And there was just the least suggestion of resentment both in his voice and in his eyes. "I hope to get a picture of a live walrus before I start any shooting," was my reply.

"You don't want to overlook the fact that this is a hunt for meat," Jim rejoined. "You can't stand up in the boat and take pictures and I don't suppose you can get 'em any other way. If you're looking for a trophy, you'd better drop that camera and stick to your rifle."

"I don't want to queer the game," I replied, "and you may rest assured that I won't stand up in this *umiak* either to shoot or to take pictures—not if I know myself."

"Well," he said, with just a touch of resignation in his voice, "it is up to you. These natives have instructions to hold off shooting until you have had your shot. I'll give you the word when your chance comes and, if you're not ready right on the dot, you'll never know whether it was your bullet or one of the hunters' that got your game for you. What sort of a contrivance is that camera of yours anyway?" he added.

I use a stereoscopic camera, with a view-finder on the side, which I have learned to hold fairly steady on a level with my eyes. I explained this to him.

"Hell's bells!" he exclaimed. "I thought it was some new-fangled pair of binoculars you had there. Can you take a picture with that outfit while you sit low down in the seat without gettin' up to focus it?" I assured him that I could. "Fine and dandy!" he rejoined. "I'll tell you when to touch her off and then you follow quick with your rifle."

·   ·   ·   ·   ·

All this time the boats hadn't moved from the ship's side. The natives were sitting there patiently with their paddles in their hands, wondering what it was all about.

Finally the signal was given and we moved away from the foot of the ship's ladder as silently as ghosts. Jim wet his finger and held it up. He then motioned to the hunters in the other boats to spread out and, keeping on the right side of the wind, each to pick the nearest floe that contained the most meat and to follow through.

While there were thousands of walrus in sight, that was less significant than it seemed at first. We were perforce obliged to pick floes lying along the edge of the pack. Had we attempted to pass any of them, we would have given a general alarm and the game would have taken to the water and disappeared. And our attack had to be simultaneous for a similar reason. Accordingly, the three skin-boats moved forward practically on a line, about a quarter of a mile apart, and all arrived at the edge of the ice pack at the same time.

No more silent paddlers could be imagined than those fifteen Eskimos. Not the slightest sound when the paddle was dipped or when it was lifted from the water. A more thoroughly organized stalk it would be difficult to imagine. The mile dwindled to a half-mile, to a quarter, to two hundred and fifty yards, to one hundred. On the floe we were approaching, we could count at least five of the monsters, all lying with their backs towards us and not a pair of tusks to be seen. How many more there were could only be conjectured. Suddenly, the one right in line with the prow of the boat lifted his head, displaying a massive pair of tusks. Simultaneously with this move, every paddler "froze." The huge creature gazed around and, apparently seeing nothing to arouse any suspicion, lurched back again.

"That's your game," whispered Jim Allen, "but not yet."

The one hundred yards shrunk to fifty and it looked as if we would beach the old *umiak* against the broad back of my walrus in another moment, when Jim gave me the word and I lifted the camera with a steadiness that was later revealed in the negative, but which I was far from feeling inwardly. I didn't take the time to reel up but gently put the instrument back on the bottom of the boat and raised my rifle. Jim had already impressed it on me that there was but one place to plant a bullet in a walrus, in order to assure immediate death—about ten inches back of the eyes, the only chance for a brain shot. The trouble in this case was that there was no eye to be seen—nor any head, for that matter. Nothing but the broad back of the neck presented itself for my consideration.

"Let 'er go," whispered Jim. "These 'Skimos won't wait another split second."

I knew there was a vertebra running somewhere through that neck and that to break it constituted my only chance for a killing shot. With more hope than certainty that my bullet might find the spot, I pressed the trigger. Shooting, as I was, from a moving boat, luck figured largely in the shot. All I could note in that mammoth pile of flesh, now scarcely more than two hundred feet ahead, was a col-

"Meanwhile the *Northland* had steamed slowly up to the big floe on which we were waiting."

The Author's 2500-lb. Walrus Coming Aboard

lapse, as if he had deflated his lungs. Otherwise, not the slightest move. My bullet had found its mark. I had broken his neck—or, rather, it would be more correct to say I had broken his back at the spot where there is usually a neck in every other animal except a walrus. And then—pandemonium!

Imagine, in the same boat with yourself, five highly excited Eskimo hunters, each armed with a high-power rifle containing six cartridges. Figure the necessity for keeping the *umiak* head-on to the ice floe, thus compelling every one of these wrought-up natives to shoot over your head. Imagine thirty bullets being fired as rapidly as those semicrazy Eskimos could pull the trigger. Each one of their deadly missiles seemed to graze my ears. No wonder Jim Allen was a bit alarmed lest I stand up in the boat to take a picture.

Notwithstanding I had five shells left in my rifle, it never occurred to me to shoot a second time. I knew I had my game and I was quite content to slither down in my seat until my head almost lay in Jim Allen's lap. I wouldn't have raised my head above the gunwale of that old *umiak* for a king's ransom. Never in all my thirty years' hunting had I been caught in such a ludicrous situation, yet fraught with such dire possibilities.

And to think of the humorous irony of it! There I was in the Arctic on a walrus hunt, for which I had brought along one hundred shells, and I had fired precisely one bullet. The sheer incongruity of the circumstances was just seeping into my bewildered brain, when a shout from Jim, right in my ear, aroused me. "Out of the boat! Quick!" Almost before I could grasp my rifle and camera and assemble my scattered senses, the big, heavy *umiak,* with its load of screeching, gesticulating natives, was high and dry on the ice floe, pulled up out of harm's way.

We had bagged ten of the monsters and nearly as many more were churning the water around the floe, some of them rising a couple of feet out of the sea in sheer rage, to see what they might get their tusks into. A final round of bullets, and the toggled spearhead secured three more. Those that got away dived deep and rose to the surface fully a hundred yards off, roaring and bellowing like so many bulls. No further attempt was made to shoot them. Off to our left we could hear the rifles cracking from the other two boats, whose occupants had also made good use of their time.

Meanwhile the *Northland* had steamed slowly up and made fast to the big floe on which we were waiting. Quite a contrast, this, to the usual native hunt, which, under other circumstances, would have been followed immediately by cutting up the carcasses on the floe and getting the meat ashore as soon as possible. In the present instance, however, all that was necessary was the donkey engine and a block and fall. Twenty-six walrus had been taken by the three boats' crews and it must be admitted they made a brave show as winter meat, piled ten to fifteen feet high on the forward deck of the ship.

The hunt had not taken more than two and a half hours and the cutter steamed back to the village of Wainwright, where the great carcasses were dropped overboard and towed ashore by the ship's launches and the *umiaks*. There the cutting-up process started and the meat was divided and stored in the underground cache of each family. These caches, being literally carved out of the frozen ground which underlies the whole Alaskan territory, make ideal refrigerators, as the temperature does not change throughout the year.

It was about eleven o'clock when the *Northland* sailed away south from Wainwright that night—the last sight the natives would have of the "Angel of the Arctic" for another year. The midnight sun was blood-red, low down on the horizon, filling the heaven with a sort of unearthly glow, sufficiently brilliant, withal, to see to read without difficulty. A half-dozen *umiaks*, filled with grateful and happy Eskimos circled around the cutter as she weighed anchor and stood out to sea.

"*Umsi-ky-ok*," they shouted—Eskimo for "Thank you" —the last word we heard as the cutter gathered way and the *umiaks* pulled for the shore. And they meant what they said, for, whether or not conditions changed during the balance of the season and the polar ice pack swung inshore or remained more or less stationary twenty-five miles out, the Wainwright natives were sure of sufficient walrus meat to carry both them and their dogs safely through another winter. As Captain Jones stated, that was "part of the *Northland's* job."

MISSING A TIGER AND SHOOTING THE SUN

Prentiss N. Gray

Although actively engaged in banking in New York City, Prentiss N. Gray has taken time from his business affairs for numerous hunting and exploration trips in the West, Alaska and Canada, and for the expedition to East Africa, the Belgian Congo and Angola which he prefaced with the interesting astronomical undertaking here related.

MISSING A TIGER AND SHOOTING THE SUN

By Prentiss N. Gray

THE *President Wilson* SAILED ON MARCH 22, 1929, taking me on my first jump to East Africa—at least, so I thought. We were hardly past the Golden Gate, out of San Francisco, when I saw three men and a woman in the smoking-room, poring over books and jotting down figures while the other passengers enjoyed the gorgeous sunshine on deck.

Each morning thereafter they were at it and most of the afternoon. From a distance I made out that the books were tables of logarithms. At last I could stand it no longer and stuck my head right into the noose by introducing myself and asking what it was all about. They were Dr. Harlan Stetson, Mr. and Mrs. Weld Arnold and Mr. Josef Johnson, members of the Harvard Solar Eclipse Expedition. I found out subsequently that they were also human beings and that my conception of astronomers as people who sat on mountain tops and talked in light-years was a bit far-fetched. In fact, they proved to be the most amusing people on board and Mrs. Arnold took first prize in the beauty parade on Easter Sunday. For some time I did not even hint that I had not known there was to be an eclipse, nor did I confess that I had borrowed an atlas from the ship's library to locate, after hours of search, the destination of the eclipse expedition, Alor Star, the capital of Kedah, in one of the unfederated states of the Malay Peninsula.

Several days after we left Honolulu, over a cool, tall drink, I dropped into conversation with Dr. Stetson, the leader of the expedition, and confessed that I was on my way to photograph the animals of Africa for the Academy of Natural Sciences of Philadelphia. He immediately showed great interest. He told me that the photographer of their expedition had fallen off a horse in Central Park a month before the date of departure and had broken his neck. The doctors did a good job in the hospital and turned him out in three weeks, alive but done up in a plaster cast. Whereupon the photographer had tumbled into matrimony and cancelled his sailing to the Orient.

This should have been my warning to change the subject, but in serene innocence I offered to display my assortment of eleven cameras decked out with telephoto lenses to entrap lion, zebra and giant sable. I did not know that scientists could shoot the sun with any of my cameras. However, it developed on the spot that mine happened to be better suited to this work than the expedition's own photographic equipment.

Then and there I was hooked. I had modestly hoped to shoot animals with my equipment. But these astronomers were after the whole works—sun, moon and stars. Only they were not very sporty about it, for they proposed to line up two of these, the sun and the moon, and get them both on one pot-shot. Of course they had some excuse, as they had to travel all around the world for less than five minutes of photographing, with the chances two to one that the day would be cloudy. I came to the conclusion that eclipse-chasing after all might be the biggest gamble in the world outside of matrimony.

For many lazy, hot days we rolled our way across the Pacific. We spent most of the time just sitting and feeling like the two old Arkansas "crackers," sitting on the store porch with their feet cocked up against a post. One said, "Bill, here comes Judge Powers' funeral down the street." Bill replied, "I sure wish I was facin t'other way, so I could see it."

.   .   .   .   .   .

At Singapore Harry Gild, who had arranged a tiger hunt for us on the properties of the Sultan of Jahore, met us at the dock and immediately plunged us into a round of shopping for helmets, khaki clothes and white suits, for it seems you must be properly dressed to meet the Sultan's tigers.

We were away in a motor the next morning at seven for the ninety-mile run up country to Batu Pahat. With every turn of the wheel Gild told us how this particular tiger, which they had surrounded in the jungle after he had carried off a native, was just yearning for one of my .465 bullets. In the middle of one of these orations we went around a sharp curve at fifty-five miles an hour and bang went a tire! In an instant we stuck our radiator into the bank and slewed the rear end completely around, as the other three tires exploded, and the car slammed against the rock wall. It was over before we could think and we pinched ourselves to see if we were alive. We were, and unhurt, but the car was a wreck. After an hour's wait, a friend of Gild's happened by and took us on to Batu Pahat in his car.

Here the rest-house maintained by the government was the pleasantest kind of surprise. We had had a vague notion that we should have to sleep in the jungle amid crawling insects and poisonous snakes, but here was a clean place with delicious food.

After luncheon we drove on another ten miles, until we found a party of thirty men at the beginning of a trail leading off into the densest sort of jungle. We were led along this path for about a mile to a small clearing, where the vegetation had been cut back a few feet for a native's garden patch. I was stationed in this clearing, with the solid wall of jungle tangle not over forty feet away. After a few minutes' wait Captain Ahmed, who was in charge of the drive, blew a trumpet and a terrific din of horns, fire-crackers and beating of tin pans arose in a half-circle in front of us about half a mile distant. It sounded like a double Chinese New Year.

For three-quarters of an hour this kept up. Sometimes the ki-yi-ing of small dogs started it off afresh if it had died down a little. It was a terrible nerve-wracking din coming out of the dark jungle and on top of it there crowded into my mind vivid stories I had read of tigers springing sud-denly out of just such a green wall as rose only a few feet away from me. I certainly was not having a good time. I glanced behind me and saw the *datok* (village chief) lean-ing nonchalantly on his Malacca stick, smoking a cigar. With no gun, no spear, he was paying my marksmanship too large a compliment. I felt I had to shoot straight or we would have a dead *datok* on our hands if the tiger ever came out.

It seemed a week that I stood there in the blazing sun, with the unseen line of beaters slowly drawing nearer. Sud-denly the brush about forty feet from me swayed. I threw up my gun and looked down my sights at a brown woolly head. My knees stopped shaking as I realized that it was one of the beaters. The drive was finished and had failed. A trumpet call brought all the beaters out of the bush. There were a hundred and twenty of them, and a worse lot of brigands I never saw. Some were armed with spears, some with swords, some with knives and some with petrol tins. They had plowed through the jungle on the orders of the Sultan, without enthusiasm, although this particular tiger was not popular with them, as, two nights before, he had carried off one of the villagers.

When they were all assembled, the Captain and the *datok* harangued them furiously for letting the tiger slip through their line. They ordered another drive at once, but neither this one nor three drives the next day produced anything but a *wa-wa* monkey and two *sambur* deer.

We could not stay a day longer, as the eclipse would not wait beyond 1.36 p.m. on May ninth, so we had to abandon the tiger hunt and return to the ship. A day later, we were dumped ashore at Penang, the port for Alor Star, and the eclipse hunt was on.

· · · · ·

We motored up to Alor Star sixty-four miles, along a road lined for the first thirty miles with rubber and coconut plantations. After that we ran out into flat country, where every inch of the land was cultivated for rice.

The field alongside the residence of the British Advisor had been chosen as the scene of operations for the eclipse expeditions. Here the British contingent from the Royal Observatory at Greenwich, under the leadership of Dr. Jackson, had labored since early March erecting their elaborate apparatus. A small part of this field had been set apart for us. We built palm shelters covering the equatorial mount for the cameras and the apparatus to be operated by our expedition.

Around the whole field were two barbed-wire fences thirty feet apart to hold back the crowd, so that the scientists could work undisturbed. The usefulness of the double-fence arrangement, with soldiers guarding the space between, was evident on the day of the eclipse, when crowds of Malays threatened to swarm over the field.

There was no hotel in the town, so the European residents had generously offered to put up the various members of the British and American expeditions. Dr. Stetson and I were quartered with Judge and Mrs. W. G. Dinsmore, as charming hosts as could be found in all Malaya.

At six o'clock on the morning of May seventh, I began to realize that sun-shooting was not all play. Stetson hauled me out of bed before daylight to work at the field. We had difficulty in setting up my cameras, constructed to photograph animals, so that they would easily panoram and tilt at just the right speed to follow the sun. We worked at this problem all day, but by night had not yet solved it. Finally we decided to put three cameras on the equatorial mount and let the clockwork of this machine keep them fixed on the sun as it moved through the heavens. Another day's work accomplished this job, despite the obstacles of balance, etc., which had to be worked out. My simple cameras, as a result of their new setting, were now dignified by the astronomical title "multiple coronagraph."

We held a rehearsal at six o'clock the next day, but the counter for the British expedition was too far off for us to hear him clearly. Each second during totality must be called out in a loud voice, as everyone in the camp has a schedule of things before him demanding prompt execution on an even second. So, when we lost the count of the British counter, we had to give up. Then we decided to get a counter of our own in the shape of a clock with a large enough second-hand to see clearly. Our schedule read something like this:

> 0 sec.—pull plate-slide
> 5 " —open shutter
> 25 " —close shutter
> 30 " —replace slide
> 35 " —change filter

etc., etc., for 299 seconds, the duration of totality.

"We built palm shelters for the cameras and apparatus."

The Author and Dr. Stetson Operating the
Multiple Coronograph

Unless we followed this schedule accurately, we were likely to do all sorts of foolish things. They tell of a photographer on one expedition, who spent a month setting up his cameras, had a fine clear day and took a dozen wonderful pictures—only to find, when he came to develop them, that he had a dozen unexposed plates. In his excitement, he had forgotten to pull the plate-slide.

The night before the eclipse, we were bidden to the Residency, to dine with the High Commissioner, Sir Hugh Clifford, and all the dignitaries of the State of Kedah. We had a hundred details still to arrange at the field, but we had to go, as the invitation was in the nature of a royal command. I had difficulty in keeping my attention on Sir Hugh, the author of "The Further Side of Silence," because my mind was busy with lenses, red filters and the prospect of a clear day for the eclipse.

All sorts of high Malayan officials were there, including the Sultan's brother, who usually represents his mentally weak, if illustrious relative. We drank the health of King George and the Sultan and lifted a dish of very rare old port to the President of the United States. With these courtesies over, we smoked.

Home about midnight, we began loading films, for this was the coolest time of the day. By four o'clock we had finished and at five were on the field, making the last adjustments on the cameras. You can imagine how anxiously we waited for dawn. Light came, to reveal a sky covered with clouds.

About nine-thirty we returned home for breakfast, a real American breakfast which our delightful hosts had planned—puffed rice, eggs, baked beans and coffee.

.   .   .   .   .

Alor Star had been a quiet little place the previous day, but long before we returned to the field the place was in a hubbub. A pilgrimage had begun from all the surrounding countryside to the grounds of the Residency. The natives apparently thought that the eclipse could not be seen from any spot in Kedah except this field. Early they lined up twenty deep against the outer barbed-wire fence, giving the soldiers all they could do to keep them from swarming over the field. Malays in gorgeous costumes and coolies with no clothes above the waist, and not much below, crowded against each other. When the Sultan arrived, he was led into the "holy of holies" within the wire enclosure, placed in a comfortable chair and surrounded by a strong guard to prevent him from being himself. The "Most High" was crazy as a loon.

During the next hour we were all on tiptoe, tuning up the instruments for the last time and making the final inspection of all the gear that had taken weeks to erect, yet would be used for less than five minutes. We cast anxious looks at the partly cloudy sky, but we saw a shadow on the ground, so everyone was immediately cheered up. Despite the clouds, my scientific colleagues were composed and their eyes seemed as full of hope as if there had been a clear blue sky overhead. Up to an hour before the eclipse started, it still looked as if we should not be able to expose a single plate. However, the sun did come out.

At nine minutes past noon the moon began to eat into the sun. Then a loud voice shouted, "First contact!" That was the signal to start. My job was to take eight pictures every ten seconds with the Akeley motion-picture camera. For an hour and a half I ground away slowly until two and a half minutes before totality, which occurred at 1.36 p.m., local time. Then I changed films and switched on the electric motor which drove the Akeley. We left this camera to run by itself, while Stetson and I exposed plates in the still cameras at varying exposures. During the partial phases heavy clouds had at times shut out the sun entirely, but, with the approach of totality, conditions had improved. We had some high cirrus clouds which, although they interfered somewhat with the scientific value of the show, did not prevent us from seeing and photographing the most awe-inspiring spectacle that nature produces.

The soldiers cautioned the crowd to make no noise, but, as the sun diminished to a thin crescent, a hum of excitement arose. When this last bright line vanished, a muffled roar broke out. The frantic waving of the soldiers' arms could not quiet the crowd. We seemed to be taking part in some rite, mystical and frightful. A Chinese set off firecrackers to scare away the dragon that was swallowing the sun. The Malay horde jammed against the wire, watching the growing dusk, the gradual cutting down of the sun, until it completely disappeared and darkness came over the face of the land. The dragon had swallowed the sun because of the sins of men.

I heard Stetson muttering to himself something about having "caught the diamond ring." I did not know anybody had dropped one. I thought that he, too, had gone mad. But months later, when I returned to America, I saw that "diamond ring." We had caught it on the moving-picture film during four-tenths of a second. At the exact moment when the moon completely covers the sun, a single ray of light shines out in a brilliant gleam through one of the valleys of the moon. At the same moment, on the opposite side of the moon, the corona breaks out and the total effect is exactly like an electric-light advertisement of a diamond ring.

During the eclipse I was too busy to see much of it except what showed on the ground glass of my camera. Once, however, I looked up during a long exposure. The sight thrilled me. The stars shone in the middle of the day and I could hear the village cocks crowing their resentment at this premature bedtime.

When the escaped sun burst forth triumphant again, I began the long grind of taking motion pictures for another hour and a half. By three o'clock I was fed up with the job and quite relieved when the call came "Last contact!"

We went home to tiffin, enjoyed a good hour's rest and then returned to the field to pack up. Next morning we left for Penang. There I boarded a steamer and continued my voyage to Africa, to put my cameras to the use for which they were designed.

A WEEK'S ADVENTURES IN GREENLAND
William H. Hobbs

Professor of geology and director of the geological laboratory at the University of Michigan and for twenty years connected with the U. S. Geological Survey, Dr. Hobbs has in recent years won recognition in another field by organizing and directing three expeditions sent to Greenland by his university principally for the study of atmospheric and meteorological conditions, a subject of increasing importance to transatlantic aviation. The eventful week here described terminated the second of these expeditions.

His travels have taken him also to the Sudan, the South Seas and the western Pacific. Besides many contributions to government reports and scientific journals, he has published *Earthquakes, an Introduction to Seismic Geology; Characteristics of Existing Glaciers; The Glacial Anticyclones, the Poles of the Atmospheric Circulation; Earth Features and Their Meaning; Cruises along Byways of the Pacific; Exploring about the North Pole of the Winds.*

A WEEK'S ADVENTURES IN GREENLAND

By *William H. Hobbs*

IN EXPLORING, AS IN MANY OTHER FIELDS OF ENDEAVOR, the "breaks," whether favorable or the reverse, seem to come bunched together. Within the brief span of a week in early September, 1928, my little exploring party in Greenland found the lost Rockford flyers, Hassell and Cramer, was shipwrecked with them on the rocks of a Greenland fjord and was rescued after three days by a small Danish relief vessel.

A few miles from our base on the Söndre Strömfjord in southwest Greenland, we had found and marked a suitable landing-field for the flyers and had wirelessed to Hassell at Rockford full instructions concerning its location. When at noon of August eighteenth he finally took off on his last hop from Cochrane in Canada, we received word of it over our radio late in the evening, when alone radio reception is possible in that region at that season. Our dispositions to receive the flyers had already been made and we had posted ourselves on the landing-field early in the afternoon. If all went well, Hassell should make his appearance in the early forenoon of the following day, which was Sunday. A field radio set had been prepared on the landing-field, so that we were in constant touch with our main radio station at the meteorological observatory on Mount Evans, eight miles away. Having no camp on the landing-field, we crowded under a sloping rock and there kept vigil while the long hours of the night wore away.

As soon as there was sufficient light, we sent up a pilot balloon and found that the wind conditions were most favorable for Hassell's arrival. Any moment now he might make his appearance. Marius, one of our Eskimo helpers, had been posted outside the observatory to watch and listen for the motor and report to Baer, our radio operator, who would relay the word to us on the field.

With ever-increasing tension, we watched throughout Sunday morning. By ten o'clock we had become anxious, for Hassell's fuel supply could not last much longer. We began to fear that he might have had engine trouble or lost his way and been forced down. The pilot, Parker Cramer, was supplied with a radio and it had been arranged that he was to sound different letters over different sections of his course, but nothing was picked up either by our watchful station or by any other. Much depressed, we at last made our way back to camp, sure that Hassell had failed and had probably perished with his pilot.

As soon as we could again establish radio communication with the outside world, we reported Hassell's non-arrival and soon after received a message from his promoter, Major L. H. Fredericks, of Rockford, expressing his belief that the flyers had come down somewhere within the wilderness of fjord and barren rock ridge lying to the southward of our station and across the Söndre Strömfjord. If the men were anywhere within that area and knew their position, they would most likely come eventually to a prominent headland of the south shore of the fjord nearly opposite our base at Mount Evans. I, therefore, sent a party under Belknap in the motor dory to take a canoe with fuel, food and a lantern and with instructions to signal the station at night. Potter, our most expert hiker, was sent first to the edge of the inland ice and, later on, with one of the Eskimos on a two-day trip into the rough country south of the Söndre Strömfjord across from our base.

A much-belated radiogram had come from the Greenland Governor at Godthaab to the effect that, on the Sunday morning when we had been awaiting the arrival of the plane at our landing-field, it had made its appearance over the little Eskimo coast settlement of Fiskenaesset, some three hundred miles to the southward, just as the Eskimos were on their way to church. The plane was flying low and the whole congregation could see even the binoculars held in the hands of the flyers. After searching about, the plane had gone off to the eastward.

Somewhat later a radiogram forwarded by *The New York Times* reported to us that the plane had been seen passing eastward over Julianehaab. Since Julianehaab is near the southern tip of Greenland, this meant that the flyers, surely nearly out of gas by this time, had flown off to sea and were probably lost. We were only later to learn that this radiogram was the same message which had come to us from the Governor over the Greenland radio system, but was reported to the world from Julianehaab, since that is the chief Greenland radio station, and reported as though the plane had been seen over that station, instead of over Fiskenaesset, more than two hundred miles away.

These messages had the effect of convincing us that Hassell and Cramer must now have perished, for they must surely have been far off their course and, not being equipped with pontoons, if they had come down either at sea or in one of the great fjords near Julianehaab and had not been quickly reported, there could be little hope that they were still alive.

On the second of September, a full two weeks after the flyers should have put in their appearance, we were making our preparations to return to the United States. The little motor sloop which had been chartered to take us down to the coast was due to reach us on the fourth. The winter party, consisting of Schneider, Carlson and Baer, had proposed a farewell dinner at the observatory. Belknap was with them, completing his map of the summit area, while Stewart, Etes and myself were busy at the fjord base of Camp Lloyd, some three miles away.

In mid-afternoon I started up to the observatory, carrying a pack, as there were always supplies to be taken up and this was our only means of transportation. A high wind was blowing in from across the wide fjord and I had just been congratulating myself that it was not necessary for any of us to be out in these treacherous waters, when, already a mile and a half from camp, there came to my ears the unmistakable hum of an outboard motor. This came as a distinct shock and I halted, straining my ears to locate the sound more accurately. Hardly a minute passed before our little Mullins steel boat, carrying two men, appeared from under the bank, rising and falling in the great seas and threatening every minute to be engulfed. Meanwhile I had been revolving in my mind the question, "What could have induced Stewart and Etes to venture out under such perilous conditions?" Then the idea flashed over me that news must have reached them from Hassell. I threw down my pack and started on a run for the landing.

Arrived there, I was surprised to be met by a group of Eskimos, who had reached the camp a half-hour or more before in an *umiak*, or large skin boat. Because of the high wind and the heavy seas, even this large boat, with its sturdy oarsmen, had hugged the opposite windward shore of the fjord until nearly opposite our camp, when, with stern wind, they had made a rapid six-mile trip across. Before leaving the other shore, their keen eyes had detected a little column of smoke rising near the shore and this observation they had at once reported to Etes and Stewart. Knowing well that the smoke must come from a camp of Hassell and Cramer—for certainly no one else could be in the region—the Mullins boat had been hastily made ready and not without great difficulty launched on the fjord with the two men aboard.

Gradually the Mullins boat made headway against the seas. It was now very slowly approaching, as we could see, the high promontory of rock which divides the great Söndre Strömfjord some two miles away, where Stewart and Etes evidently planned to make a landing. With the greatest anxiety we watched them, the boat going out of sight frequently in the heavy seas, only to rise again high on the crest of a wave. With our binoculars we were at last able to make out that they had effected a landing under the lee of the point.

After a considerable rest at the point, the two men were seen again putting out in the boat. Now they were steering directly for the point where the smoke had been seen. We continued to watch them with a good deal of anxiety, though the seas they encountered were without doubt a good deal less heavy as they neared the windward shore. It was already growing dark as we made out their apparently safe landing at their destination.

An Eskimo had long before been dispatched to the observatory to report the probable early rescue of the flyers, cancel the farewell dinner and recall Belknap for use at the lower base. Before leaving the observatory, Belknap arranged a preconcerted signal with Schneider, the aerologist there, that, if the rescue should be effected after dark, as seemed likely, we were to signal by flashlight the words, "Hassell safe."

A lantern was now set up above the shore station to guide the boat on its return. It was well after dark when drifting flashlight signals told us that the boat was starting back from the farther shore. Again it made its way toward the high promontory in the fork of the fjord, but now, with the wind on the quarter, at a much more rapid pace. Arrived there, signals which we could not clearly make out were flashed and, after some delay, intermittent lights indicated that the boat was starting out again, but now apparently getting too far east to reach the landing.

One of our Eskimos suggested that he go out in the motor dory with Belknap and guide the other boat to the landing with a flashlight. Belknap agreed and they started out, the two boats now flashing signals to each other. This had the desired effect and we could see that Stewart's boat had changed its course and was steering toward us. Before long the beats of the two motors became noticeable as both were racing for the landing. As the increasing hum of the more distant motor indicated it was getting nearer, we strained our eyes to make out the number of its crew. The dark patch above the gunwale appeared to indicate more freight than the two men who went out. Yes, there can now no longer be any doubt. We make out distinctly four men in the little boat. As the boat's keel grates on the shingle beach, we step into the water and lend a hand to the two rescued men.

Slowly and painfully with our help the two men make their way up the bank to the dining tent. Hot soup is ready. Caribou steaks are there to broil if the men are in condition for such food, but we soon learn that they have been on starvation rations for the two weeks of their wandering and so they wisely hold themselves down to the soup.

Professor Hobbs, with Parker D. Cramer on His
Right and Bert Hassell on His Left

Arrival of the Rescuers, with the Wreck in the Background

While they eat, I dig out their story. As soon as the outlines of the narrative are clear, I make my way with a lantern up over the three miles of stony trail to the observatory. Belknap has meanwhile flashed his signals "Hassell safe," and Schneider on the watch has carried the message to Baer at the radio transmitter. At once the call "2UO, URGENT" has gone out. Dick Hilferty, on duty at the radio station of *The New York Times,* hears his station call and stands by, awaiting my arrival with the story.

Through foresight in arranging the preconcerted signals, together with some good fortune in the quick establishment of contact with the *Times,* the outline of Hassell's story was in the *Times* office within three hours after his rescue and on the front page the following morning. Hassell was able, not without difficulty, to climb to the observatory the following day and send the *Times* a fuller account of his experiences.

. . . . .

On the next day, September fourth, Hassell and Cramer, with Belknap, Stewart, Potter and myself, started for the coast on the little motor sloop *Nakuak,* which had arrived during the early morning in charge of an Eskimo skipper and had given us a busy day discharging cargo for the station and taking on our supplies. We bade farewell to our winter staff, Schneider, Carlson and Baer, and weighed anchor in the late afternoon.

The great fjord down which we were to sail to the sea —one of the greatest in the entire world, since it is one hundred and twenty miles in length—we were to navigate during the night. On the average the fjord is about two miles in width and of a depth sufficient for the passage of an ocean liner. We retired early, Belknap, Cramer and I opening out our sleeping-bags in the narrow space of the little cabin, Hassell and his old friend Etes laying theirs on the cargo in the hold. Stewart and Potter chose to sleep on deck, while our three Eskimos joined their compatriots of the crew in the little forecastle. The Eskimo skipper was competent and knew the course, so we left to him the entire responsibility. Tired after a heavy day and after late hours since the rescue, we went early to sleep, though Cramer suffered much from his stomach, which had protested against some indiscretion in eating since his recent starvation régime.

A little before dawn we were all awakened by a sudden heavy shock to the little vessel. Crawling quickly out of my sleeping-bag, I climbed the little ladder to the deck. I could see in the faint light a towering rock cliff close at hand. An Eskimo head was poked out of the engine-room. Cries now came simultaneously from the cabin and the hold that the ship was filling with water. As the skipper threw the helm over and steered for the rocks, I dove back into the cabin, fished my boots out of a foot of water and, emerging again, took bags and other duffle that was now being passed up to the deck from both the cabin and the hold. Steam issued in volume from the engine-room and showed that the engine was already in part under water.

The ship now struck a second time and seemed to be firmly perched on a reef. The dinghy was therefore brought alongside and we began piling our stuff into it. Etes got in and paddled the loaded boat to the cliff, some thirty feet away, and in the darkness succeeded in getting a precarious foothold on the slippery rocks. But now the sloop began to settle slowly by the stern and threatened to slide off into deep water. It was therefore necessary to suspend our salvaging operations until we were able to get an anchor ashore with one of its flukes securely set in a cleft of rock, after which our Eskimos worked at the winch until the ship was held from further slipping. A little more deliberation was now possible in getting our equipment ashore. By half daylight we were all on shore with our boxes and bags, more or less soaked with sea water, piled about in disarray on shelves of the rock, wherever a secure lodgment was possible.

We could now take some account of stock. We had a fair amount of light food, also some tin cases of pemmican, kerosene fuel and a Mannlicher rifle with very little ammunition. Stewart had with him his rod and line.

We were fortunate in finding a little spring of water close by and at once set about preparing a good breakfast. Over our coffee we discussed our chances of getting away. The Eskimo skipper confessed to us that the accident had occurred because he had fallen asleep at the helm and had awakened only when the sloop struck the reef. He volunteered with one of his crew to take the little dinghy and make an attempt to reach the small fishing settlement of Kangamiut, some fifty miles down the Greenland coast. As the wind was now very high, we postponed consideration of this until later.

I had climbed to a little shelf of rock above our landing-place and had made out without difficulty the peculiar form of the Simiutak (Eskimo for "stopper"), a striking mountain mass occupying an island which partly blocks the wide entrance to the fjord. We were therefore able to fix our position as on the north cliff of the fjord, about twenty miles in from the mouth.

The salvage of the *Nakuak,* so far as we were now concerned, was not to be thought of, for her hull was evidently badly damaged and she had gone on the reef at extreme low tide. Had she gone on at high tide, the range of tide is here so large that she would have been left high and dry, giving us some opportunity for repairs to her hull.

We had still another possible means of transportation to

some settlement on the coast. The *umiak,* with the Eskimos who had reported Hassell's camp and led us to the rescue, had started out from our base a day in advance of us and our crew reported that we had passed them during the night. They were, therefore, somewhere up the fjord and must eventually pass our camp. They were carrying out a full cargo of caribou meat, but, should they come past us in the daytime, they must see our wrecked vessel and would no doubt be willing for a consideration to cache their cargo on the shore long enough to take us out to some Eskimo settlement, where we should be able to arrange for further transportation by either motorboat or *umiak.* If they should go by in the night, we would hardly see them unless a watch was set and this was forthwith arranged. Our Eskimo, Peter, had keen eyes and was very reliable, so it was arranged that he was to sit up and watch for the *umiak.*

At noon, as the wind had somewhat abated, our Eskimo skipper and his single companion started out in the dinghy, carrying a note from me to the Danish manager of the little settlement of Kangamiut. In the afternoon Potter, our hardiest climber, undertook to ascend to the top of the high rock cliff in order to get a look around. He was thus able to see a camp only a few miles above us on the fjord, but separated by a dangerous rocky promontory which it would have been foolhardy to attempt to climb over at the time, for it was already late in the afternoon and growing dark. We trusted to our watch and the next morning Potter succeeded in reaching the camp, only to find that the Eskimos had left in the night and had escaped Peter's vigilance. We were thus left solely dependent on the success of our Eskimo messengers in getting through to Kangamiut.

Potter had reported seeing arctic hare on his climb to the summit and it was highly probable that there were fish in the fjord. Moreover, after a sufficient delay, the failure of the *Nakuak* to return would cause anxiety and another sloop would certainly be sent out in search of her. We hoped, however, that we should not be compelled to depend on any such means of rescue, as we would thus be almost certain to lose the means of getting back to civilization before winter. On the second day we established a watch at intervals along the fjord to report any rescue vessel, but, when three days had passed, we began to fear that our boat had failed to win out.

I now considered the necessity of putting our party on strict rations and making a definite effort to increase our food supply. I had left my tent to announce this to the party, when, glancing down the fjord, my eye fell on a motor sloop coming toward us. Our Eskimos had won out and the manager of the little fishing settlement, Bestyrer Alexander Goettbergsen, had started out to our rescue.

One of the Eskimos of the crew was sent in his *kayak* down the fjord and up the coast to Holstensborg to report the wreck of the *Nakuak* and have a motor boat sent to bring back our Eskimos. The rest of us were soon aboard the sloop and late that night we arrived at Kangamiut, where we sat down to a great feast of good things, provided by our genial host.

Later, we were fortunate enough to find a tramp freighter, whose captain generously took us aboard, on condition that we "feed and sleep" ourselves. In this manner we were able to reach Europe.

AN EYE FOR AN EYE

F. W. Hodge

Born in England but brought to this country while a child, Dr. Hodge embarked in early youth on the career that has made him one of the leading authorities of the world on the American Indian.

At twenty he entered the U. S. Geological Survey and two years later became field secretary of the Hemenway Expedition, which conducted archeological researches in Arizona and New Mexico. Returning to Washington, he was appointed to the Bureau of American Ethnology and during the next eleven years pursued field studies of the Indians and their remains in the Southwest.

In 1900 he accepted an administrative post in the Smithsonian Institution, which he resigned ten years later, becoming ethnologist-in-charge of the Bureau of American Ethnology. He left this position in 1918 to join the scientific staff of the Museum of the American Indian, in New York City.

Under the auspices of the last-named institution, he conducted (1918-1923) archeological excavations in the ruins of the Zuñi pueblo of Hawikuh, New Mexico, one of the so-called "Seven Cities of Cibola." The expense of this research was borne by the late Harmon W. Hendricks, a member of The Explorers Club, who also provided funds for the publication of its results, an extended report of which is in preparation.

Dr. Hodge has held important offices in a number of scientific and historical organizations and has written many papers on Southwestern archeology and ethnology and on the early contact of the Indians of that region with the Spaniards. He has served in several editorial positions, his *magnum opus* being the two-volume *Handbook of the American Indians North of Mexico,* which stands as an enduring monument to his tireless industry and fine scholarship.

AN EYE FOR AN EYE

By F. W. Hodge

THE BLIGHTING SANDSTORMS WHICH PRECEDE THE coming of springtime in Zuñiland had at last died away; the Indians were departing from the mother *pueblo* to their farms at Nutria, Pescado and Ojo Caliente; prayer sticks had been planted in the fields and rain gods were the subject of daily invocation. Old Kúhni, hoe in hand, had dropped in for a chat on the way to his farm at Pescado. Zuñi had settled to its humdrum life, the aged and those whose little cornfields were near by being now its chief occupants.

White men were busy, too—the kind that were none too welcome to the decent folk of New Mexico. Cattle and horse rustlers. A couple of their ilk had drifted into our camp on a well timed visit for the midday meal, and how they ate! Then they were off, each riding a pony, with a rifle slung across the saddle, and each with a well laden pack-horse trailed with a *reata*. They said they were on a search for the "lost Adams mine" in the northern country, but we observed that they started on the eastward trail and continued in that direction until they passed out of sight.

The next we heard of these 'Melicanos was when word reached the *pueblo* that a Zuñi youth on a good horse and wearing a six-shooter had been approached by two rough-looking men on the road to Fort Wingate, a few miles west of Pescado; that one of the men tried to snatch the gun, but the boy had veered his horse in time to save it and had made off for Pescado lickety-split to inform the men there of the occurrence. The Indian boy did not fire, for were there not two against him, and with rifles, too?

Incensed at the tale the young Indian related, the men of Pescado immediately rounded up their horses, seized their arms and followed the trail of the rustlers, while messengers were despatched to the other settlements for aid. The white men were almost overtaken before reaching the Box S cattle ranch among the pines of the Zuñi mountains, where they took refuge in a log house. The only other occupant at the time was a Chinese cook.

The Indians, eighteen or twenty of them, deployed at what they regarded as points of vantage. Hopeless of either taking the rustlers alive or killing them in their impregnable fort, the besiegers adopted the policy of drawing the enemy's fire and thereby exhausting their ammunition. But the white men were too well stocked for such tactics to succeed.

In the hope that their firing might have some effect through the windows and the chinks between the logs of the cabin, the Zuñis changed position from time to time. Kúhni, behind a giant pine, waved his blanket slightly beyond the tree, until it became a rag from the expert marksmanship of the whites. Then Kúhni became a little reckless, for, in exposing his blanket once more, his face got a little beyond the protection of the tree and his lower jaw was shot entirely away. About the same time Capitán Lóchi, in trying to pass on all fours from one *arroyo* to another, was shot through the hips.

Such was the news that reached us at Zuñi late in the evening. Meanwhile Lóchi, paralyzed, together with what remained of Kúhni, had been recovered in the darkness and conveyed to the *pueblo,* amid the death wailing of the

Dr. Frederick W. Hodge, in the Library of The Explorers Club

Dr. Hodge and Tsínahe, a Zuñi Assistant

women and the howling of scores of dogs which took up the refrain. To make the occasion seem more eerie, one horseman after another galloped by our camphouse across the little river from the *pueblo*, dashed into the stream and clattered up the opposite bank. Things were doing in Zuñi.

About half-past ten that night, I had a visit from young Túmako, otherwise known as Zuñi Nick, the only man in the tribe at that time who could speak English, which had been taught him by Douglas D. Graham, the trader. Graham had departed only that morning for Fort Wingate, forty-five miles by road, on his way to Albuquerque.

Nick's attitude lacked the friendliness which usually characterized him; indeed, he addressed me rather brusquely and without waste of words.

"Téluli, I want to borrow a horse."

"Yes? Well, why don't you get one of your own horses?"

"They're all out on the range and I could not find them in the dark; besides, I'm in a great hurry."

"Why do you wish a horse anyway?"

"I want to go to Fort Wingate to see Tsiponkwin" (Black Moustache, Mr. Graham). "There's trouble at the *pueblo*. The war priests are holding a council and they threaten to kill off all the Americans for murdering our men in the mountains."

I did not regard Nick very seriously, yet knew that, while not an aggressive people, the Zuñis were wont to resort to the well established *lex talionis* in such difficulties as the present one. I do not recall whether I thought of it at the time, but I might have recalled the story of how the Zuñis once settled all old scores against the Navahos by inviting them to witness a performance in a small plaza of the *pueblo*. While the affair was in full swing, they fell on their luckless guests and killed them to a man, fifty of them. They were likely to do such things on the spur of the moment.

At any rate, I went to the corral with Nick and gave him a horse. It did not occur to me at the moment as strange that Nick should wish so particularly to borrow a horse from me when horses galore had been arriving at Zuñi from the outlying villages and fields throughout the evening.

In our camp at the time were two white men, members of our party, two ladies, two men visitors (the late Lorenzo Hubbell and a respectable cattle dealer), and Titskimatski, known also as Squint Eyes, a Cheyenne employed as our herder. As a matter of precaution, I took Titskimatski with me to the Presbyterian mission school on the other side of the *pueblo,* roused the two ladies from their slumbers and escorted them to our camp for safety, with two little Indian girls whom they had adopted. How they were to be protected by us, however, was another question, for it chanced that, on the day before, we had fired all our cartridges in rifle practice, totally unaware, of course, that any emergency such as the present one could possibly arise.

The wailing and the howling finally died away and we joined Hubbell and the other visitor in slumber.

Before daylight the next morning Nick reached Fort Wingate, aroused Graham and told him of the trouble. The newspapers called it an "outbreak." The guest of Commandant Bradley, Graham was somewhat alarmed at what might happen and recommended that a troop of cavalry be despatched at once. At the Box S ranch, the two rustlers were placed under arrest by Lieut. John J. Pershing and taken to the fort, while the other troopers under Lieut. Alonzo Gray continued to Zuñi.

The effect of the troops was magical. The Indians had been surly to a degree, not even deigning to respond to our

morning greetings and not venturing near our camp—not
even those whom we regarded as among our best friends.
But on the arrival of the soldiers, who imparted the knowledge that the two killers had been arrested and taken to
the guardhouse, the attitude of the Zuñis instantly changed.

During the day I was asked to go to the *pueblo* to see
what I could do to relieve the wounded Capitán Lóchi. I
examined the wounds and removed the gobs of *piñon* gum
with which a medicine man had sealed them to repel all
evil influence, but, although I ministered to him in every
way I could during the ensuing fortnight, the poor fellow
died. The next morning I was visited by a relative of the
departed, who kindly informed me that the family did not
hold me culpable for Lóchi's death. I informed the emis-
sary that the message was deeply appreciated.

As for the rustlers, they were turned over to the civil
authorities and, when placed under trial at Los Lunas
months later, their appearance had been so transformed by
a local tonsorial artist that the Indian witnesses were not
sure of their identity and they were acquitted. In their
packs had been found moccasins with reversed soles—the
toe-ends where the heels should have been, in order to de-
ceive pursuers.

.   .   .   .   .   .

During the years to follow, Nick led a varied career.
Charged with witchcraft, he was once hanged by the
thumbs, his feet free of the ground, resulting in great torture. A troop of cavalry came, followed by the arrest and
conviction of two of those held responsible for inflicting the
punishment customary in crimes against the tribal com-
monweal. Later he was honored by election first as lieu-
tenant-governor, then as governor, of the tribe. There's
nothing narrow about the Zuñis!

Thirty-four years later, while we were concluding our

excavations at the Zuñi ruin of Hawikuh in 1923, Nick
came to me one day and said:

"Téluli, do you remember the Box S killing many
years ago, when I came to you at night and borrowed a
horse?"

"And I lent it to you, didn't I?"

"Yes, you lent it to me, all right. Do you know why I
wanted to borrow that horse?"

"Of course," said I. "You wanted to go to Fort Wingate
to see Mr. Graham."

"Naw, I didn't have to see Tsiponkwin. Besides, there
were plenty of other horses around, weren't there? Do you
remember that I told you that the Pithlanshiwani were
holding a war council and were talking about killing all
the white people?"

"Oh, yes, I remember that quite distinctly."

"Well, they sent for me and told me to go over to the
camp and ask you to lend me a horse. If you refused, they
would know you were a friend of the two murderers, who
had had dinner with you that day, and the Zuñis would
come over and kill all the white people in your camp."

This would have been a prompt and efficient way of
carrying out the Zuñi law of "a life for a life," but, as our
luck would have it, the warriors bided their time and,
when the opportunity came, murdered the cattle dealer
who had spent that uncanny night with us, and later took
the life of a young Mexican shepherd.

Our own precious scalps had been saved, but the score
was settled.

CAMP NOTHING

John P. Holman

Southern Alaska and British Columbia
have been John P. Holman's favorite
haunts and the goal of several journeys.
In the course of one of them, as here told,
he prospected for platinum at the base
of Mount McKinley, in company with
Professor Herschel C. Parker, a charter
member of The Explorers Club.

He was for five years editor of *Forest
and Stream* and spent several seasons in
Louisiana, where he established for the
National Association of Audubon Societies the Rainey Wild Life Sanctuary.

CAMP NOTHING

By *John P. Holman*

JOHN MADSON REALLY WAS TO BLAME FOR THE WHOLE thing. He had told the Professor that there was gold to be found at Pincher Creek, on the Kenai Peninsula, Alaska, and the Professor had brooded over it until he saw, not only gold, but also platinum, free platinum, churning and concentrating on the bars and benches of the lonely little stream that for centuries had gurgled and worn its way through the wilderness of the Kenai Flats.

The Professor let me into the secret one beautiful spring morning, as we sat on the deck of the steamship *Alameda,* which was twisting and turning through the tortuous channels of the Inside Passage to Alaska, whither we were bound on a mining mission to the region adjoining Mount McKinley.

"You see," said the Professor, "we might be delayed in getting up the Susitna River on account of the ice and we could easily take a side trip and run over to the Chickaloon Flats. There are lots of brown bear over there and maybe you could get some good shooting. John Madson said he had heard from someone who had heard from someone else that someone had once found gold on Pincher Creek and it might be a good plan to look into this."

I gazed out over the deep blue waters of Icy Strait, which we were just entering, to the glorious mountain ranges rising tier on tier into the limitless sky, all bathed in

sunshine and resplendent in garments of white. Truly it
was a land of dreams that stretched ahead and, somehow,
Pincher Creek seemed to fit into my dreaming with marvelous ease. I, too, began to picture the lonely shore, the
gurgling mountain stream and the glittering gold. The
more we talked about it, the more firmly it became fixed in
our minds that Pincher Creek was well worth looking up.
On our arrival at Anchorage, at the head of Cook Inlet,
a week or so later, we were more than ever obsessed with
the idea.

We talked the matter over with Bill Julian and Bert
McDowell, Alaskans of wide experience, and finally decided that we would see Nick Gykama, of the launch *Swan,*
and ask him to take the four of us, Bill, Bert, the Professor
and myself, across Turnagain Arm and put us ashore at the
mouth of Pincher Creek. He readily fell in with the plan,
as almost everyone in Alaska seems to fall in with any plan
anybody ever suggests, and, as the ice was still hard and
fast in the Susitna River and our trip in that direction was
barred for at least a week or two, we decided to start the
next morning.

.   .   .   .   .

We spent the remainder of the day getting together our
supplies. You who have been there know what that means
—the fever of it, the sheer joy of anticipation, as you go
from store to store picking up and checking off the things
you must have. We got a tent at a secondhand store, a
stove, an outfit of dishes, pick, pan and shovel for prospecting, groceries and so on down the list.

In a little while, we had all our newly acquired possessions checked off and sent down to the *Swan,* which was
tied to the government dock across Ship Creek. Early the
next morning, Redword, of the Crescent Hotel, got us out
of bed and we started down to the dock, filing along in the

cool morning air, sniffing the adventure to come with eager relish. Nick was waiting for us, the tide was right and we were off. Anchorage faded into a blur at the foot of the Chugach Mountains, whose rugged peaks pierced the morning mist in majestic grandeur. Turnagain Arm was shining ahead in one of its rare moods of quiet acquiescence, so we made good time, slipping easily along on the fast outgoing tide, down to Fire Island.

Here we had to anchor and wait for the incoming tide to take us up the Arm and over to Pincher Creek, so we utilized the time in eating lunch. Bill Julian lapsed into reminiscent mood, talking of old Klondike days, and kept us all laughing as we lay about the cabin and smoked away the noontide hours, until the floating blocks of ice began to hesitate and turn back in the opposite direction. Then Nick pulled up the mud-hook and we chugged slowly along the rugged coast of Point Possession.

Late in the afternoon we came to a break in the cliffs that lined the shore and located a stream dashing down a steep ravine. "This is the spot," said the Professor. Accordingly we anchored and, filling the dory with our duffle, landed on the "stern and rockbound coast." Three trips of the little dory sufficed to land the entire expedition on a great ice-pan at the mouth of Pincher Creek. Nick blew a short whistle of farewell and we watched the *Swan* fade out to sea, but Nick had given his solemn promise to return in ten days' time. "That will be long enough to see all that's to be seen here, I guess," said Bill, with a faint suggestion of a twinkle in his eye.

We fell to work and cleared a site for our tent as close to Pincher Creek as we could get it, "because it needs watching," Bert said, staggering across a log with the stove under one arm and a bag of flour under the other. The Professor had already started to prospect along the shore.

In an hour's time we had the tent up and the stove jointed, a fire going and prospects showing up pretty well, as far as dinner was concerned.

It surely was a wild spot we had chosen for our ten days' banishment. The roar of the creek, the boom of the ice, crashing and breaking up along the shore, the continual swish of the sea as it beat in rhythmic swells on the beach, all blended in the mighty music of the wild. The cliff rose perpendicularly a hundred feet or more above the ice-fringed shore, stretching in unbroken formation for miles in either direction, a barren waste of shore line, sky and water. Across the Arm lay the mountain ranges, solid snow from base to summit, white and solemn. To the north rose Mount Susitna, guardian of the marshes, and beyond, in a misty pall of sunset pink, towered mighty McKinley, the wondrous mountain of the lonely northland, clear-cut against the sky of night.

.   .   .   .   .

When everything had been finally made shipshape around our camp, the Professor returned with the startling information that he had discovered a "colmer" about a mile up the beach. "Gee!" said Bill, "I'm glad I brought my automatic." "You see," the Professor continued, ignoring Bill's remark, "this formation about here is probably a continuation of the formation found about Mount McKinley and contains the same kind of platinum-bearing clay. I have examined some of it under my glass and I can see little colmers of irridium and other platinum metals. There is no doubt that this whole country is one vast treasure-house, containing hundreds of millions of dollars' worth of platinum and gold."

"Well, that ought to be enough," said Bill. "Let's see what we have in the way of dinner."

After a hearty meal we stretched out in comfort and

smoked. The Professor continued his oration on the precious metals of Alaska, Pincher Creek gurgled and roared down to the sea and the tide lapped lazily along the ice-fringed shore. The fire died down in the stove and presently we crawled into our sleeping-bags and sleep came with the dim twilight of the northern spring.

The next day was one of exploration. We pushed back into the country a few miles and discovered a series of lakes, still bound in the fetters of winter, with only a little piece of open water near the mouth of each. The land was just awakening to the first faint call of spring. A few ducks circled overhead and settled down into some little patch of open water. Wild geese winged their strong flight northward. Under foot the soggy ground oozed and bubbled, as the snow patches gave way to the new grass of another year. All about the edges of the lakes moose tracks showed in great profusion, some decidedly new, clear-cut and fresh —others fast fading into the mould of other days. It was great to be in the heart of the wilderness again and to breathe the scent of the silent places.

Returning, we reached camp about noon. After lunch Bill and Bert took a number of pans of gravel at Pincher Creek and prospected for gold, but got only a trace of color, not enough to bring even the faint suggestion of a smile to a miser's face. It looked as though the Professor's estimate had been a little exaggerated, but we bore our disappointment with fortitude and the Professor explained with just as much gusto why it was that we didn't find any gold.

And this is the wonder of the northland—no matter what the actual outcome may be, an expedition is always successful. The country is so large and has so many prospects—and, anyway, it is always well to know what a certain part of it does not contain—so that, provided the food holds out, the trip is bound to be a success. But the great joy of it all lies in the wonderful lure of the unknown places, the strong desire to see what lies beyond.

.   .   .   .   .

All that evening the Professor brooded over the disturbing result of our day's prospecting. We could see that it worried him. Bill talked away about similar expeditions he had been on, when the gold he sought seemed to have evaded the issue, but the Professor sat by himself in a corner of the tent, studiously occupied with his magnifying glass, examining some samples he had gathered during the afternoon.

"Well, I guess I've got it now!" he finally exclaimed, after an hour of close study. "Got what—the measles?" asked Bill. "No, platinum," exclaimed the Professor, as he held up a big piece of hardened clay. "Beautiful! Magnificent! I can see platinum sticking out all over it! It's in colloidal form," he continued, "but it's there." And then he went on and explained how he had discovered it.

When we went to sleep that night, we felt convinced that, although we had found but little trace of gold near Pincher Creek, we were pretty close to the greatest source of platinum in the world and that the next few days would surely reveal some startling secrets in a get-rich-quick plan which old Solomon had overlooked.

Early the next morning the Professor led us up the beach a mile or two and we gathered a fine crop of rusty-looking specimens from the face of the cliff, carefully placing them in a canvas bag, under the watchful eyes of our mentor.

"I have found out," said the Professor, "that the ordinary method of panning is not reliable when you prospect this kind of ore; it has to be treated in an entirely different manner." "How do you treat it?" asked Bill eagerly. "With respect," said Bert, as he carefully placed a piece of the substance in the bag.

We carried the precious ore back to camp, the Professor expatiating upon the volatilization method of treatment, which would extract our new-found wealth from the earth and make us all rich beyond the dreams of Midas. It was truly a wonderful discovery. All you had to do was to roast the ore, stir in some chemical, distill the residue, roast again, stir in some water, catch the distillate, sell the stock, roast the investors, catch the money—and you had the secret.

"I've been twenty years in Alaska," said Bill, "and I never knew that platinum was so easy to find. I must have scraped enough off my boots to make the deposit in the Ural Mountains ashamed of itself."

"And then," resumed the Professor, "after we exhaust the supply of ore in this part of Alaska we can move our plant up the Susitna River and volatilize the Alaskan range. Then Siberia will undoubtedly open up another great field of endeavor."

"Yes," said Bert, "maybe we could sell it to the government railway for rails. Platinum rails would surely last longer than steel ones and steel is so high now, anyway."

"Well," said Bill, "as long as we have so much platinum, it's no use looking for any more gold. Let's go down to the flats tomorrow morning and see if we can get some geese. I don't think they would feel out of place in this company—only we would feel like cannibals eating them."

So the next morning we left the Professor to his dreams of untold wealth and Bert to his chores about the camp, while Bill and I started for the Chickaloon Flats, which lay about seven miles down the Arm, a great country of wonderful marshes that stretched for many miles, until they gradually faded into the purple haze of the Kenai Mountains. It was the summer home of countless wild fowl. Long before we had really entered into its deep loneliness, we felt its magic charm and heard the voices of the birds faintly borne to us on the breeze of the quiet morning. All the world was steeped in the joyous life of springtime. Walking along the shore, following the curve of the tide, revelling in the glorious sunshine, we experienced one of those rare moods when mind and body are in perfect tune and the joy of life is clear and distinct—no clouded visions to warp our thoughts, but an open path in the land of heart's desire.

We passed a long grove of spruce trees strung out along the shore, fringing the base of the cliffs above us, from which we caught the notes of songbirds resonant with the happy renewal of life. For many long months all this land had lain in the dark silence of relentless winter and now it was awakening to a glorious resurrection.

At last we came to the end of the beach. Beyond stretched a wilderness of flats and slews. I took off my shoe-packs and pulled on a pair of hip boots which I had brought from camp and, while Bill gathered some drift-wood and built a fire among the rocks, I trudged on alone to explore the marshes. Large flocks of geese were swinging in from the sea. Plump mallards splashed up from among the reeds and sped away on swift wings. Plover, snipe, cur-lew, almost every variety of water bird whistled and darted in endless profusion, all joining in a mighty chorus of notes, the music of the marshes.

I walked a number of miles into the heart of the swamp, sat down on a dead log, took out my glasses and spent a couple of hours in a most fascinating study. The little water birds were especially interesting. They were so quick and active in all their doings, restlessly swimming and quarrel-ling among themselves, as they wandered from pond to pond, and seemed to take such delight in life. I picked up a flock of Canada geese feeding in battle array, as skirmishers, spread out in a long line, advancing slowly over the drier parts of the flats. As I was returning to where Bill was sitting, I heard a number of shots in rapid succession coming from his direction and saw a flock of geese flying low, coming in from the sea. Bill was emptying his automatic pistol, in the hope of winning a fat goose for dinner.

I crouched low in the grasses when the flock spread out and turned in my direction. I had a little single-barrel shotgun. When the leader swung over my head, I stood up and fired. Down he came and landed with a great thud almost at my feet. I watched the others part and swing off, honking wildly, and sighed for another barrel in my gun, as I noted what a nice double I might have made. I reloaded quickly, but they were too far away to try another shot. As I was picking up my prize, a lone mallard sneaked across the sky. I swung my gun after him and he, too, curved to the ground. Two more geese turned and came back and one fell to a long shot. Then a sprigtail crumpled up and splashed into a shallow pond.

"Well, we have our Sunday dinner anyway," said Bill, as I came up to where he was sitting by the driftwood fire. We ate our lunch and smoked awhile and then trudged wearily back to camp along the shore.

We found the Professor and Bert busily engaged in getting supper. The bag of platinum specimens stood in one corner of the tent undisturbed and, although we breathed an atmosphere of great wealth, we felt that the supreme test of value must await our return to civilization, so we occupied the remainder of our term of banishment with matters of lesser import.

The next day we walked along the shore in the other direction a number of miles, climbed the cliff and stood on Point Possession, looking out across the great moose pastures of the Kenai, a wilderness of lakes and streams, thick forests and open swales and marshes. The mighty sweep of Cook's Inlet opened up around us, and beyond, to the north and east, stretched the dim ranges of the everlasting mountains, still clothed in the white garb of winter. The high tides were breaking up and carrying away the great pans of shore ice and the flood was dotted with bergs drifting out to sea.

That night a storm blew in from the east and the waters of the Arm were lashed to fury, while the waves beat in a smother of foam along the beach. We sat warm and secure in our little tent, with the stove burning cheerily, while the dim twilight of the stormy night wrapt us in a mantle of deep and brooding contentment.

Early one morning a faint whistle disturbed our slumbers. The Professor, looking out through the tent opening, perceived the *Swan* bravely chugging in toward the beach. We were all up in short order and, after a hasty breakfast, broke camp and soon had all our duffle on the beach. A few trips of the little dinghy sufficed to put it all aboard the launch. An hour later we were steaming away toward Anchorage on the fast-receding tide. "Goodbye, Camp Nothing," said Bill, as he watched the cliffs fade into the dim horizon.

Thus our voluntary exile on Point Possession came to an end, as did also John Madson's wild dream of gold on Pincher Creek. Results proved later that the colloidal form of platinum still awaits a master chemist.

We had found no gold, but something that was far more valuable—quiet companionship with the untrammeled solitudes of the great outdoors.

BULLWHACKING ACROSS THE PLAINS

W. H. Jackson

It is doubtful if anyone has done more than W. H. Jackson to preserve a pictorial record, with camera, brush and pencil, of pioneer times in the West.

Reaching Salt Lake City in 1866 in the manner he so graphically describes in the following story, he made his way through to California as a mule-team driver and then back to Omaha with a herd of broncos for the eastern market.

Here he began many years of work as a landscape photographer, first along the route of the Union Pacific until its completion and later on other railway lines from the Atlantic to the Pacific and down into Mexico. For ten years he was photographer for the famous "Hayden Survey."

In 1894-1896 he carried his camera over portions of North Africa, Asia and Australia and crossed Siberia in winter by sledge, photographing scenes for *Harper's Weekly*.

Although now in his eighty-ninth year, he is energetically cooperating in the work of the Oregon Trail Memorial Association and takes an active interest in any movement to perpetuate the story of the Old West.

In addition to numerous reports, he is the author of *The Pioneer Photographer,* written in conjunction with Howard R. Driggs.

BULLWHACKING ACROSS THE PLAINS

By W. H. Jackson

B ULLWHACK," AS DEFINED BY STANDARD DICTIONARIES, IS "a long heavy whip with short handle" and "bullwhacker" is a "driver of oxen." (Colloquial, western U. S.)

In the vernacular of the Old West all oxen are "bulls." The bullwhacker was found at his best in large commercial or military freighting outfits. The characteristic of his profession was a skillful use of the "long heavy whip with short handle."

Years ago I bullwhacked my way across plains and over mountains into the Far West. It was an experience that turned out to be well worth the hardships encountered, for it led first to my becoming an itinerant photographer, reproducing the scenes of my recent travels, and then quite naturally into the service of the U. S. Geological Survey (Dr. Hayden). For nearly ten years, with a pack-mule load of wet-plate equipment, I explored the wilds of the Rocky Mountains for pictures in places that had hitherto known only the Indian, the trapper or the prospector.

It all came about in an unpremeditated way, my going West. In April, 1866, I was getting on fairly well in Burlington, Vermont, and was engaged to be married in June. The engagement was broken, and I took the matter so seriously that from that moment I was possessed with the one purpose of going away from that place as quickly and as far as I could.

With only the money I happened to have in my pocket, I took the first train out of town and the next day landed in New York City. There I unexpectedly ran across a comrade of Civil War days, who happened to be out of work, broke and as ready as I for any enterprise, if far enough away from all former associations. The prominence given at that time to reports of the gold stampede to Montana decided the matter and there we would go, perhaps to gain much wealth!

With small means for such an undertaking, we left New York on April twenty-first, and two months later arrived at St. Jo, Missouri, then the end of railway transportation westward. During those two months we worked at odd jobs, going from one city to another, frequently separated but coming together again by arrangement, each time a little farther on our way, until finally, at the Missouri River, we were on the threshold of our adventure.

We had been advised by mining companies in New York before leaving that at the Missouri River landings we would find trains leaving daily for the Far West, among which it would not be difficult to get employment or passage to our destination. Sure enough, St. Jo was alive with the activities of forwarding companies sending out long trains of horse, mule and "bull" outfits into the Rocky Mountain region. In the city were also many young men thrown upon the country after the disbanding of the northern and southern armies, and various others seeking employment like ourselves.

We arrived at St. Jo with barely enough money to pay for a breakfast. A job must be had at once. An advertisement in the morning's paper caught our eyes—100 *Teamsters Wanted for the Plains. Apply at the Intelligence Office on Francis Street bet. 2nd and 3rd.* An immediate application revealed that "bullwhackers" were wanted to drive

from Nebraska City, Nebraska, to Virginia City, Montana,
at $20 a month—fee for the job, $1.50 each.

That was just what we were looking for, except that the
fee business stumped us for the time being and we retired
to see what could be done about it. First, we made the
rounds of the corrals and other places where trains were
outfitted, looking for other opportunities. We were dressed
about the same as when we left New York, which included
stovepipe hats—then customary headgear in the East. This,
with our obvious "tenderfoot" appearance, failed to impress favorably the hardboiled wagon bosses and teamsters
we interviewed. We soon realized that there was no chance
whatever for us with the horse-and-mule outfits, where
some degree of experience was required. Not so, however,
for bullwhackers, as was indicated by the low scale of wages
as compared with more than double the amount for "mule
skinners."

But how to raise those three dollars? Each of us went
about it in his own way, my comrade Rock to scrape acquaintance with other boys applying for the same job, who
might possibly be "touched" for a small loan, and I to sell
or pawn something. The only thing I had of any value for
that purpose was a box of colors, which was worth three or
four times what I asked for it. In an all-day canvass among
those having use for such colors, I failed—most fortunately,
as it turned out—to get a raise of any amount, and rejoined
my comrade discouraged with the prospect.

But my discouragement was changed to joy when Rock
waved a five-dollar bill in my face in proof that our money
troubles were over, at least for the time being. He had
won the confidence of one of the boys who said he was as
hard up as we, but finally dug up a little roll that he had
hidden away, almost from himself. That evening all who

had signed up, about two dozen, went aboard a river packet leaving at sunrise next morning for Nebraska City.

. . . . . .

Provided only with deck passage, we found our prospective quarters occupied by and overflowing with some three hundred Mormon immigrants on their way to the new Zion in Utah. In this dilemma, we were assigned the upper, or hurricane, deck, with an injunction not to intrude on the sacred precincts of the cabin deck. During the forty-eight hours of chugging up the "Big Muddy," we found the open deck delightfully cool and pleasant for sleeping, but a very inferno when the sun beat down on its unprotected surface in daytime.

The overseas immigrants, however, as observed from above, engaged most of our attention. If we did not care, or were not allowed, to go down among them, there was no hesitation on their part, young or old, in coming up to our deck in the cool of the evening. Among them were some pretty young girls, proselytes of the Church, who were the objects of much rivalry among the adventurous youths of our party in pressing their attentions, which in some cases were carried on to a degree where vigilant *duennas* unceremoniously packed off their charges to the lower deck again.

Aside from interesting conversations with the older immigrants about their former life and the hopes and aspirations which had brought them to America, we made acquaintance with members of our own party, with whom we were to be associated during the next few months. There were, of course, all kinds and conditions, from the professional of "Pike County, Missouri," to the "tenderfoot" from the East like ourselves; but among them were some fine young fellows of natural refinement and good education.

One of those boys, of a good Philadelphia family, who

went out with a train following ours, came West well supplied with money, bought a wagon and a team of mules and
intended to make the trip independently. He was persuaded, however, for safety as well as economy, to sell his
outfit and go bullwhacking. Two months later he was
killed, not by Indians, but by a stroke of lightning, and was
buried out on the Sweetwater under the shadow of the
Devil's Gate. Accidents were much more frequent than
killings.

We arrived at Nebraska City at two o'clock in the morning, the Mormons going a few miles farther up river to
another landing. The town was dark and silent; no one met
us, but, walking up into the business section, we slept away
the rest of the night on sidewalks and porches. An agent
then appeared, and, after a good breakfast, we were taken
to an outfitting house and permitted to purchase, as a
charge against wages, whatever we wished in the way of
personal equipment for the journey. Besides necessary
clothing, arms and ammunition were of most concern, for
it was predicted that troublesome times were to be expected
out on the plains and it was wise to be "well heeled." With
these preliminaries cared for, we were marched out some
three or four miles to the outskirts of the city, where our
train, the wagons corralled in a great circle, was already
loaded and awaiting only the arrival of its drivers to pull
out.

Nebraska City at that time was the chief point of departure for the West, particularly for freighting outfits, as
it was the most direct route, with fewer river crossings than
those usually associated with the trail to Oregon. With its
outfitting activities, it was a busy place. Only recently I
found in an ancient file of *The Nebraska News,* of the date
of our departure, that "a total of 184 wagons, each drawn
by six yoke of oxen, left Nebraska City in one day." It was

the last year of overland travel from the "River" by wagons, as the transcontinental railroad was then well under way in a feverish rush to beat its rival from the Pacific Coast into the Salt Lake Valley.

Our outfit, one of the many engaged in this freighting business, consisted of twenty-five wagons with trailers, drawn by six yoke of oxen, with from seven to eight thousand pounds of general groceries as the average load, all consigned to Virginia City, Montana. The personnel of the train was composed of two wagon masters (invariably called wagon bosses), a clerk, night herders, one or two extras and the twenty-five drivers. After being assigned to our wagons, with the yokes, whips, chains and other requisites for driving, we retired to our wagons to rest up for the ordeal of the next day.

. . . . . .

Before it was quite daylight we were roused from our sleep by the night watchman persistently pounding the wagon sheets and shouting, "Roll Out! Roll Out! The bulls are coming!" My first sight of them as they were driven in was not reassuring. Fresh from the freedom of the range for a long season, they came in bellowing, pawing the earth and raising a big dust generally. But there was no time to think about it, one way or another. No time, either, for breakfast. The business of yoking up began at once. The wagon boss, perched on a wheel, pointed out the ox each one was to take (which must thereafter be recognized out of its three hundred fellows for the same place in his team), and the liveliest experience I ever had was under way.

A six-yoke team was made up of leaders, three yoke in the swing, pointers and wheelers. The procedure was first to yoke the wheelers and hitch them temporarily to a wagon wheel; then, beginning with the leaders and hitching them to another wheel, the four other yoke were added in order, connected by chains running from yoke to yoke. The wagons being parked facing outward, the wheelers were first taken out and put on the tongue; then the long string of five yoke followed and were hitched on ahead of the wheelers.

It would make a long story if I should tell all that happened in that first yoking-up. Most of those engaged in it had never seen an ox yoked, much less driven one. The corral was crowded to the limit, many of the oxen were unbroken, others had forgotten all about it in running the range and some of the more refractory ones had to be lariated and drawn up to a wagon wheel to be yoked. The wagon bosses helped as much as possible and occasionally an old-timer lent a hand. But about all that could be done in individual cases was to have the ox pointed out to the prospective bullwhacker, and then let him go about it as best he could.

The wheelers were little trouble, for they were selected from the well broken standbys; but with the swing it was a merry scrimmage all the way through. The most difficult part of it came in the attempt to drive out this long string of five yoke to be hitched to the tongue. The contradictory "gees" and "haws" and the natural cussedness in the cattle themselves, bolting this way and that and getting into snarls with other teams, to the exasperation of their drivers, brought about a situation only straightened out by the bosses and others taking a hand in it. It was nearly high noon when all were hitched up and the bosses began starting out the teams for us, one after another.

Trailing each other closely, we went along fairly well for awhile. Our wagons, however, were not provided with brakes and at each considerable descent in the road, the team of oxen had to be stopped and a chain-lock thrown around one of the wheels. Coming to the brow of a rather steep hill, I attempted to stop my team. The wheelers held back all right, but the others pressed on and, overcoming the wheelers, raced down the hill to keep ahead of the heavily loaded wagon, which I expected to see tumbling over them in a wreck. But by good luck more than anything else the bottom was reached without a smash-up and we went on to camp and breakfast without further incident.

So much for the first day. Two weeks later and some two hundred miles on our way, we were at Fort Kearny. Matters had improved greatly in the meantime, as shown by the progress made. Our wagon boss had been wonderfully patient with his lot of green drivers, who by this time had become fairly efficient bullwhackers. The daily program was to be routed out of our wagons at daybreak, yoke up and pull out by sunrise, drive until 10 o'clock and then corral for breakfast. The noon lay-over lasted until about three o'clock, when the cattle were again driven in and the morning's work repeated. The afternoon drive continued until a good camping-place was reached, which meant water and grass, usually about sundown, but often much later.

We were divided into three messes, from which one was chosen or volunteered as cook, in consideration of being excused from other camp duties, such as greasing up and day herding. The other members of the mess took turns in providing fuel and water. Fuel was the greater problem, as over a large part of the way there was no wood of any kind and the only substitute was "buffalo chips," the dried and hard manure of the plains. The driver providing fuel for the day usually hung a gunny sack on his wagon and during the day's drive picked up enough chips along the road to meet all requirements. The fare, ample in quantity but not always of the best quality, was flour, bacon and coffee, occasionally diversified with beans and dried apples.

At Fort Kearny we came under military inspection as to

our preparedness against Indian attacks, and it was shown
that, besides individual equipment, the train itself was provided with a number of carbines. There also had to be not
less than thirty wagons in each train permitted to pass
farther up the Platte Valley route. A small train that had
been held up at Fort Kearny now joined us, and we traveled
together throughout most of the trip. Reports and rumors
of uprisings were continually coming in. All along the road
were frequent evidences of the raids of 1865, the most serious on the Plains, when stations and ranches were destroyed and travel entirely suspended for a time.

The prevailing rumor was that the Indians intended
making a clean sweep of the whole Platte Valley within the
next ten days. We had seen nothing of them, except a small
band of Oto Indians, who exacted a tobacco tribute from
some of the drivers. It was said that this was a bad sign and
that plenty of them were back in the hills watching the
road, and meant mischief.

Passing through Old Julesburg, rebuilt since its burning by Indians the year before, we soon came to the Upper
California crossing of the South Fork of the Platte. The
river at that time was more than a half-mile wide, and running swiftly over a shifting, sandy bottom. The greatest
depth at the ford was about four feet, but with many shal-
lows and sand-bars in mid-stream.

Other trains besides ours were engaged in crossing at
the same time. I can hardly do justice to the scene that was
being enacted before my eyes. The Platte was filled from
bank to bank with moving wagons, one to two dozen oxen
to each, passing back and forth. Removing most of their
clothing, the drivers were in the water up to their shoulders, lined up alongside their teams. The first plunge from
off the bank was the most exciting moment.

The cattle were nervous and reluctant to enter the

water and, when in, it was hard work to make them string out for a steady pull. As I have said, the river bed was a shifty quicksand and, unless the wagon was kept moving, it quickly settled down and became almost unmovable. When this was about to happen, there ensued a pandemonium of shouting, with snapping of whips and beating with sticks in urging the floundering oxen back into line, so that there would be no pause or slackening.

And so it goes, all the way over. The current is swift and strong in the deeper channels, sometimes taking the smaller cattle off their feet, until pulled back into line by the others. It took about two hours to make one trip and, as there were many recrossings, we were a day and a half getting our fifty separate wagons over.

Into this hurly-burly came a band of some fifty Indians returning from a great pow-wow at Fort Laramie. They began crossing at the same time—big braves on little ponies, squaws leading the packs, dogs and papooses perched on top, with other juveniles wading through in nature's garments only. Among them, coming through on foot, was a proud old man, whose only raiment except his breech-clout was a brass-buttoned officer's coat and cocked hat, both of which had probably seen service in the Mexican War. Both sides of the river were lined with corralled wagons, while groups of bullwhackers, soldiers from the near-by post and Indians were engaged in what was going on, or stood as onlookers along its banks.

. . . . .

From there on to Fort Laramie the driving became more arduous, and the landscape changed. Instead of level plains, we encountered steep hills, deep gulches and clogging sands, which drew heavily on the endurance of men and beasts in the hard grind of each day's drive. On the way we passed groups of Indians returning from the re-

cently disbanded treaty conference at the fort, from which
Red Cloud and his affiliated bands had withdrawn in pro-
test against the building and occupation of army posts in
their last hunting-grounds by an expedition that had just
preceded us from Fort Kearny. But at the fort all was quiet
enough.

Winding our way over the rugged foot-hills of the
Laramie range, then called the Black Hills, we halted for a
time at the "Junction" of the new Powder River cut-off
for Virginia City, Montana, by which the distance was some
five hundred miles shorter than along the old route by way
of South Pass. It was optional with our wagon boss which
road to take and we started out with the expectation of
going over the cut-off; but, in view of the disturbed condition of the country and the massing of hostiles in the
Powder River region, it was decided to keep to the longer
route. Of the few outfits venturing the other way, none got
through without loss, and some did not get through at all.

It was along here that we again encountered our Mormon companions of the boat ride from St. Jo to Nebraska
City. The composition of their train was novel and interesting in its variety of equipment. There was nearly every
kind of vehicle that ever rolled on wheels, from a single ox,
drawing a cart, to the prairie schooner with its six- or seven-
yoke team, with the same diversity in horse and mule outfits. They strung out on the road in a long procession, a few
of the more hardy or adventurous ones a long way in advance, but the larger number walking along with the
wagons.

Passing one of their encampments after nightfall, we
first saw numerous little campfires, inside and outside of the
corralled wagons, glimmering out of the dusk, from a distance resembling a military bivouac. Passing nearer, the
aroma from coffee pots and frying-pans greeted the senses;

and when the weather was favorable, the strains of music from violin and banjo could be heard, with much frolicking and dancing among the younger "Saints."

The region about Fort Caspar and from there to the Sweetwater was said to be the most dangerous on the road. Just after pulling out from Deer Creek for the Platte Bridge crossing at Fort Caspar, we were overtaken by the telegraph operator and mail carrier, flinging back word, as they dashed by on horseback, that the station had been attacked and burned, and some of the employees killed. Later we met three six-mule teams, the wagon boxes filled with soldiers and line repairers, tearing down the road like mad, bound for the scene of action. Keeping on our way, we never heard what really happened.

Soldiers at Fort Caspar gave alarming accounts of the Indian situation, but we saw nothing more of it as we traveled up the Sweetwater, over South Pass and down to the parting of the ways on Ham's Fork, where the road to Salt Lake branched off to the Southwest. At one of the Sweetwater stations I lost my New York comrade, who left the train to join the telegraph line service. I never afterward heard from him. In the meantime I lost all interest in Montana and decided that Salt Lake held greater attractions than a mining camp.

Here, at the parting of the ways, the matter had to be decided. Half a dozen others were of the same mind, but all backed out except Bill Maddern, who joined me in notifying the wagon boss of our intention to quit. Then there was the devil to pay at once. Both wagon bosses took a hand in threatening to have us arrested and sent to Fort Bridger. Despite further threats that they would see that we never got to Salt Lake or any other place, we stuck to our purpose and were allowed to depart, surrendering of course all wages due, and leaving the train as poor as when we joined it.

No trains for Salt Lake coming along just then, we were offered a job by a Mormon who had a contract to supply the Overland Stage Line with hay. From the hayfields five or six miles up Ham's Fork, we hauled it with ox teams, first to Granger, where we put up sixty tons, and then another stack of the same amount at South Bend station. We were at it three weeks for a dollar a day and an understanding that we were to be taken into the city at the end of the job. But the Mormon was a canny old codger.

When the day of settlement came, he said he had no money with him, and would pay when we got to the city, but, if we didn't care to wait, he would give us "store pay" on the little trading ranch at the ferry. Not caring for their goods, we preferred waiting, although, as my boots were about worn out, I did get a pair of moccasins. A train coming along just then, bound for Salt Lake City with two drivers short, our old employer interested himself in getting the job for us, suggesting that we would thereby be that much better off and, as he was going in at the same time, we could easily find him at his home address. We never did find him, however, and again had only experience for our pains.

.   .   .   .   .

Our new train consisted of fourteen wagons, but large ones, without trailers, and the usual six-yoke teams. We were twenty-three days en route, much of the way over mountainous roads. Fortunately, good weather prevailed until almost within sight of Salt Lake Valley, when we ran into the very worst weather and road conditions of the whole season.

On October twelfth we began climbing the Wasatch Mountains, the eastern boundary of Salt Lake Valley. Next day in Parley Park, near the summit, we lay over a day on account of rain. The following day was still dark and gloomy, but the train pulled out for the summit, everyone anxious to get over before conditions became worse. The road, however, could not have been worse. It was a new grade, hardly finished, and the long soaking of the day before had made the surface as treacherous as wet clay can be.

With our tremendously big, heavily laden wagons, we had little control. On downgrades all went with a rush, the wagons skidding dangerously over the banks, with drivers and cattle floundering around in the deep mud. The steeper upgrades were made only by the last ounce of effort on the part of men and cattle. By doubling teams, one wing of the train was pulled up to near the summit and left there.

The other half of the train remained at Ferguson's. During the night, snow began falling, and by morning was several inches deep. It was freezing cold when I was called early to go out on day herd until we pulled out, the night herder coming in at daylight. My only footwear at the time was the moccasins I had bought at Granger, already well used up and of little use in running around through snow and sagebrush.

After breakfast we took the remaining wing of the train right through to the summit, but not without a tremendous amount of hard work. At first the mud was frozen quite hard, but with the passing of cattle and wagons it was soon cut deeper than ever, some of the wagons sinking in to the hubs. The amount of punishment those poor bulls had to endure was something awful; some were so exhausted as to be hardly able to stand on their feet.

In the worst places half a dozen drivers, with the bosses lined up on each side of a team and with snapping of whips, shouting and pounding, urged the poor brutes on until

they were ready to drop in their tracks. With twenty-four
oxen to a team, it was nip and tuck all the way. My wagon,
one of the largest and most heavily laden, became so deeply
stalled that it was left behind. The last quarter-mile was the
hardest, but one by one the wagons crept up, until at nightfall only mine and another remained.

My thin moccasins, of course, did not hold out long
under those conditions and, before the day was over, I was
running around practically on bare feet. I was still on day-
herd duty and with another driver had to take the cattle,
as soon as unyoked, some two or three miles below, where
there was better feed and shelter for them, until the night
herder came out—and he was in no hurry about it. I got
back to our wagons about nine o'clock, finding the campfires all out, and only the remains of bread, bacon and
coffee for a late, cold supper. Bunking in at once, I did not
get out of that wagon again for three days, my feet being so
sore and swollen that I could not possibly stand on them.

Next day the two remaining wagons were extricated
from the frozen mud, after being entirely unloaded, and
then hauled up with the rest. For two days more, in descending Parley Canyon, I was bumped around in my
wagon like corn in a popper, but on the last day was able to
get out at the mouth of the canyon and drive into Salt Lake
City, ending my bullwhacking experiences for all time by
being docked for the time I had been laid up.

A LEAP IN THE DARK

Charles A. Lindbergh

To Colonel Lindbergh's world-renowned achievements in practical aviation need merely be added here the mention of his aerial survey of the Maya territory in Mexico and Central America, which was one of the earliest applications of the airplane to archeological exploration.

He is an Honorary Member of The Explorers Club.

A LEAP IN THE DARK

By Charles A. Lindbergh

I TOOK OFF FROM LAMBERT (ST. LOUIS) FIELD, SEPTEMBER 16, 1926, at 4:25 p.m. and, after an uneventful trip, arrived at Springfield, Ill., at 5:10 p.m. and Peoria at 5:55 p.m. I took off from the Peoria Field at 6:10 p.m. There was a light ground haze, but the sky was practically clear, containing only scattered cumulus clouds.

Darkness set in about twenty-five miles northeast of Peoria and I took up a compass course, checking on the lights of the town below, until a low fog rolled in under me a few miles northeast of Marseilles and the Illinois River. The fog extended from the ground up to about six hundred feet and, as I was unable to fly under it, I turned back and attempted to drop a flare and land, but the flare did not function and I again headed for Maywood, hoping to find a break in the fog over the field. Upon examination I discovered that the cause of the flare failure was the short length of the release lever and that the flare might still be used by pulling out the release cable.

I continued on a compass course of fifty degrees until 7:15 p.m., when I saw a dull glow on the top of the fog, indicating a town below. There were several of these light patches on the fog, visible only when looking away from the moon, and I knew them to be the towns bordering the Maywood Field. At no time, however, was I able to locate the exact position of the field, although I understand that

205

the searchlights were directed upward and two barrels of gasoline were burned in an endeavor to attract my attention.

Several times I descended to the top of the fog, which was eight to nine hundred feet high according to my altimeter. The sky above was clear, with the exception of scattered clouds, and the moon and stars were shining brightly.

After circling around for thirty-five minutes, I headed west, to be sure of clearing Lake Michigan and in an attempt to pick up one of the lights on the transcontinental line. After flying west for fifteen minutes and seeing no break in the fog, I turned southwest, hoping to strike the edge of the fog south of the Illinois River.

My motor cut out at 8:20 p.m. and I cut in the reserve. I was at that time only 1,500 feet high and, as the motor did not pick up as soon as I expected, I shoved the flashlight in my belt and was about to release the parachute flare and jump when the engine finally took hold again. A second trial showed the main tank to be dry and accordingly a maximum of twenty minutes' flying-time left.

There were no openings in the fog and I decided to leave the ship as soon as the reserve tank was exhausted. I tried to get the mail pit open, with the idea of throwing out the mail sacks and then jumping, but was unable to open the front buckle.

I knew that the risk of fire, with no gasoline in the tanks, was very slight and began to climb for altitude when I saw a light on the ground for several seconds. This was the first light I had seen for nearly two hours and, as almost enough gasoline for fifteen minutes' flying remained in the reserve, I glided down to twelve hundred feet and pulled out the flare-release cable, as nearly as I could judge over the spot where the light had appeared. This time the flare functioned, but only to illuminate the top of a solid bank of fog, into which it soon disappeared without showing any trace of the ground.

Seven minutes' gasoline remained in the gravity tank. Seeing the glow of a town through the fog, I turned towards open country and nosed the plane up. At 5,000 feet the motor sputtered and died. I stepped up on the cowling and out over the right side of the cockpit, pulling the rip-cord after about a hundred-foot fall. The parachute, an Irvin seat-service type, functioned perfectly; I was falling head downward when the risers jerked me into an upright position and the chute opened. This time I saved the rip-cord.

I pulled the flashlight from my belt and was playing it down towards the top of the fog when I heard the plane's motor pick up. When I jumped, the motor had practically stopped dead and I had neglected to cut the switches. Apparently, when the ship nosed down, an additional supply of gasoline drained down to the carburetor. Soon the ship came into sight, about a quarter-mile away and headed in the general direction of my parachute. I put the flashlight in a pocket of my flying suit, preparatory to slipping the parachute out of the way, if necessary. The plane was making a left spiral of about a mile diameter and passed approximately three hundred yards away from my chute, leaving me on the outside of the circle.

I was undecided as to whether the plane or I was descending more rapidly and glided my chute away from the spiral path of the ship as rapidly as I could.

The ship passed completely out of sight, but reappeared again in a few seconds, its rate of descent being about the same as that of the parachute. I counted five spirals, each one a little further away than the last, before reaching the top of the fog-bank.

When I settled into the fog-bank, I knew that the ground was within 1,000 feet and I reached for the flashlight, but found it to be missing. I could see neither earth nor stars and had no idea what kind of territory was below. I crossed my legs to keep from straddling a branch or wire, guarded my face with my hands and waited.

Presently I saw the outline of the ground and a moment later was down in a cornfield. The corn was over my head and the chute was lying on top of the cornstalks. I hurriedly packed it and started down a corn row. The ground visibility was about one hundred yards.

In a few minutes I came to a stubble field and some wagon tracks, which I followed to a farmyard a quarter-mile away. After reaching the farmyard, I noticed auto headlights and a spotlight playing over the roadside. Thinking that someone might have located the wreck of the plane, I walked over to the car. The occupants asked whether I had heard an airplane crash and it required some time to explain to them that I had been piloting the plane and was searching for it myself. I had to display the parachute as evidence before they were thoroughly convinced. The farmer was sure, as were most others in a three-mile radius, that the ship had just missed his house and crashed near by. In fact, he could locate within a few rods the spot where he heard it hit the ground, and we spent an unsuccessful quarter-hour hunting for the wreck in that vicinity before going to the farmhouse to arrange for a searching party and telephone St. Louis and Chicago.

I had just put in the long-distance calls when the phone rang and we were notified that the plane had been found in a cornfield over two miles away.

It took several minutes to reach the site of the crash, due to the necessity of slow driving through the fog. A small crowd had already assembled when we arrived.

The plane was wound up in a ball-shaped mass. It had narrowly missed one farmhouse and had hooked its left wing in a grain shock a quarter-mile beyond. The ship had landed on the left wing and wheel and had skidded along the ground for eighty yards, going through one fence before coming to rest in the edge of a cornfield, about a hundred yards short of a barn. The mail pit was laid open and one sack of mail was on the ground. The mail however, was uninjured.

The sheriff from Ottawa arrived and we took the mail to the Ottawa post office, to be entrained at 3:30 a.m. for Chicago.

MANEUVERING IN MATTO GROSSO
John Lindsay

After graduating as a civil engineer from the University of Pennsylvania, John Lindsay spent two years as field observer for the Department of Research in Terrestrial Magnetism of the Carnegie Institution of Washington, during which time he traveled over every country in Central and South America, Mexico and the Falkland Islands, crossing the Andes five times and traversing Matto Grosso, as related in the accompanying story.

He lives at present in Porto Rico and travels extensively in the West Indies.

MANEUVERING IN MATTO GROSSO

By John Lindsay

I ARRIVED BY RIVER BOAT AT CORUMBA, THE BACK DOOR
of Brazil. Dr. Rodriguez Albes, the Brazilian Minister at
Asunción, had supplied me with letters of introduction to
the *aduana,* or customs, officials and to the President of
Matto Grosso, so that, on arriving at Corumba, I had no
difficulty in getting through the customs. Baggage, instruments and gear were soon on the way up the hill to the
hotel in a small donkey cart.

In my room, with six-foot-high partitions and the circulating air above, eavesdropping was unavoidable. The
half-Indian, half-Portuguese garble was unintelligible to
my unaccustomed ear, when to my amazement in perfect
English I heard, "That looks like an American's baggage
below." My immediate reply was "Righto!" and into the
room burst Gow-Smith, the explorer. Our dramatic meeting over with, I persuaded Gow-Smith to join my expedition as far as the capital of Goyaz.

By then I had gathered information about the feasibil-
ity of the overland trip from Cuyaba to Goyaz, through
unexplored Matto Grosso. One or two men who had been
to Cuyaba spoke of the impossibility of one man making
the trip. There was unanimous accord on the uncertainty
of even a party getting through. This was proven in the
unsolved mystery of the Fawcett party.

We planned to journey up the Cuyaba River to the

town of Cuyaba, jump off civilization and follow the earth's magnetic equator, my object being to establish a set of magnetic stations along the zero magnetic latitude and to make solar observations for position, while Gow-Smith, who had come down from the Explorers Club of New York, would make a study of the Indians and unexplored territory in the heart of Brazil. If we could not get through overland, we would go down either the Xingu or the River of Death. I shall never forget that conference, as the plans we formulated led to startling consequences later.

No explorer passes that section of the world without meeting Ramsay, the once-famous Texas sheriff, now two-gun cattle and ranch owner at Descalvados, one of the most interesting characters in the world, a friend of Roosevelt and arch-enemy of the cattle thieves of that section. We had to pass on and refuse his prolonged hospitality. His last words to me were:

"Never draw a gun unless you mean to kill. In fact, never draw a gun under any circumstances. Shoot from the hip and be sure you kill."

. . . . .

The boat trip to Cuyaba was to take nine days. The boat was poor and extremely dirty. The heat was intense. Mosquitoes were thick. If the heat had not kept us from using the small cabin we had obtained, it would have been impossible to sleep in it anyway on account of the fleas and numerous other insects which infested the place, not to mention the smells from the scullery and the continual grinding of the wood-burning engines. We therefore used it to store our instruments, rifles and equipment, while we slung our hammocks on the deck.

Most of the other passengers were soldiers. There were, however, several civilians, including two women. They spent their entire time in discussing the revolution which

was reported to be in full swing near Cuyaba. Meanwhile
Gow-Smith and I discussed our probable route and spent
the remaining hours in playing checkers on a board we
had made, using cartridges for men, trying thus to forget
the intense heat and the continual insect pest.

On the thirteenth day we reached the San Lorenzo
River and the following day entered the Cuyaba River.
Here our troubles commenced. The river was extremely
low, there being only a few feet of water. Our boat no
sooner got clear of one sand bank than it stuck on a second.
This necessitated several of the crew wading out with a
cable, attaching it to a tree further up and across the stream
and, by means of a small donkey engine, dragging the boat
several hundred feet further up the river. It was a slow,
monotonous process.

By this time the food supply was getting low and we
were reduced to the usual rice and beans and supplied with
a kind of hardtack to take the place of bread. We had
reached wild country. The brush was quite dense along
the banks of the river and *jacaré* could be seen basking in
the sun along the shore. Beautiful-colored birds flew from
tree to tree, while monkeys swung from one limb to another.

A bullet through the body of a *jacaré* or small croco-
dile, simply causes it to dive and from all accounts it ap-.
parently recovers. If one can judge the relative position
of the eye as they come sailing through the water, with
only a periscope showing, the bullet is not wasted.

On the eighteenth day our system of cabling up the
river proved useless, the water being only four feet deep.
We were permanently established on the sand. The next
day we transferred all our belongings to a small motor
boat, which had come down from Cuyaba, and continued
our journey northward. By three p.m. the motor boat

stuck, so that we had to change again, this time to a native canoe. It proved to be very precarious traveling, as the least sideward movement meant that Gow-Smith and I, as well as baggage and instruments, would be in the water. However, by midnight we reached a place on the bank that our paddlers told us was the Cuyaba landing. It was pitch-dark. The landing proved to be some rocks at the water's edge. After much confusion and shouting, someone brought a lantern and we arranged for transportation which took us to the "Great Hotel Gamma." Tired and hungry, we reached the hotel, to find that no rooms were available. After much discussion with the proprietor, I obtained permission to sling my hammock in the room of a Turk and obtained a disturbed, although much-needed sleep.

Arranging for a *comitiva,* or pack-train, proved to be extremely difficult. Almost all the desirable mules had been taken over by the government and the few remaining ones were being held by the owners at a prohibitive price. Finally we were fortunate in meeting Colonel Jao Albino, who had been one of Roosevelt's guides on his historic trip and who was at that time the owner of several good mules. After lengthy negotiations he consented to let us have six animals. We then secured the services of an Indian named Militao, bought the necessary gear, such as saddles and camp equipment, and, taking a supply of rice, beans and coffee, rode off from the last point of civilization for our trip into the little-known territory of Matto Grosso.

We felt secure until an advance-guard of cut-throats, murderers and bandits caught up with us at Rio Manso. Former lieutenants of the diamond king, Colonel Morbeck, they had been turned loose at Cuyaba on their promise to "finish" the colonel. Taking a good look at our rifles and goodly supply of ammunition, they "invited" us to accompany them on their mission. Our three-day ride in their company does not form a part of this story, but, when one of the band who had taken a personal liking to us, warned us that we should get away as soon as possible, we fortunately were able to bid them a hospitable adieu, continuing northeast while they took a southern direction. Every one of the band was killed a week later by Morbeck's men.

. . . . .

We followed the Rio Manso closely for days. One morning, after Militao had captured the mules, we got an exceptionally early start. We were now nearing the Indian territory. Fortune had been with us and I had managed to obtain excellent observations toward completing the magnetic map of the world.

Gow-Smith rode on ahead. I agreed to follow his tracks. Since an almost disastrous experience with Militao and our not-so-sure-footed mule, I had decided to remain at the comparatively slow pace of the *comitiva,* keeping an eye on the instruments and our rapidly diminishing food supply. We had to reach water; without it, the animals were lost and it would be only a question of time before we would ourselves give out. We were out of the thicker brush and had reached a sort of plateau, which, however, was far from level and meant some pretty rough climbing for the animals and picking the best possible track.

Gow-Smith was now far ahead. No usual stop for rest and *almuerzo* while the sun passed the zenith. It was a matter of ride on and on until we reached water.

Late that afternoon the tracks of Gow-Smith's mule became fainter and fainter and finally, due to the rocky nature of the ground, it was almost a matter of guesswork. Militao showed no signs of fatigue, the animals were still keeping their follow-the-leader movement, but their pace became noticeably slower as the day wore on. I personally felt fine and not more tired than usual from a day's hard ride, but certainly could have done with a stop for food and water. I knew that this would mean disaster, however, for, if once we stopped and unpacked the mules, it would be the latter's final resting-place.

Finally a division of possible routes. Had Gow-Smith gone on the northern or the southern track? I left Militao with the animals while I rode on about half a league along the southern trail to see if there were any possible chances of picking up the lost hoofprints. Not a sign. A decision must be made and the wrong one meant possible end to our exploration and ourselves.

I was worried about Gow-Smith. He had no food with him, although plenty of ammunition. The Chevantes? Just how far north were we? I had not taken a solar observation for several days, but knew that the territory I was in was the Indian No Man's Land, the fighting ground of the Chevantes and Bororos. The latter I could take a chance on, but to encounter the former on the warpath might mean anything. I must go on. I am not superstitious, but how was one to decide? I took out my Oaxaca knife and twirled it in the air. It fell pointing directly along the northern side of the divide. We went north.

Down, down the slope I went, scanning all around for thicker, greener growth, a sign of water. The sun was sinking fast, but a beautiful sunset held no thrill for me that afternoon. League after league. It grew dark. I rode a little ahead of the *comitiva*. The shrubbery became thicker. I pulled out a flashlight and examined the ground thoroughly—nothing.

Finally I came across the print of a deer. More shrubbery, thicker and thicker. It was ten o'clock and I could hear Militao swearing and urging on the tired animals. At last tracks and plenty of them, only not those of Gow-

Smith's mule, but those of *oncas* (Brazilian spotted leopard). My hopes rose, as I knew we were now certainly approaching water. I awaited Militao and the *comitiva*. At last their cursing broke the stillness of the night, growing louder and louder as they approached.

We held a conference. I decided to make a last try for Gow-Smith by firing my rifle. The first shot rang out with a thundering echo. No response. Another and another, until I had used five precious cartridges. I had no sooner told Militao that we would strike out again and keep on till water was reached, when the heavens seemed to open and we got too much water. We unpacked the animals and turned them loose, but it was too heavy a rain to undo the packs. Therefore we simply covered tent, instruments and gear with the pack-skins, swung hammocks and turned in. A fire was impossible, which of itself would not have been particularly sad but I had seen too many *onca* tracks to feel easy and also I knew that, when I fired my rifle, I was inviting trouble from the Chevantes tribe, if they happened to be on the warpath that particular evening and on the lookout for their "friends," the Bororos.

I was afraid to sleep that night, as we would make an excellent meal for hungry *oncas*. My vigilance was not un-rewarded, for, just as the rays of dawn appeared, I saw two gleaming, malevolent green eyes about ten yards away from my hammock. Unnerved, I fired—and missed. The brute sprang but fell dead just short of Militao, as I had instinctively pulled the trigger again and had plugged the leopard through the brain.

By morning the rain had stopped and we prepared a breakfast of rice, beans and most welcome coffee. When the sun had reached a height of ten degrees above the horizon, I took a shot at it and found we were much farther north than I had planned, actually in the heart of what was thought to be Chevante Indian territory. We wasted no time. Mules cornered and packed, I led the *comitiva* toward the mountain range. Up and up we went.

Toward mid-afternoon I looked back at the camp we had left and saw smoke curling above the jungle growth— not a pleasant sight, as it brought to mind the poisoned arrows of the Chevantes. Militao had also seen it, for he was now urging the animals on with renewed vigor. We continued over the welcome crest and down again into the next valley. An uneventful night and we were heading for the second range.

.   .   .   .   .

The sun stood at about eleven when I took my first look over the peak and, instead of seeing only the wilderness I had expected, there, directly in our path and within shouting distance, were a group of about twenty of the best-looking, apparently wild Indians I had ever seen. All were gathered about one man, who appeared to be their leader. He was naked except for a large head-dress. Immediately they spotted the *comitiva*, as we must have been beautifully outlined against the sky. No time for thought, maneuver I must.

Calling Militao, I instructed him to unload the instruments immediately. Never had that tripod and theodolite been set up so quickly. I cannot swear to my accuracy, but leveling did not matter, and the earth's horizontal intensity to five decimal places would not have stopped a well thrown spear or counteracted the prick of an arrow point. I had the sun's image on the colored glass as they came up, filled with curiosity. Waving my arms, I immediately invited the man in the prominent headgear to look. This did not have the desired effect. He did not appear interested in the sun's image but kept staring at me in a manner which did not add to my peace of mind.

Oddly enough, Militao, who had been standing by, spoke up in a peculiar tongue, which was most startling to me, as I had supposed until that moment that I had fully mastered his complete vocabulary. There was instant response from the Indians. Militao explained that the leader had been particularly taken with my field-glasses. After negotiating, I made a trade for his headgear, a gorgeous affair of macaw feathers, trimmed with small paraquita feathers near the band. The Indians were hunters from the semi-civilized Bororo tribe.

No, they had not seen Gow-Smith. However, they explained hopefully that they had been away from their village for several days and others of their number might have picked up his trail. A day's ride with the Bororos for guides and we came upon a sight I shall never forget. In the midst of the wilderness, where even the natives would not venture, was a well planned village and, as we approached, out of a main building came a figure in clerical garb.

It was a *padre* from the Colonía Corazón Jésus. For twenty years these Italian priests had given up their lives in the aiding of the Bororos. There was no need for more maneuvering now, for five minutes later Gow-Smith rode up, accompanied by the Father in charge.

After five delightful days with the *padres,* Gow-Smith and I, with the faithful Militao, set out again into the jungle to continue our work and finally reached Goyaz.

RESCUED FROM THE "DEATH TRAP" OF
THE ARCTIC

Burt M. McConnell

Arctic exploration, gold mining, aviation, and writing have been Burt McConnell's principal occupations to date.

In 1913-1914 he was meteorologist and secretary to the commander of Stefansson's third arctic expedition and, as he here relates, organized the rescue of the *Karluk* survivors, marooned on Wrangel Island.

Then followed a year as assistant editor of *Recreation Magazine,* two of war service, and ten on the editorial staff of *The Literary Digest,* with a special interest in aviation and the air mail.

In 1929 he went into the woods of northern Quebec, sixty miles from the nearest known inhabitant, without food, clothing, matches, weapons or shelter, and maintained himself by bow and arrow for two months (September 21-November 26) just to show that it could be done.

RESCUED FROM THE "DEATH TRAP" OF THE ARCTIC

By Burt M. McConnell

T HE MAN SITTING OPPOSITE ME HAD JUST FINISHED HIS first square meal in seven months. For five months, each seemingly longer than a year, he had been marooned on Wrangel Island, a hundred miles off the coast of northeastern Siberia, with never a sight of sail or a smudge of smoke. His shaggy, matted hair streamed down over his eyes in wild disorder. His grimy face was streaked and furrowed with lines and wrinkles. His caribou-skin clothes were begrimed with seal oil, blood and dirt and were in tatters. The color of his skin could not have been judged from a look at his hands, so stained were they. His full, unkempt beard effectually hid the emaciation of his cheeks, but his sunken eyes told of suffering and want.

This was John Munro, chief engineer of the *Karluk,* flagship of the Canadian Arctic Expedition of 1913.

The story of the dramatic rescue of Munro and his eleven companions is a narrative to stir one's blood. It is the story of a comparatively unknown arctic tragedy— a sturdy whaling vessel, with twenty-two men, one Eskimo woman and her two children on board, caught in the drifting ice fields north of Alaska and carried westward for fifteen hundred miles, only to be sunk by the shifting floes; the dogged retreat of the shipwrecked lot over a hundred miles of chaotic pressure ridges; the needless loss of eight lives before the party reached Wrangel Island; the seven-months' wait by the survivors, camped in flimsy tents, while two of their number pressed southward over another hundred miles of ice to Siberia in search of aid; the death of one castaway by accident and two from scurvy; hardship and starvation; finally, the heroic rescue of the nine men, the woman and the two Eskimo children after they had abandoned all hope. A small amount of seal meat and a few arctic fox carcasses were the sum total of their food supply. Munro had but twelve cartridges left with which to sustain himself and his companions throughout the winter. Long ago they had given up hope of ever being rescued. They knew only too well Wrangel Island's inaccessibility. They had matches, but their clothing was insufficient for another winter. These survivors of the shipwreck must have perished, had they not been rescued.

In February of that year they had been fairly well clad in caribou-skin shirts and trousers and sealskin boots, but after working, hunting and sleeping for more than six months in these garments, their bedraggled appearance can better be imagined than described. The nerve-wracking suspense suffered by the castaways while waiting for relief must have been terrible. They had no way whatever of knowing whether or not Captain Bartlett had been able to reach the mainland, and very few ships ever pass near enough to distinguish even a smoke signal on the island.

Their rations, even with the strictest economy, had lasted only until the first week in June, for the three months previous to our arrival they had subsisted on whatever they could obtain.

Wood was plentiful and fresh water could be had by melting snow or pieces of year-old salt-water ice that had been exposed to the rays of the sun and thus made into fresh ice. Tobacco, tea, coffee, salt, sugar, flour and other luxuries they had not known for several months, but still they were alive and well.

. . . . . .

". . . You came just in time," Munro was saying. "I had only a dozen cartridges left with which to kill game enough to last us through the winter. We'd have starved to death long ago if it hadn't been for Mr. Stefansson's Mannlicher rifle. One day, after our food supply had become exhausted and we were wondering where the next meal was coming from, I saw a seal out on the ice. I managed to creep to within a hundred yards of him before being compelled to stop to steady my nerves. It seemed to me that the seal must hear the beating of my heart.

"While resting, this thought came to me: if you miss him, you will starve! For seals were very scarce, and we had seen no other game in several days.

"The seal was basking in the sunlight, unaware of his peril. I crept to an advantageous position, set the hair trigger of my rifle and took deliberate aim—or tried to. I think I drew a bead on the head of that seal for at least two minutes, then almost collapsed when I realized that my hand was too unsteady to make my aim certain. Here was meat enough for all of us for a week, our very lives were at stake, and yet here was I with an acute attack of something akin to buck fever! It was a terrible predicament. I lay back on the ice, trying to regain my composure. But then came the thought that, if I waited too long, the seal might disappear into the water.

"I aimed again, but my nervousness still frustrated me; in that state I could not have hit a barn, so I waited. During this wait I kept saying to myself, through my clenched teeth, 'I'll get you!' and calling the poor seal all sorts of names. I was a caveman for a few moments. Then, when I had talked myself into a state of comparative calm and had convinced myself that I simply could not miss, I fired. The seal gave one convulsive shudder and lay still. For the time being, our troubles were over. But you came just in time."

. . . .

Stefansson, with a scientific staff of nine, of which the writer was a member, and a ship's crew of fourteen, four Eskimo men, one Eskimo seamstress and her two girls— thirty-one persons in all—had set out in the whaler *Karluk* in the summer of 1913, under the auspices of the Canadian Government, to explore as much as possible of the area lying between Alaska and the North Pole. While Stefansson, Wilkins (now Sir Hubert), Jenness and I, with two Eskimo dog drivers, were ashore hunting caribou on the north coast of Alaska, the ice in which the ship was imprisoned, eighteen miles from land, broke away under the influence of an unprecedented northeast gale and carried the helpless *Karluk* westward toward Siberia. There, sixty miles north of Herald Island, she was crushed like an eggshell some four months later. Meanwhile we hunters were left marooned on the north coast of Alaska, but we managed to make our way to Point Barrow. It was not until a year later that the rescue party, of which I was a member, reached the survivors on Wrangel Island. It was a stirring story that the castaways had to tell. . . .

A phonograph concert was being given in the after cabin of the *Karluk* when the first warning of disaster came —a tremendous groan from the vessel's staunch timbers as the ice field closed in. Everyone worked desperately to save the necessary articles that had been left on board until the last moment should come. Every care was taken to secure the twenty-seven dogs, for only by their aid would retreat over the treacherous ice fields be possible. It was a weird and dreadful night for the twenty-two men, the Eskimo woman and her two little girls of eight and four years.

Presently to the creaking of the *Karluk's* timbers as they were smashed like pencils by the irresistible pressure was added the touching sight of her actual writhings as she twisted and turned like an animal in a trap. Then came the rush of in-going water. A few hours later the ice field which had sealed her doom receded at the whim of an unknown current and the place where lately a gallant ship had floated became a mere blot of black water, strongly contrasted against the spotless white of the surrounding ice and snow.

Nothing like this had ever happened before in the Arctic. True, more than a hundred ships have been caught in its icy grasp and hundreds of adventurous young men have gone down with their vessels or lost their lives in the retreat over the ice to shore, but never in history had a crew been compelled to abandon a crushed and sinking vessel in the midst of the long arctic night, with the temperature thirty-five degrees below zero and a raging blizzard blowing from the northeast.

Captain Bartlett, Peary's ice navigator, was in command; Stefansson and the five of us who made up the hunting party were marooned between Point Barrow and the Mackenzie delta, a thousand miles from the scene of the disaster. Fortunately Bartlett, in anticipation of the crushing of the ship, had removed several months' provisions to a comparatively safe place on the ice. Here, at Shipwreck Camp the twenty-five castaways settled themselves to wait for the end of the arctic night and the return of the sun, so that they might retreat to Wrangel Island, a hundred miles away.

As the hours of daylight lengthened, Captain Bartlett began preparations for the grim race against starvation and the elements. First, an advance party of seven men and two sleds was sent to cut a trail with picks, over which the retreat might be made. Theirs was a heart-breaking task; often it was necessary to haul the sleds up steep acclivities with ropes and let them down on the opposite side in similar manner. Finally, when they arrived at what they believed was Wrangel Island (but which was in reality Herald Island, a forbidding mass of rock rearing itself abruptly out of the sea) they found their way blocked by three miles of open water. Electing to wait until the ice on which they stood drifted ashore, First Officer Anderson and Second Officer Barker, with two seamen—all inexperienced in arctic travel—piled their provisions on the ice, pitched their tent alongside and sent the other three men and the two dog teams back to Shipwreck Camp.

The officers and seamen who stayed with the provisions were never seen again; the shifting ice fields probably carried them off into that region marked "Unknown" on maps of the Arctic. These four were the first pawns to be sacrificed on that white chessboard that has claimed perhaps seven hundred lives since explorers first attempted to find a Northwest Passage to China.

Against Captain Bartlett's wishes and contrary to the advice of their companions, another party of four—three scientists and one sailor, departed from the base camp, poorly equipped and pulling their own sleds. This was composed of Dr. A. Forbes Mackay, Oceanographer James Murray, Anthropologist Henri Beuchat and Seaman Morris. Both Murray and Mackay had been with Shackleton's Antarctic expedition, but their experience was no match for the furious blizzards that frosted their feet and hands and broke up the ice over which they laboriously made their way. Impatience to reach Wrangel Island ahead of the others cost them their lives. Their bleached bones were found some twelve years later on the wind-swept shore of Herald Island. Four more were thus added to the death list, making eight in all.

The main party, under Bartlett, set out and in three weeks reached Wrangel Island. Their slow advance was marked by innumerable hardships. For five days in succession a blizzard compelled taking refuge in the tents. Trails had to be chopped with picks and spears through rough ice piled into chaotic ridges. Vast floes had been tumbled about and thrust upward into barricades by pressure, as if by the hands of a giant.

On reaching Wrangel Island, a comfortable camp was first established. Then Captain Bartlett and Katarktovik, the youngest Eskimo hunter, set out over the ice toward the mainland of Siberia, a hundred miles away, with seven dogs and a sled. It was a terribly difficult journey, during which Bartlett and the Eskimo lost several dogs and broke through the ice many times. Later in the spring the trip could have been made safely in Eskimo *umiaks,* but none of these sturdy walrus-hide boats had been brought from the wreck.

Reaching the mainland, the two travelers continued to East Cape and thence to Emma Harbor, a distance of several hundred miles. They were then taken on the whaler *Herman* (Capt. Pedersen) to St. Michael, Alaska, at the mouth of the Yukon, where Bartlett was able to communicate with the Canadian government by telegraph. At its request the United States government sent the Revenue Cutter *Bear* to the rescue.

On her first journey the *Bear* was only able to get within twenty miles of the ice-encrusted island. The Russian government, which also responded to Canada's appeal for aid, sent two ice-breakers, but Fate played another trick on the castaways—war was declared and Russia recalled her vessels by wireless. An effort was also made by an American whaler to reach the survivors, but, blocked by heavy and densely packed ice, they were unable to make a landing. At least three other whaling ships would have made the attempt from Point Barrow, but everyone seemed to feel sure that the *Bear* would be able to reach Wrangel Island on her first voyage.

Meanwhile, I had reached Point Barrow. When the *Bear* did not succeed, I became alarmed for the safety of the shipwrecked party, came down to Nome on a schooner, and telegraphed to the Canadian government, suggesting that it charter a vessel to proceed independently of the *Bear* and approach the island from a different angle where, presumably, there would be no ice. When this suggestion was rejected, I went to talk the matter over with Olaf Swenson, an old friend, owner of the *King and Winge,* a tiny trading schooner, and urged him to attempt the rescue. He agreed to join in the race and invited me to go with him.

. . . . .

We left Nome for Wrangel Island, six hundred miles away, on September third. September fourth we reached East Cape, Siberia, where Swenson engaged fifteen Eskimos and secured an *umiak*. This was for use in case the schooner should find herself, like the revenue cutter, unable to get near the island. Light in weight and covered with walrus hide, this Eskimo boat could be dragged over the ice which might surround the island, and launched in the open water beyond. On September fifth we sighted loose ice fields and the next day entered the pack within a hundred miles of our goal.

We were not in serious peril, save as anyone entering an ice pack is in peril. An ice field is a danger zone; it is always in motion and at the mercy of winds, tides and unknown currents. The possibility of having your ship crushed by the ice or frozen in for the winter, when you have only two months' provisions on board, is not pleasant to contemplate. Therefore, in undertaking this rescue, Swenson did a fine and admirable thing. In the Arctic he is known as a "white man."

First came several hours of ice bucking. The staunch little vessel, only one hundred feet long, but with excellent engines of 140 horse-power, forged her way through seemingly impassable fields. When Captain Jochimsen, the ice pilot, encountered an ice field through which the schooner could not force her way, he skirted its edge until he found an opening. His fearless and skillful seamanship and uncanny knowledge of ice conditions contributed largely to our ultimate success.

The ice was moving all this time under the influence of a southwest wind, which made the situation all the more dangerous for the *King and Winge*. The field became heavier and more densely packed as we neared the island. We passed pressure ridges almost as high as the masts of the schooner. Sometimes, when sent full speed into the ice, she would slide clamberingly up on the floe, like a polar bear struggling out of the water, and break it down with her sheer weight.

At midnight, when it became too dark to see clearly, the fight was postponed until daylight and Captain Jochimsen, who had been on deck for more than twenty-four hours, retired for a three-hour nap. Progress was resumed with the coming of dawn, and slow and discouraging it was.

After three hours of bumping, crashing and grinding against the densely packed ice, we emerged from the hundred-mile field within sight of the precipitous granite cliffs and the sandy beach near Rodgers Harbor, where Captain Bartlett had told us the survivors would be found. Within five miles of the beach open water appeared, after which the approach became a comparatively simple matter.

When we were within two miles of shore, a tent was sighted by the lookout in the crow's nest and, as we came nearer under full speed, a flag-pole and a cross could be seen near the tent. When within half a mile of the camp, Captain Jochimsen began blowing the ship's siren at intervals. When no one appeared in answer to its blasts, our spirits fell. We had expected to find twenty-three people at this place, yet we could discern only a dilapidated four-man tent, a flag-pole and a cross. No sleds or dogs were to be seen.

Suddenly a man emerged from the tent on hands and knees. I shall never forget his actions. He did not show signs of joy. He did not wave his arms and shout for sheer happiness when he sighted the ship, as some of us had expected the survivors would do. He did not run up and down the beach to attract our attention, but rose and stood rigidly beside the tent, gazing at us as if dazed.

It was plain enough that he at first refused to believe the evidence of his eyes, as he had first refused to believe the evidence of his ears when he heard the sound of the siren. Indeed, he brushed his hands across his eyes more than once, as if to clear away something which might be there, deceiving him, before he finally decided that the *King and Winge* was a real ship come to rescue him.

As soon as he reached this conclusion, apparently, he turned abruptly and entered the tent without another look toward us or even a friendly wave of the hand. Almost immediately, however, he reappeared, bringing with him a British flag, which he raised to half-mast. This confirmed the news conveyed by the cross—someone had perished. At first we were apprehensive that the entire party, with the exception of the one man we saw, had died, but this gloomy possibility was dispelled presently by the appearance of two other men. But still we were wondering. Could it be possible that but three remained of the twenty-three?

None of this strange trio made any demonstration. Each seemed dazed by his sudden good fortune and stood near the tent and stared at us.

The first mate hastened the launching of the Eskimo *umiak*. When it came within a hundred yards of the beach, the man whom we had seen first started toward us, taking a rifle from its case as he came. He seemed to be loading the magazine with cartridges, at which our Siberian natives became greatly frightened. They pointed to their foreheads and muttered, "That man long time not much eat; him crazy." Swenson quieted their fears, however, and they kept on paddling.

.   .   .   .   .

The greatest moment in Swenson's life and mine came when we landed upon the beach and advanced to meet this strange individual, who proved to be Munro.

"How many are left, Chief?" I asked, almost timidly.

"There are nine at Cape Waring, all well the last I heard, but Mamen and Malloch died last spring and are buried near the tent over there." He pointed. These men had been my best friends in the whole party. With no means of procuring fresh meat, they had fallen a prey to a form of scurvy.

But there was no time for reflection, for Fred W. Maurer, one of the *Karluk's* firemen, then came up. He was pale, weak and emaciated. I did not recognize him until Munro spoke his name. Templeman, the steward, next appeared. He was gaunt and very pale. The caribou-skin clothing of these two men was in the same condition as Munro's; they had worn it and slept in it for seven months.

The belongings of the rescued men were collected in a

very few minutes, while I sat in the tent and wrote a message for any rescue vessel that might arrive later. The tent was left standing to serve as a beacon. We then hastened aboard the ship, which was immediately headed for Cape Waring, thirty miles to the eastward. After breakfast I played the phonograph for the three guests and gave them a glad surprise when I played "Pierrot's Serenade," a violin solo by Kubelik, which had been our favorite record on the *Karluk*. I had bought this record in Nome, just before starting, for this very occasion. That shows how much confidence I had in Swenson and Captain Jochimsen.

Although Munro had lost about thirty pounds in weight in the preceding months, he was found to be in remarkably good condition and insisted on piloting the schooner to the other camp. He was soon coaxed below, however. Our obliging Japanese steward prepared a delicious breakfast for the castaways, who consumed quarts of coffee in a few hours, huge spoonfuls of both sugar and condensed milk going into each cupful. An hour after a meal they were hungry again. It seemed impossible to fill their long-neglected stomachs. Each man devoured a whole can of condensed milk with a spoon, as though it were ice cream.

On the way to Cape Waring each survivor indulged in a bath—a luxury they had not known in six months or more. They were given clothing from the ship's stores and by almost everyone on the ship. Their tattered skin garments were thrown overboard.

We reached Cape Waring almost before we were aware of it. With the aid of glasses we could see two tents on shore and near them little black figures running up and down the beach to attract our attention. These survivors were regarding our arrival with far more manifestation of excitement than had been made by the Rodgers Harbor group.

We were again able to take the schooner to within two

miles of shore before being blocked by the ice. Kurraluk, the expedition's best Eskimo hunter, fearing that we would not see the tiny tents, had gone out over the ice to intercept us. His look of wonder and astonishment at seeing me was laughable; he thought Stefansson and his hunting party had been lost in the same gale which carried the *Karluk* to the westward. As he shook hands with me, he muttered to himself and insisted on feeling my arms and shoulders to see if I really were flesh and blood.

The early morning had been cold and clear, but now snow began to fall so thickly that the schooner could not be seen at a distance of a quarter of a mile. Several of the marooned men rushed out upon the ice to meet us. They had hunted every day, we were told, but had not been able always to kill enough game, so that at times the little band had gone hungry. They were in a desperate plight when we arrived and had abandoned hope of rescue for that year. They had but forty cartridges left—forty cartridges with which to provide meat for nine hungry mouths for a whole year! Their flimsy tents were torn and full of holes, and their food supply was almost exhausted. George Breddy, fireman, we learned, had accidentally shot himself and was buried on the hill near the camp. They had intended to move their camp that day to the north side of the island, where driftwood was known to be comparatively plentiful. They would have done this but for the snowstorm, in which event we would have been compelled to search the island for them.

. . . . . .

Thus twelve of the original ship's company were rescued; three were known to be dead and eight were missing, while Captain Bartlett and one Eskimo reached Siberia safely. Such was the fate of this section of the most elaborately equipped expedition that ever went into the Arctic.

Only three dogs out of twenty were left and but one sled of their original three. The rest had been lost, with their loads, in the water between Wrangel Island and Herald Island. The survivors had a plentiful supply of matches, but their clothing was woefully inadequate. One man had frozen the great toe of his foot in March and it had been amputated with a butcher knife and tin-shears. Another man had fallen into the water, and had frosted the heel of one foot; he was still limping. They made a weird-looking procession as they walked out to the *King and Winge,* by twos, with the Eskimo baby on her father's sled. They climbed aboard the little rescue ship and we sailed away in the direction of Herald Island, where we hoped we might sight some of the eight missing men. But a solid field of heavy ice barred our progress and, although we skirted its edge for forty miles, no sign of the missing adventurers was to be found.

The next afternoon we met the revenue cutter *Bear,* on which Captain Bartlett was a passenger. Bartlett boarded the *King and Winge* and, after thanking Swenson for the trouble he had taken, ordered the survivors to transfer to the *Bear.* So the revenue cutter, instead of the *King and Winge,* still gets credit for the rescue. Captain Cochran, of the *Bear,* took me also to Nome, where we arrived September thirteenth, gratified with our success, but feeling only too keenly the lose of three members of the expedition and our inability to find any trace of the eight missing men. Their names, with the names of the three who perished on Wrangel Island, are to be added to the staggering toll which the Arctic has taken from the ranks of adventurers since the fourteenth century.

MALOS HOMBRES

Gordon MacCreagh

At seventeen Gordon MacCreagh ran away from home and went to India. This was the start of a migratory period crowded with interest and variety.

After trying his hand at sundry odd jobs, he turned to gathering butterflies and other insects in Nepal and Bhutan for the British Museum and trophies of the hunt for visiting sportsmen to palm off as their own "bag."

And then, with another American as partner, he carried an open-air moving-picture show to the back-country villages of the Shan States and the northeastern frontier of Burma. For lack of other currency, admissions were paid in chickens and pigeons; a patron tendering a goat at the box office would receive a ticket and five chickens in change.

Surveying work in Burma and the Yun-nan province of China was followed by travel in Straits Settlements, Siam and the Dutch East Indies, including a daring trip across the island of Borneo.

He then transferred his activities to South America, crossing the Andes from the west coast in 1924 with the Mulford Expedition to explore the Upper Amazon basin, as entertainingly recounted in his *White Waters and Black*. The following year he led the Amazon Film Expedition up the Amazon and the Rio Negro to the headwaters of the Uaupés.

Still moving eastward, he made two trips to Abyssinia and wrote an interesting book about that interesting country, *The Last of Free Africa*.

MALOS HOMBRES

By Gordon MacCreagh

IN THE SPRING OF 1923, "THE WEST COAST LEADER," AN enterprising weekly newspaper published in Lima, Peru, printed a hurried note to this effect:

It is reported that a revolt has broken out among the Aymara Indians of the Bolivian highland. Indians are massing on the heights overlooking La Paz. The city is surrounded and all railway communication has been suspended. The situation is said to be serious.

For some people, Fate means life cast in a pleasant mold and fortune attendant upon their ways. For others it means just cussed luck. It was my kind of Fate to be in the midst of that uprising.

La Paz is topographically, as well as in many other ways, a very unexpected city. In the high Bolivian plateau, thirteen thousand-odd feet up in the air, flat as a midwestern plain and immeasurably more dreary because that elevation is high above the timber line and nothing grows there except a sparse, wiry bunch grass, there appears a sudden deep gash in the ground, an immense oval bowl.

One has been told to expect a quite abrupt arrival, but no one ever realizes the sheer suddenness of the thing. The snow line of the Cordillera Real crawls slowly nearer till one seems to have arrived at its very foot; and still one wonders, looking across the desert plain, where this mysterious city can be hiding—till the train is suddenly crawling along the very brink and one looks down the sides of craggy, Grand-Canyon-colored cliffs, a startling thousand feet onto the close-clustered, red-tile roofs of the city.

A city easy to surround. A city horribly easy to roll huge boulders into from the lip of the chasm.

. . . . .

On this particular spring morning the anxious question in the citizens' minds was, when would the Indians muster up courage and initiative enough to begin to roll boulders? And would the military storm the heights and dislodge the Indians?

Through the field glasses one could see bands of them on the surrounding height—painted, match-stick rows of them silhouetted along the abrupt edge, and gaudy, poncho-wrapped masses of them where the slope was not so steep. Thousands of them, silent, sullen, incuriously inert, as the Aymara usually are.

They required only a leader, some strong man with decision and initiative enough to appropriate to his own use their persistent legend about a Redeemer, a Messiah who would free them from the white man's yoke—a leader to release their smouldering resentment and fan it to a flare of screaming, maniac slaughter. Up till now they had lacked just that one man—and, as a matter of fact, they continued to lack him to the very end of their fiasco.

For the Aymara are a people who have been. Long years ago, they were a sturdy warrior people, whom the Incas could not conquer, so they made honorable treaty and lived as tributary allies. Today they retain only the stout limbs and barrel chests of a mountain people living in a thin and chilly atmosphere.

Serfs of the soil they are, broken under the white man's yoke. Their country has been split up into vast estates, measured by the thousand acres, owned by *haciendéros* who seldom come to their *haciendas*. Most of the people belong upon the soil where they live; they go with the estate—"so many acres and so many families." They subsist, under incredible climatic hardships, upon tiny potatoes, absurd nubbins of corn, beans and barley that never ripens; they herd undernourished sheep and llamas on their barren hills—and for most of them two days of labor in every week must be given without remuneration to the *haciendéro* on whose estate they happen to have been born.

They are hopeless, helpless, broken, sullen—and they hate.

One dim hope remains to them—that the Redeemer, the promised Messiah of their legend, will some day actually come. It seems that all oppressed peoples must have some such legend in order to continue to live. For their Messiah the Aymara wait with the furtive, scowling patience of caged creatures.

One relaxation they have—fiesta. On the forgotten vestiges of their bloodthirsty religion have been grafted the dates and dogmas of a hazy Catholic Christianity. The ancient worship of the miracle of an evergreen tree in mid-winter has become Christmas; the bloody human sacrifices of the new spring have been translated into Easter—and so forth.

Thus it happens that, at the major festivals of the Christian church, the Aymara are in the mood to expect portents; and in their somber, sodden manner they make merry.

How can a broken people make merry except by drowning their sorrows? So the Aymara send ponderous, logy reed rafts across Lake Titicaca, over the Peruvian border, and smuggle in Standard Oil kerosene cans full of excoriating alcohol. And they drink that desperate spirit by the pannikin-full and go into amazing, involved ceremonial dances, the meanings of which they have long ago forgotten, and they lurch and stagger and shout and fight.

Gods of the fiery sun, how ferociously they fight! Not a fiesta passes but there are killings throughout the scattered villages. It is at fiesta time that the Aymara become potentially dangerous.

The citizens of La Paz knew all these things, knew to a hair just how potentially dangerous the Aymara might be, given a leader able to stir up mass indignation in the same way that individual fighting rage was aroused. And those citizens were very properly nervous.

What they did not know was how the military garrison would respond. For the whisper was that the unrest had been engineered by the *politicos*, by the ever-existent anti-government, or revolutionary, party, the plot being to cause a diversion from without the city by stirring up the Indians to throw off the yoke, while they won over (so the rumor ran) certain leaders of the city garrison.

As for the diverting Indians, the *revolucionistas* retained the cheering knowledge that, once they had grabbed the reins of government, they would come along with a few regiments of riflemen and slap the yoke right back, and the only ultimate difference to the Indian would be that the master of the *hacienda* for whom he labored, instead of Don Carramba, would be Don Sacramento.

. . . . .

All these things were told to me. I was not in the surrounded city, with its garrison of doubtful soldiers, menaced by Indians on the heights. My fate was to be a lone *Americano* in the middle of this unrest in an Aymara mud village called Chapalto, near Tiahuanaco.

Tiahuanaco is an ancient place of extraordinary interest. A great pyramid mound, with a hollow top filled by a lake and enormous carved monoliths are relics of a pre-Inca civilization about which nobody knows anything very much.

A railway, built by British capital, passes close to Tiahuanaco on its way to the capital. At Tiahuanaco is an ancient Spanish church, which displays, built into its sturdy walls, the anomalous vandalism of great blocks of pre-Inca stones, carved with symbols of a lost sun worship. A quite modern and utterly inexcusable crime it is that, for a mile or so on either side of the splendor that once was, the railway has utilized convenient carved monoliths for building its culverts.

I was in Chapalta, a few miles from Tiahuanaco, to see what strange and ancient things I might dig out of the ground. With me was a Bolivian Cholo half-breed, who acted as interpreter and who, in spite of the many things that have been said about Latin-American half-breeds, was a strong man of his hands and a staunch *compañero*. He was as dark as any Aymara and he had the broad nose and high cheek bones of an Inca idol. But he wore pants and a coat, so to the Indians he was just another cursed *blanco* who imposed the yoke.

This being Easter, a benign and overworked Catholic priest was making his semi-annual rounds of the back-country villages, performing the ceremony of open-air mass, to remind the angry people that they were Christians.

The Cholo half-breed and I were guests at the priest's hut for dinner. We dined sumptuously on the best that the land afforded—*charque,* which is dried mutton full of weevils; *chuno,* which are frozen potatoes and the most horrible vegetable in the world; and broad beans with leathery shells, which are very good for mules.

We knew nothing about what was going on in the distant city. No trains had run for a week. There was no news.

We were isolated. Rumors came. Only rumors. The talk was that La Paz had been stormed by hordes of Indians —which we disbelieved. There was a story that a neighboring *hacienda* had been burned—which we thought might be true. A horribly circumstantial detail that the Indians had nailed the *corregidor* of the next district to the adobe wall of his own office and had disembowelled his Chola wife before his expiring eyes later turned out to be true.

For fact we knew nothing. The priest smiled with weary patience and shook his head.

"These people are children," he said. "If one knows what un-understandable things a child may suddenly do, one may know what these people might, or might not, do. Sometimes—alas, most of the time—they are bad children. But children they are and, until they have learnt, their doings must be forgiven."

Which was all very well and right and proper for a priest, but was thin comfort for a godless American who had come to dig ancient pottery and heathen gods out of the ground.

"Sacred shoes!" swore the Cholo half-breed. "What they do concerns me not so much as what they have. Drunken Indians are *malos hombres,* but they can be handled. But I have heard talk that some of these people have an old shotgun or two hidden away, stolen from the railroad-building time."

The priest nodded somberly. He had been hearing that story for years.

The day was Saturday, the day between Good Friday and Easter Sunday. The Aymara were holding high fiesta. Tiahuanaco is close to Lake Titicaca. Raw alcohol was therefore plentiful. A few minor fights had already broken out, but no knives or *machetes* as yet.

We *blancos,* as I have said, knew nothing. We were utterly isolated, cut off from all communication. We knew only that trouble was in the air and that it had reached the point of violence in other places. Our locality was, so far, comparatively peaceful. We looked to our guns and we—the priest—prayed.

Toward us the Indians had shown no direct hostility. Sullen looks and mumbled curses had been the worst. There was an atmosphere of expectation. Something was going to happen, something unusual, upon which much would hinge.

.   .   .   .   .

An uncomfortable afternoon passed. Outside, the Indians howled as they lurched around their dances and screamed as they fought. Then a sudden extra-frenzied howling announced we did not know what—we thought, perhaps, an onslaught.

An Aymara lad, a faithful convert of the priest's, came in anxious perturbation and told us, "It is the condor dance."

The priest explained. On certain occasions, rare and only when matters of the greatest import were on hand, an old *brujo,* a witch doctor, came down from his hermit hole on the high slopes of the Cordillera and performed the mystic Dance of the Condor. The priest did not know the significance or the symbolism of the dance. Probably the laymen of the Aymara had forgotten. But the occasion of the dance always meant something of unusual importance and excitement, and the Indians were always especially unruly upon these occasions.

"*Qué diablo,* we must look at this," said the Cholo. "We may learn something of what is happening."

But nothing was to be learned. If the Indians really

knew or understood, they were in no mood to tell a *blanco* —they had never told any *blanco*.

The *brujo* was a man with an extraordinarily leering mephistophelian face, who wore the skin of an immense condor over his shoulders and manipulated the ten-foot wing-spread with his arms. He strutted and leaped and crowed, evidently imitating the doings of a condor; and each time he flapped the enormous wings and leaped high in the air and then made the gesture of rending flesh with his great beak, the sullen Indians surged round him and yelled with excitement.

The Cholo, boldly enough, caught an Indian less drunk than most by his poncho and offered him money to explain what it was all about.

Ordinarily these people, who seldom see cash money, would have traded at least words—if only subterfuges—for a silver coin. But this attempt, as well as another following it, evoked only a mask of dull stupidity and lowered eyes.

A screaming mob of dancers whirled and lurched towards us. We dropped hands to our guns—for my part, because there was no place to run to. But the mob broke up, to show us in its center another wizened ancient, who jigged with a dried snake and a stuffed animal that looked like a weasel.

As he hopped, he leered and muttered things at us, and the Indians howled appreciation. One drunken fellow jostled us.

"We'd better get out of this," I told the Cholo. "Our presence isn't doing anybody any good."

A solid jam of staggering dancers filled the village square and cut us off from the priest's house. So we retired down a mud alley to the hut that we had rented from the local realtor for our stay for two *bolivianos* (30 cents) and hoped that the horde would all get sufficiently drunk to forget about us.

Why didn't we there and then run away, while the running was good? For one reason, night was upon us. And for another, where should we run? The whole countryside was making fiesta. Disturbance was everywhere—in other places, as far as we knew, worse than here. Better the devils we knew than the devils who might be yet drunker somewhere else.

So we shoved the wooden bolt of the slab door into its hole in the adobe wall and hoped that the good priest's prayers would be effective.

In about an hour a hurried scratching on the door made us open. The priest's convert lad scuttled in with fearsome caution, to tell us that the *padre* had sent him to warn us about the news.

The condor witch doctor's manipulations had resulted in signs and portents. The omens were good for abolishing all white men from the land. The long-promised Redeemer was at hand. And tonight, the tenth day of the month of the condor, was the night set by the ancient gods for the first great stroke.

The *padre* thought, continued the boy, that, as long as he kept out of the way, he might be safe, for he hoped— fond man—that his people would remember his many ministrations to them. But we, *blancos extranjeros,* must be warned to lock ourselves in, to hide, to run away, to take whatsoever futile precautions we might think of.

The precaution that appealed to me was to steal out— dash out, maybe—make our way—fight our way, possibly— to the Tiahuanaco railway station five miles away, where we thought we had seen a hand-car.

That, said the convert lad, would be a very good thing

250 TOLD AT THE EXPLORERS CLUB

to do, only the Tiahuanaco station agent had thought of
the same precaution four days before.

The Cholo offered a craftily desperate plan.

"Muerte de Dios," he growled. "The alley is empty. All
are in the square, listening to the devil bird. Maybe we
can sneak out and break into some other hut, where they
won't think to look for us. There will be only women; we
can quiet them. We may have to kill some screeching hag;
but, *cien diablos,* we must protect ourselves."

The idea had its merit. With extreme luck one might
find a hut the inhabitants of which were all assisting at the
orgy in the village square. Failing that, one might have to
overpower and perhaps gag the decrepit occupants and
remain in close hiding. The flaw in the plan was that the
other residents of the hut would eventually come home.

Hurriedly we debated the possibilities. When the other
residents should finally come, we speculated hopefully that
perhaps everybody would be so befuddled with that excoriating alcohol that no attention would be paid to the
noise we might make in subduing the newcomers.

The thing might be pulled off; we were desperate
enough to attempt it. The only alternative was to flee into
the darkness and be overtaken by daylight in the open
country, surrounded by a maze of little Indian villages.

.   .   .   .   .

I don't know what might have been our decision or
what the outcome. Decision was taken out of our hands
by a crescendo outburst of yells from the village square
and, after much confused shouting, a shot. With horrible
menace the thing seemed to crash out beyond all normal
proportion above the bedlam of ferocious yells. I felt as
chillingly cold in the stomach and as chokingly dry in the
throat as I hope never to be again.

"So that settles it," said the Cholo, with grim fatalism.

"There's the gun I was afraid about. The only question now is, how many do we get first?"

He broke his revolver and, with a certain nervous determination, spun the barrel to see if it was loaded.

"Fastest place I know for a reload is to carry them in the mouth," he muttered. And, like a bill-poster with tacks, he stuffed a half-dozen verdigris-covered, greasy cartridges into his cheek.

Myself, I had a Luger seven-millimeter, with an extra clip in the holster, so I was provided with all that I could ever hope to use in case of a rush.

The only question remained, how much shooting would drink-crazed Indians stomach before they broke? Or would they keep on coming?

With the first reverberation of the shot the convert had moaned, "Here they come!" and darted out of the hut, away from our unsafe company, into the night.

There ensued more confused shouting and argument down in the square—a delay in the expected rush for our hut. We, crouching in the dark, interpreting every sound with tense anxiety, judged that the meaning of the lull was just another drink of Dutch courage all round before the screaming mad rush to the massacre of the whites.

It seemed so. Presently a babel of shouts and yells broke out again and with it the confused sound of men moving drunkenly.

"This is it," I thought to myself. "Aim for their stomachs, *amigo*," I told the half-breed. "No fancy shooting."

With startling affright another gun-shot crashed out in the further dark. More howls. Drunken yells of triumph. Two more shots. Shrieks. Another shot. Shouts. Yelps. Howls.

"*Sangre Cristo!*" the Cholo swore in nervous irritation. "They need to work up some more courage yet. I wish they would come and get it over with, one way or the other."

But the ferocious clamor remained only a clamor. And the clamor presently—miracle!—lulled and died down and sublimated to a maudlin mumbling.

Strangely futile and devoid of menace. No more belligerent yells, no movement in our direction, no rush of murderous maniacs. Nothing. Heavy silence. A stertorous silence, if one may say so, after the night's animal howling.

We in our stuffy hut began to breathe with less tremor in our inhalations. The half-breed interpreted the silence.

"The leaders quarrelled in their cups over how to set about us and somebody who has the say-so got hurt. *Carallos*, if we get through till morning, we'll grab that gun and handle this soused mob."

· · · · ·

Morning dawned on a subdued and very sick village. We walked unmolested through lanes of sad and sorry Indians, to join forces with the priest once more. Some of the shrieking maniacs of the night before now sat on their doorsteps in the cool morning air, holding their heads in their hands. We picked our steps over the sprawling bodies of others. Nobody looked at us.

The *padre* told us the news of the night.

"The good God has delivered you, my friends," he rejoiced, and blessed us. "He has heard my prayers and the end justifies the inscrutable means. Listen now and I will tell you."

It appeared that a combination of circumstances had all worked together toward inflaming the murderous intent of the night—the general unrest, of course; the condor wizard; a rumor that the long awaited Aymara Redeemer had appeared on Mount Illimani, the tutelary deity of La Paz.

And then a most extraordinary combination of events

—a miracle, almost—had occurred to dissipate the determination to slaughter.

This was Easter, you remember, the Saturday between Good Friday and Easter Sunday. Observe now how the simple savage accepts the deeper mysteries of Christianity.

The Aymara have absorbed just enough of the Easter doctrine to know that, during the period of Good Friday to Sunday, God is dead—He has been crucified and has not yet risen again, you see.

So here is a splendid opportunity to work off any outstanding grudges, for God can't see the evil-doer and mark it up against him in the big, black sin-book for future hellfire. Hence the Aymara have developed the custom of saving up their particularly ferocious yearnings for revenge till the Easter fiesta and giving full vent to them during the interregnum while God can't chalk it up against them.

An astounding and fascinating thought!

What better opportunity for a massacre could be desired? Naturally then, as the liquor soaked in, certain of the more turbulent bad "injuns" decided to inaugurate a St. Bartholomew's Eve against the hated *blancos*.

By the sheer intervention of Providence, however, it had come into the fuddled mind of the ringleader—he who possessed the stolen gun—that he might as well take advantage of God's interregnum to pay off an old score that he had been saving up against an enemy a little way down the block; it would be a good beginning to the massacre anyhow.

So he went with all his gang to his enemy's house, shoved the unsteady muzzle of his scatter-gun against the man's chest and blew the whole of his enemy's back out with both barrels at once.

That was the first resounding crash we had heard. The drunken gang yelled their success and howled to the rest of the populace to come and see what manner of men they were, and they all celebrated the favorable omen of their enterprise with another kerosene can full of liquor.

Then another man in the gang, stimulated by the spirit of emulation, remembered that he, too, had an enemy. So they all went round together and shot the wretched man and his son and a couple of women who happened to be in the house.

For which further success they had to celebrate riotously once more. After which, by the grace of God, they were too besodden drunk to move, and the massacre died in the horrible throes of its birth.

So the good *padre* was able to reiterate piously, "So you see, my friends, prayer is answered!"

And the Cholo crossed himself and said fervently:

"*Válgame Dios! Qué libramiento!* What a deliverance! Come, *amigo,* let us consummate this saving of our lives. Let us find an *Indio* sober enough so that we may beat some intelligence into him and find out where that gun is and let us immediately grab it."

Which we forthwith most expeditiously did. And we spent the rest of the morning looting the Indians' huts of supplies of food and barricading the priest's house against an indefinite siege.

Which fortunately did not materialize. The promised Indian Messiah failed to put in an appearance. The political *coup* in the city was a fiasco. Presently trains ran again. Soldiers marched through the land. The turbulent Aymara reverted to their accustomed dull, sullen subjection.

And I dug some rare bronze godlings out of the ground.

BURIED ALIVE

Warren King Moorehead

Director of the Department of American Archaeology at Phillips Academy, Andover, Mass., Dr. Moorehead has devoted many years to archeological exploration in New England, the Ohio Valley, the southern states and the Southwest.

He is a member of the U. S. Board of Indian Commissioners, is an authority on the mound-builders of America and has published many scientific books and papers.

BURIED ALIVE

By Warren King Moorehead

DURING THE SUMMER OF 1888 I WAS EXPLORING INDIAN tumuli in Ross County, Ohio. In my college days I was a long-distance runner and very strong. In fact, in 1885 I ran what would now be called a Marathon—from the college buildings (Denison University, Granville, Ohio) down a long hill, through the valley, up high hills southward, to the Baltimore and Ohio Railroad tracks, up the track to East Newark and back over the same route, a distance of more than twenty-two miles. These strenuous runnings put me in excellent physical condition and my survival of the adventure about to be described is probably due to this training.

We were excavating a mound eleven feet in height, located near Austin. Our pit extended to the base line. As the men continued their trench, they threw the earth back of them. The wall in front was high, the side walls somewhat lower. Naturally, the loose earth to the rear sloped upward, there being the usual cleared space of five or six feet between the edge of this earth and the front wall. In these early days of mound exploration it was customary to undermine slightly the face of the trench, then the men would go on top, insert their shovels and throw down a large section of mound wall. Today different and more pretentious methods are employed.

The workmen, having accomplished their task, were

257

sent to the top of the mound and, as they prepared to cave off a section, I observed a small bone protruding at the base line and jumped down into the pit with my hand trowel. I was in a crouching position; above me towered eleven feet of wall. Suddenly, without warning, a mass of earth extending from the floor to the summit and probably eighteen or twenty inches in thickness fell. It started with a slight noise sufficient to warn me. I leaped backwards and landed on soft earth to the rear in such a position that my head and shoulders were rather higher than the rest of my body.

Had I had but another second, I might have escaped, being very athletic, as I have stated, but the mass of falling earth caught me in an instant. The first sensation was of darkness and then came intense pressure. Even to this day I can recall vividly the cold earth against my face and body and the never-ending pressure. My arms were extended, legs somewhat apart. I had fallen on a heavy clod of burnt earth and this pressed against the lumbar vertebrae, pushing two of them out of line, so that I was paralyzed from the waist down for five or six weeks.

My mouth opened and I remember the unpleasant sensation of trying to dislodge earth. I was held absolutely. I recall that it was impossible to move even a finger, although I tried. I wore a very light field costume, with a watch in the left pocket of my thin shirt. Two ribs under this watch were broken, as was the crystal. The watch chain was fastened across from left to right side. It was pressed into the flesh and left a red mark across my chest. A straw hat was jammed down over my forehead and for several days afterwards I bore a stamped pattern of the braided straw.

Clinton Cowen, a college classmate, who afterwards became an engineer, was in charge of the workmen and his testimony is to the effect that I was buried about a minute—some of the men thought a little longer. Our laborers threw earth aside frantically with their shovels and dug down nearly three feet before they reached my head. I recall a slight movement of earth above me, then a shovel struck my scalp, which under other circumstances would have been rather painful, but was a most welcome blow! At once they uncovered me down to the chest. One of the first things I observed was that the men were panting and streaming with perspiration. Cowen was wont to comment on a rather uncanny sight, that black head protruding from the earth! He also said that, having exposed the head and shoulders, they stopped for a moment and he observed that earth pressure on the body was forcing the blood up, the veins standing out prominently on my neck and head. I could not breathe, the air having been forced out of my lungs, and Cowen pressed with his hands on each side of my chest. I remember that this sudden intake of air was very painful.

They carried me out and laid me on a mass of oat sheaves, which furnished a very soft bed. I recall a small, wild canary perched on a high thistle which sang a sweet song and flitted away as the men approached, also that the sky seemed unusually blue and bright. Some farmers came, one brought a farm wagon, numbers of oat sheaves were thrown in and the team proceeded to the residence of Strawder James. Mr. and Mrs. James kindly gave me their own room, located on the first floor of their residence, and I was put to bed for several weeks until I could be transported on a cot in a baggage car, to my home in Xenia, Ohio.

Mr. James was a very kind-hearted man. In Cincinnati he had purchased a small music box which played three tunes. He used to set this on a table near the head of my bed each morning and wind it up before he departed for his work. At noon he would repeat the process and also in the evening. Mr. Cowen, years afterwards, one evening when we were in camp at Cahokia, declared that, after a month of this musical entertainment, I was able to whistle the three tunes backwards as well as forwards!

In later years my work necessitated entering caverns and rock shelters, but I could never bring myself to explore with any degree of satisfaction underground. There always seemed to be impending danger.

The vertebrae have probably adjusted themselves, but doctors in subsequent years, examining me for life insurance, paid particular attention to that portion of the spine and reported adversely on my application.

In 1897 pulmonary tuberculosis began to develop and my physician sent me to Arizona. There a specialist, observing the condition, told Mrs. Moorehead that she should take me to Dr. G———, spinal expert, New York City. He thought that I had tuberculosis of the spine and added the cheerful information that I might not live more than a year. He placed me in a straightjacket to throw the weight of the upper body on the hips and thus relieve the spine. This aggravated the pulmonary tuberculosis and I went to the Adirondacks where I remained two years and ten months under Dr. E. L. Trudeau's care.

An interesting correspondence ensued between Trudeau and G———, both savants in their respective callings, Trudeau maintaining that, since I was suffering from severe hemorrhages of the lungs and breathing was hampered by the straightjacket, I would die from pulmonary tuberculosis unless "said jacket was removed." G———, true to his training, retorted that I would die of spinal trouble unless the jacket treatment was continued! According to the diagnosis of these two eminent authorities there was no hope—

absolutely none. They finally compromised by taking the jacket off and putting me on a cot for many months.

There is a grim humor in this entire incident. Both Trudeau and G—— have gone to their rewards. They were wonderful men and I have no criticism to offer. Two skillful examiners from two of the largest life insurance companies of this country turned me down as a doubly bad risk because of "spine and lungs" and have "gone West" while I, rejected by the experts and condemned by the physicians, am still alive and able to carry on!

MONGOLIAN INTERLUDE

William J. Morden

William J. Morden is field associate in the Department of Mammalogy of the American Museum of Natural History. His record of work in Africa and Asia makes an impressive exhibit of scientific activity crowded into a short space of time.

In 1922 he led an expedition to East Africa, Uganda and the Sudan; the following year he headed another to Baltistan, Ladakh, Kishtwar and Kashmir, and in 1924 one to Nepal and Upper Burma. He organized and led the Morden-Clark Asiatic Expedition of the American Museum of Natural History in 1926, of which the story that follows tells the most dramatic episode. He left Kashmir April first; collected in the Russian Pamirs; crossed Kashgaria; collected zoological specimens in the Thian Shan Mountains; crossed the Great Turfan Depression, the Dzungarian plains and western Outer Mongolia, and made a new crossing of the Dzungarian plains and the Mongolian Altai, traveling eight thousand miles and obtaining a comprehensive series of *Ovis poli*, Thian Shan ibex and roe-deer, besides specimens of other fauna of the various regions. The full story is told in his *Across Asia's Snows and Deserts*.

In 1929-1930 he led the Morden-Graves North Asiatic Expedition for the same institution, spending eight months in Russia, Tashkent, Samarkand, Bokhara and eastern Siberia, and covering about seven hundred miles by camel caravan on the steppes of Kazakstan, obtaining a series of the saiga antelope and making a general collection of the fauna of the region. He spent the winter in the forests of the Amur River country, getting three fine specimens of the "long-haired" Siberian tiger, as well as a comprehensive general collection.

MONGOLIAN INTERLUDE

By William J. Morden

CONTRARY TO POPULAR IMPRESSION, MOST OF THOSE WHO go into distant and little-known lands in the interests of science, those who explore unknown areas or who collect specimens in far places, are not impelled by a desire for "adventure." I do not mean that they do not enjoy pitting themselves against and overcoming difficulties encountered. What I mean is that their purpose is to procure their information and collect their specimens with as little labor, as little danger and as little "adventure" as possible. I have heard several explorers say that, if they find themselves facing a situation against which they have not prepared and which seems likely to bring their work and possibly their lives to an end, then they have been guilty of an error. Carefulness in making plans and in working out the major details of a project should cover every contingency, so that, should danger arise, an expedition will have within itself means of eliminating or overcoming the difficulty.

But, no matter how carefully plans and preparations have been made, now and then a situation may arise where a desired result can be obtained only through a course which involves risk. As an instance of this I will relate a story of an "adventure" which occurred in Central Asia in 1926.

I was the leader of the Morden-Clark Asiatic Expedition of the American Museum of Natural History. My companion was James L. Clark, assistant director in charge of the Department of Preparation at the Museum. Clark and I left Kashmir on the first of April, crossed the Himalaya and Karakoram ranges, collected *Ovis poli* in the Russian Pamirs during May and then traveled northward to Kashgar in Chinese Turkestan.

My original program, worked out in conjunction with Roy Chapman Andrews, had been to make contact with his Central Asiatic Expedition at the town of Hami, in Eastern Chinese Turkestan. Clark and I were to collect ibex, roe-deer and other specimens in the Tian Shan Mountains during the summer. The Central Asiatic Expedition expected to be working in the western Gobi that year and the plan was for one or more of the expedition's cars to push through to Hami, where Clark and I would join them on the first of September. Unfortunately, a civil war raging around Peking prevented Andrews from taking the field that season. A message from him, received by us at Kashgar in June, made it necessary to re-arrange our plans.

For several reasons, I wished to cross Mongolia. First and foremost was the possibility of collecting specimens of saiga antelope, a rapidly disappearing species. A few of these little animals are still to be found in part of Mongolia and I hoped we might be fortunate enough to locate their limited range. Another reason was that the American Museum wished Clark to study the Mongolian Plains, as his department was charged with the preparation of the zoological collections of the Central Asiatic Expeditions from that region. Should we turn back and retrace our steps to Kashmir, after completing our work in the Tian Shan, neither of these objectives would be attained. We considered the matter for several days and decided to attempt to cross the Gobi to Urga with a camel caravan.

We could get little information in Turkestan. The

Chinese could tell us almost nothing, nor could the Soviet consuls at Kashgar and Urumchi give us much help. Chinese domination over Outer Mongolia had ended some years before and, although Russian influence, we understood, was in the ascendency in that country, the Russian consuls themselves could tell us little about conditions at the moment. They did, however, offer to advise Moscow that we were starting and ask that Soviet representatives in Mongolia be instructed to assist us where possible.

There was no Mongolian representative in Chinese Turkestan, so it was impossible to procure Mongolian credentials before entering the country. Our proposed route across the Dzungarian plains had never been traversed by white men, though it was occasionally used by native caravans. We knew that we were taking a chance, but the results to be obtained seemed worth the risk.

On arrival at Kuchengtze, the starting-point for caravan travel across the Gobi, we had with us one assistant, Mohamed Rahim, who had been with us several months. Although he spoke no English, his Hindustani was excellent. In addition, he spoke Turki, the language of Turkestan, and a useful amount of Chinese.

I had expected no difficulty in hiring camels at Kuchengtze, but, when the Chinese caravan agencies learned that we intended to enter Outer Mongolia, there were suddenly no camels available. At last, however, we obtained a native caravan of thirty camels, together with a caravan *bashi*, or leader, and five men. We hired a guide who was said to know the route to Urga and to speak fluent Mongolian. There was no way of checking up on this individual, so we had to take him more or less on faith. As it turned out, he had been over part of the route several years before and, when not excited, could speak some dozen or so words of Mongolian. Under stress, he could not only speak no Mongolian but little of anything else.

We left Kuchengtze on October twenty-third. Immediately the weather broke and, from then on, snowstorms were of almost daily occurrence, with the temperature much of the time considerably below zero. Plainly, winter was under way.

About three days out, one of the caravan men stole a horse and deserted. We were pretty angry about it at the time, but, looking back, we decided that he was the only one of the party with good sense.

Most caravan travel in Central Asia is done by night, for the Bactrian camel is a cold-weather animal and travels best during the cooler hours. On halting, it is customary to picket the camels until daybreak and then turn them loose to graze. Our marches usually began some time in the afternoon and continued into the early morning.

At dusk one evening, our caravan *bashi* rode ahead to try to locate a Mongol post known to be somewhere near by. Shortly after dark we came upon him, sitting on his horse and looking intently down a slope to the right. While questioning him, we heard voices below and three dark figures rode rapidly up the hill. The first was a bare-headed individual, who began to shout in a gruff voice at our party. We could not understand what he said, but his tone gave us the feeling that all was not well.

Clark and I thought it time to show ourselves and explain that we were white men on our way to Uliassutai and that we wished to find the post; so we called the interpreter and instructed him to tell who we were. One of us took out a spotlight and we flashed it on our faces to show that we were not natives. The fellow was evidently startled, for he blinked in the light, then lighted a match and by its flickering rays scrutinized us closely. He was a repulsive-looking

individual with a badly scarred face. As he wore no uniform, we wondered if we had not met some Mongol
bandits, instead of Mongol soldiers. Then several more
horsemen came tearing up from different directions and
we realized that unawares we had been well surrounded.

In the starlight, I could see that the newcomers wore
the winter headgear of the Red Army, peak-topped felt
helmets with Soviet stars in front. All carried rifles slung
over their shoulders and rode active little Mongol ponies.
They seemed a wild lot, but the fact that they had uniforms
of a sort reassured us and we felt certain that, as soon as we
located the commanding officer and told him who and
what we were, everything would be all right. We instructed
our guide to tell them that we wished to go to the post
with our whole caravan. A guttural reply and a gesture
indicated that we were to turn down a steep slope to the
right. On the way, they surrounded us closely and evidently
commented on the fact that we were armed, which seemed
to displease them, though there was little opportunity to
do more than notice their expressions.

So far as we could see in the darkness, the post consisted
of two yurts. Into one of these we were hurried by our
escort. Inside the yurt, about a dozen savage-looking individuals were seated around a small dung fire, while a
single bowl of grease with a floating wick gave a dim light,
which but added to the gloom. All wore sheepskin coats and
pointed felt helmets with red stars in front. Some wore
heavy felt boots with leather soles, others Mongol leather
boots with toes turned upward. Around the wall hung belts,
rifles and various articles of equipment.

We had brought three of our men along and we five,
added to the dozen or so already there, crowded the small
yurt nearly to capacity. Lowering looks met us as we
entered, but a place was made in the circle around the fire

and we were motioned to sit. Through the interpreter I asked for the commanding officer, but it appeared that there was no officer present. We tried to explain who and what we were, where we were coming from and where we wished to go, but they took no interest in our explanations. I produced our papers, which included passports, letters in Russian from Soviet authorities and a number of documents with large red and gold seals on them. The latter had never failed to impress local officials in Turkestan. We endeavored to explain the papers, emphasizing the Russian permits and a personal letter of introduction to the Russian consul in Kobdo.

We said we were Americans, but it was quite evident that they had never heard the word. One unfriendly individual, who seemed to have a good deal to say, asked us if we were Russians. Fearing someone might speak Russian, I answered that we were not, but said that we had many friends among them. That, however, made no impression on their stolidity. One of them suddenly asked if we had Mongolian passports and, when I replied that we had not but expected to get them through a Soviet consul, there were ugly looks and whisperings. Then we began to sense trouble ahead.

• • • • • •

One by one, Mongols left the yurt, until but a single man remained by the door. In spite of our distinctly hostile reception, it seemed best to pretend that we felt sure of ourselves, though we were far from it. We supposed, however, that we would at least be free to make camp over night, so, when we heard the caravan outside, we arose and moved toward the door. Mohamed, who was nearest the entrance, went first. As he neared the door, the Mongol standing by it struck him in the face and knocked him down. Then he growled what seemed to be an order and pointed to the floor, which probably meant that we were to sit down. That we did not do so at once may have been one reason for what followed. We had not yet realized what sort of savages we had met and probably a bit of the "dominant white man" feeling still remained. But not for long.

The guard shouted and the whole crowd came pouring into the yurt. Several carried ropes and, before we knew what was happening, they set upon us in overwhelming numbers and we went to the ground under a mass of Mongols. Probably in normal moments we would have realized that resistance was useless, but at the time coherent thought was suspended and we fought our assailants as best we could in the crowded yurt. But we never had a chance and our struggles only served to infuriate them. As I lay on my back, I saw a Mongol take a vessel of boiling water from the fire and start to pour it on my face. I rolled my head to the side and closed my eyes. Fortunately the water went wide of its mark.

We finally ceased the unequal battle and lay back, while they forced our arms in front of us and passed ropes around our crossed wrists. Then we were jerked to a sitting position and the ropes tightened. Men seated themselves on each side of us and, with feet braced against our wrists, jerked the ropes as tight as possible. The pain was pretty severe. I felt my wrist crack and thought it was broken. During the struggle, the back of my right hand was torn by a rope and this was very painful. When they had us bound, the ropes were soaked with water, so that they would draw even tighter. The whole mob shouted continually in a sort of excited frenzy and each seemed anxious to take a hand.

Completely trussed up, we were roughly thrown on our backs, our pockets were turned inside out and our clothes torn open in a very thorough search. It was not a gentle process, either, for we were rolled over and over on the ground and each roll caused a hard jerk on the rope stretched between us. During the search, one chap kept his foot on my head.

When the fracas started, Clark was smoking a pipe and this a Mongol knocked clear across the yurt. I was chewing a bit of gum but fortunately no one noticed it; before I finished with it, that was probably the hardest chewed piece of gum in history. They took everything from our pockets and clothing and tossed the articles across the yurt, where they were tied up in one of our handkerchiefs. We were searched twice before we were permitted to sit up. Even then, we were not allowed to warm our fast-numbing hands over the tiny fire. I tried to do so a couple of times, but on each occasion was struck in the face and knocked back. One big savage seemed to take a particular dislike to me and lost no opportunity to get in an extra bit of unpleasantness.

Our three men were tied up at the same time as ourselves and were badly beaten in the operation. Mohamed received a worse pounding than the others and his cries of pain were not pleasant to hear. The beating of our men was pure savagery on the part of the Mongols, for they did not struggle when being tied.

For some reason our captors did not prevent our speaking together, so we were able to discuss things. There could be no doubt that we were in a very serious fix. I asked Mohamed if he had learned anything from the interpreter. Mohamed, a bit dazed, moaned and replied that the interpreter had overhead the Mongols saying that we were to be shot. I asked him whether it was to be at once or in the morning, but he had learned nothing beyond the fact that we were to be shot.

It was quite evident that, as matters stood, we could

expect no mercy. The only thing we could do, lacking some break in our luck, was to take whatever might come as stoically as possible and not give our captors the satisfaction of seeing us weaken. Clark and I talked now and then, but not very hopefully. There seemed little chance that we would come out alive. We wondered how long we could stand the probable torture.

A series of rather disconnected thoughts passed through our minds but, except for the natural dread of torture, we both agreed that we felt no actual fear of death. Neither Clark nor I was particularly frightened at the thought of being shot. To both, however, it seemed such a futile thing to be shot by a group of savages on mere suspicion.

The things which caused me the most concern were: first, the terrible period of waiting and the anxiety which my wife must go through when we did not arrive in Peking and the equally distressing interval that must be spent in trying to find out what had happened to us; secondly, a very sincere hope that the Mongols would make it quick and short. I had no panorama of my past life, such as I have read comes to one facing practically certain death. As for the future, there was a complete blank; it had ceased to interest me.

By and by a newcomer entered the yurt. Apparently, this individual was not a soldier, for he was dressed in a blue coat instead of the usual sheepskin. He and Mohamed talked in low tones and I could catch enough to gather that Mohamed was carefully explaining who we were, where we had come from and what we had been doing and, as I had told him to do, strongly emphasizing the fact that we had many friends among the Russians. The fellow seemed interested and understanding; his attitude was noticeably different from that of the soldiers. At first I thought he might be their officer, but Mohamed told me that he was just a Mongol civilian who could speak Chinese and was thereby able to converse directly with Mohamed. Our interpreter was practically useless, for, while he had not been badly injured during the *mêlée,* he was thoroughly frightened and spent his entire time kneeling on the ground, mumbling prayers interspersed by deep groans. The Chinese-speaking Mongol went out after a while and we were left to our thoughts, with several armed soldiers standing guard over us.

. . . . . .

How long they kept us in the yurt we had no means of knowing. After what seemed an age, during which time our hands grew more and more swollen and painful, several of the group entered and motioned us out through the yurt door. Our three men went first, then Clark and I followed, with the rope dragging between our bound hands. In the starlight we saw several dark figures with rifles. We felt sure they were leading us out to a firing squad. Clark and I said goodbye to each other.

We were led off into the gloom, fully expecting to be halted and shot at any moment. A dim shape, appearing vaguely in the light of the stars, resolved itself into a small caravan tent. We were roughly thrust inside the entrance and again thrown to the ground. Our big dogskin helmets were put on our heads and these came so far down over our eyes that we were practically blindfolded. Moving feet were all we could see. Presently we were dragged to the rear of the tent and forced into a sitting position back to back against the tent-pole. Our arms were trussed to the pole by a rope passed around the two of us.

After we were tied so tightly that movement of arms or bodies was impossible, they again pushed our caps low on our heads and threw a few sheepskins over our legs. It was away below freezing in the tent—how cold we did not know, but certainly close to zero.

It looked as though we were there for the night. That was worse than being shot, for it was certain that, even should we live, there was little chance that we would ever again have the use of our hands. Even though they did not freeze—which they probably would—with circulation entirely stopped for many hours, they would undoubtedly be paralyzed by morning. We were hundreds of miles from any possible medical attention and, though we might be finally released, there seemed nothing ahead but a most unpleasant lingering death by blood poisoning. It was a thought I tried to keep out of my mind.

Now and then the soldiers felt our hands, though at the time we could not understand why. It occurred to us that they might know how long the hands could remain bound before numbness would intervene and the pain no longer be felt. The fact that they covered our feet and legs with sheepskins simply meant to us that we were to be tied up in that position until morning, in which case our hands would be lost and little else would matter.

That period seemed endless. At first we hoped that they might loosen our bonds for the night but, as time passed, we were in too much pain even to hope. We could not move our fingers and there was no sensation in the hands when the Mongols touched them, although, curiously enough, they burned as though scalded; sudden pains shot through them now and then and flashed up wrists and arms. By the dim light I tried to see my hands each time they were examined, but could only tell that they were badly swollen and out of shape.

The last time the man felt my hands, he must have decided that they had reached the limit, for he said something to the others and they at once began to untie us. He tried to loosen my rope himself, but it was so tight that he had to call for assistance. When at last it was off, I felt a surge of blood down my wrists and into my hands. I had expected it to be painful when the rope was loosened, but it was not; on the contrary, it was decidedly pleasant.

The removal of our bonds was like an unexpected present. One moment we had been without hope; the next, though it still seemed likely that we would be shot, at least we were not to be tortured to death. We were probably closer to fainting just then than at any other time. Before, we had rather hoped we might.

After freeing our wrists, the Mongols gave us our goatskin coats. Then, seated back to back, we were again bound to the tent post by ropes which passed about our arms and bodies. The wrists of our three men were unlashed and their arms were tied by ropes above the elbows, but they were not otherwise bound. Sheepskins tucked about our legs and feet made us fairly comfortable, though we were so limp by then that we could only lie back and rest. Nothing to eat since early morning, added to the strain of the last few hours, had weakened us badly.

A little later, the Mongols brought us bowls of their tea, a rather dirty and most unpleasant concoction made of brick tea and salt. But it was hot, so we gulped it down. Shortly afterward we were agreeably surprised to have them put a couple of our own cigarettes in our mouths and light them for us. Certainly that cigarette tasted better than any other I ever smoked.

The sudden change from pure savagery to more humane treatment was bewildering. We talked it over but could not understand the motives for either the original outburst of ferocity or the change. At all events, for the present our hands had been saved and the night ahead promised to be less unpleasant than we had expected.

The Author after Being Released by His Mongol Captors

"They seemed a wild lot, but the fact that they had
uniforms of a sort reassured us."

Our hands still hurt severely; in fact, bruised nerves gave us trouble for many days. The rope burn on the back of my right hand became infected and it was a month before I finally got it under control.

All night Mongols wandered in and out of the tent, squatted by us, scrutinized us closely, felt our clothing and generally satisfied their curiosity. A guard was always seated at the tent door with a rifle across his knees. One of these chaps amused himself now and then by aiming his rifle at one of us and curling his finger suggestively around the trigger. He would hold the position for several seconds, then put the rifle down and laugh uproariously. He evidently enjoyed his little joke.

· · · · · ·

The night dragged on and on, for we were still in suspense regarding the outcome. With no means of keeping track of time, we could only watch a tiny bit of sky visible through the tent door and hope for the dawn. We managed to slip our ropes down the post until we could lie partly stretched out and ease the strain on our backs. We even slept in snatches.

Shortly after daylight we were taken outside, with our arms still bound above the elbows. Several soldiers stood guard with rifles at the ready. Where they expected us to run in that open country, with our arms tied, was a mystery, but each time any of us were taken out of the tent for a moment, one or more soldiers always had their rifles pointed in our direction. It was really funny, though the future was too uncertain for us fully to appreciate the humor.

Later our caravan men, who had not been molested and had made camp near by, were allowed to bring us some of their tea and hard bread. The tea, while not good, was far ahead of the salty Mongol variety and, by soaking the bread, we could soften it enough to obtain a little much-needed nourishment.

Sometime during the morning Mohamed was led out of the tent. Almost immediately we heard two shots. I said to Clark, "There goes poor Mohamed. I wonder who's next." For two hours we waited in suspense; then, to our amazement, Mohamed was led back to the tent. He had merely been taken out to open our boxes, so that the Mongols could examine the contents. The shots had been fired by someone experimenting with my automatic pistol.

Late in the afternoon a snappy-looking stranger rode up. His long coat was of blue silk, lined with sheepskin and tied with a yellow sash. Mongol boots with turned-up toes and decorative stitching of red and green, a closely fitting leather cap and sheepskin trousers completed his clothing, while a large Mauser automatic pistol hung prominently in its wooden holder at his side. With him came a younger man who spoke Turki and acted as interpreter.

The newcomer, very evidently a Buriat, was of a much higher type than the soldiers we had hitherto seen. He proved to be in command of the post and, about an hour after his arrival, we were conducted to the yurt. Our papers, which had been taken from us with everything else, were opened and examined, though it was quickly apparent that the officer could not read them. He seemed to have control of the situation, however, and the soldiers did not have so much to say as formerly. We found our firearms, field-glasses and other articles of kit piled in the yurt.

After the commander had asked a number of questions, we were taken back to the tent, still bound and with no information as to what was to happen. Nothing was told us, nor were any of our questions answered. The one-sided conversation between the officer and me was carried on through Mohamed and the young Mongol interpreter.

Our own interpreter was still worthless, for what little Mongolian he could speak originally he had lost completely in his fright. He did, however, tell us that we were thought to be spies and that a patrol had been sent back along our trail to learn if we were the advance party of some invading force. Again, he said that the real commanding officer of the post was at a place some two days north, that a messenger had been sent for him and that we would be kept prisoners until he arrived. All sorts of stories were passed on to us. Probably none of them were true, though anything seemed possible. The Mongols themselves treated our inquiries with insolent indifference.

Shortly after we re-entered the prison tent, a big bowl of rice and meat was brought in by one of our caravan men. We had had practically no food since breakfast the day before, so the whole five of us pitched into the rice. Clark and I ate native fashion. Squatted by the bowl with the men, we dipped our hands into the sticky mess and made the rice into balls. With arms still tied at the elbows, it was impossible to reach our mouths, but we threw balls of rice at our mouths and inhaled deeply to catch as much as possible of the precious food. It was a wonderful picture— two white men, three Turkis and a couple of Mongols feeding noisily in the dimly lighted, filthy tent. It was getting pretty close to nature—a bit too close—but the rice and meat were good and strengthened us considerably.

That night was even colder than the previous one and, as the Mongols had taken away many of the sheepskins for their own use, we were so chilled that we got little sleep. Much of the time we just lay and shivered. It had been a bit of good fortune that, when captured, we both happened to be wearing felt boots. Had we been wearing leather footgear, our feet would have frozen, for certainly our captors would not have permitted us to get our heavy boots from the caravan. My injured hand throbbed and ached, but my request to be allowed to get something for it from the medicine kit with the caravan stores was curtly refused.

Our boxes already had been opened and our arms and ammunition, of course, had been confiscated. During the day our two pistols had been proudly worn by various soldiers, who took a huge delight in strutting past us. The officer later took these to himself and appeared, wearing his own Mauser and both our revolvers.

The next morning the commander came in and looked us over. Shortly after that the ropes were removed and we were ordered to go to our camels and make camp. After being bound in the freezing tent for thirty-six hours, it was a great relief to be out in the air and free to move about again. We put up a tent and attempted reorganization of our much-scattered belongings. The officer had made one inspection of our kit the day before; that morning he inspected it again, to the great edification of a group of curious soldiers, who fingered everything and constantly pushed us out of the way so that they might better see what was going on. All that day we were bothered by soldiers who sat about our tent and followed us everywhere.

Later in the day we were again called into the main yurt, where another inspection of our papers and the contents of our saddle-bags was made. A few small articles were given back to us, but most of our possessions, such as field-glasses, compasses, thermometers and extra camera lenses, were not returned. It was interesting that the Mongols seemed anxious to have us take their photographs. We doubted if they knew what the cameras were, but they liked to stand in front of the buzzing Eyemo and hear the hand cameras click.

Our experiences in the yurt and prison tent began to seem unreal and dream-like—the sort of thing one reads about, but which makes little impression because it could never actually happen. My infected hand, however, which I had at last been able to bandage, was a constant reminder of stern reality. After our release the Mongols were not aggressively unfriendly, although they treated us as their inferiors and felt free to come into our tent at any time and demand cigarettes.

.   .   .   .   .

In the days following we were sent from one post to another. Evidently no one knew what to do with us. Each post passed us along to another one, always under armed guard. At each post a further examination of our baggage and papers was made. We asked to be sent to Uliassutai, as that was on our route to Urga and China. This was curtly refused. We asked to be allowed to return to Turkestan. That was also refused. We were finally informed that we were to go under guard to Kobdo, which is the headquarters of Western Mongolia.

It was a most unpleasant march of some two hundred and seventy miles across the Mongolian Altai, by a trail which I do not think has ever been traveled by white men and which in winter is not even used by Mongols for camel caravans. After struggling for twelve days to force our tired camels and horses through deep snow, up and down steep slopes and across several passes, near the end of November we arrived at Kobdo.

I had hoped that we might persuade the authorities there to allow us to continue our journey to Uliassutai and Urga, but this they flatly refused to do. Eventually, with the assistance of some friendly Russians and the Soviet consul, we made our way by wagon and sleigh to a branch of the Trans-Siberian Railroad at Biisk, a distance of about six hundred miles. From there it was a week's journey by train to Peking.

As nearly as I have been able to determine, the Mongols thought we were spies, and it seems that their code calls for spies to be executed first and investigated afterwards. Apparently, the civilian Mongol who spent some time conversing in Chinese with Mohamed, believed that we had influential Russian friends. This information, passed along to the soldiers, probably convinced them that it might be safer to await the arrival of an officer before shooting us, as Soviet influence was paramount in Outer Mongolia. The officer, with more intelligence and a greater feeling of responsibility than the soldiers, decided that for the moment, at least, we were not dangerous, and thought it best to shift the responsibility to the shoulders of his superiors.

At the time we were at a loss to understand the ferocity of the Mongolians and the seemingly needless agony of the first few hours. Months later I learned from Roy Chapman Andrews that the binding of a prisoner's hands until circulation is stopped is a recognized form of torture among Mongols. Andrews told me that he had seen it practised in the jails at Urga. Clark and I can testify that it is a most effective method.

It would seem that the application of torture was intended to frighten us. Very probably its use was dictated by a feeling of uncertainty and fear on the part of the Mongols themselves. We had arrived unannounced at their post at night from the direction of Chinese Turkestan; we were armed; they could not read our credentials and were suspicious of us. It is quite possible that our interpreter's story about our being considered an advance party of a larger invading force was true. The outburst of savagery was the natural consequence of suspicion and fear, engendered by our unheralded arrival.

Frankly, I am not particularly proud of the foregoing recital, for I agree with others that "adventure" has no place in the work of a scientific expedition. I have been asked, however, to describe the incident and, inasmuch as the specimens and film, which were the objectives of the expedition, came through undamaged, I relate the story as an example of what can happen, regardless of the most careful plans and preparation.

ARCTIC GHOST

Felix Riesenberg

Felix Riesenberg earned his title of "Captain" by fifteen years' active service at sea. He is a master mariner in sail and steam, his last command having been the *Newport*, then serving as the New York State nautical schoolship. He is also a graduate of Columbia University and an engineer.

He was a member of the Wellman Polar Expedition of 1906-1907 and spent that winter in charge of the camp established on Danes Island, on the north shore of Spitsbergen, where occurred the nerve-racking experience here described.

In September, 1907, he took part in the first attempt to fly over the polar regions in a dirigible balloon. On account of poor material and adverse weather conditions, the venture met with failure, the balloon being blown back and wrecked on Foul Glacier, in northwest Spitsbergen.

He is the author of twelve books, among them *Standard Seamanship* (used throughout the English-speaking merchant service), *East Side, West Side; Endless River; Shipmates; Red Horses; Under Sail.*

ARCTIC GHOST

By Felix Riesenberg

IT SEEMS TO BE A PRINCIPLE, IF THERE ARE PRINCIPLES
other than those conjured by imagination, that quick
existence, if I may so qualify it, is possible only between the
poles of birth and death. But we do know that there is pre-
extension of these limits so far as birth is concerned, but
just where does this begin? We do definitely know that life
starts before parturition, that intention, of some kind, pre-
cedes conception, and that a marvelous complication of
circumstances leads to the event called life. We may also
conceive of a continuation of the result of this elaborate beginning, following the sudden snuffing-out of material
motion. The hereafter, yes—but still here if we only knew.
Why should things that take so long to start end with sudden abruptness? Do the things that are absolutely not of the
flesh, such as the conscience and the will, do these things
evaporate in an instant, or before the dissolution of their
earthly shell? Is memory a thing of mud? Is love a mere
assemblage of cells? Is one skull exactly like another? Can
we assay the value of a brain by weight or size? There must
be something other than the burial of the body to attend
the cessation of life. This process is not completed in an
hour, or in a day, if there is such an entity as time in the
realm of ghosts.

Such speculations are disquieting in the growing gloom
of an approaching polar night. And under such condi-

tions there were naïve arguments between us as to the vitality of such things as bones, or entire skeletons, once most intimate parts of living men. In other words (if those more fit to discuss this will permit) do the preserved remains carry with them an allegiance of the spirit? Do mummies, tortured and distorted, still demand attendance on the part of their life principle? Is not the flesh and bone an equal, or let us say, a necessary partner with the soul? Is one *nothing* and the other *all?* The ancient Egyptians seemed to think so. And what are a few centuries, or a thousand or more years, in the scale of all time? May not the spirit cling to the bone and play havoc with weak mortality, adjacent in the living, shivering flesh? Even the stoutest might hesitate to sleep among the headstones of a cemetery through an interminable night.

Fear is as great as faith. The mind, grown out of mystery, unable to pierce the unknowable, totters on the brink of chaos when we revolve it on an inward orbit, searching secrets. Even with all of our jumbled heap of practical learning, how little do we know!

One might hesitate to tell the whole truth in matters of unusual moment, even if it were possible to achieve complete expression or to reveal emotion too poignant for words. Who can convey the utter terror of a small child screaming in the dark at the apparition of a shadow on the wall? Perhaps that child is voicing something only a young soul is tuned to fear. And here it may be said that I do not believe in ghosts—I have repeated this to myself over and over again.

Well, this is the beginning, or at least it is the explanation, or the excuse, for the story to follow. Still there is something more to be added before the matter is set forth. If the departed come back, we must be certain that they were there, and suffered, and sinned, and served, and died. Even the most willing mind can hardly conceive of a virgin planet peopled with ghosts.

. . . . .

I spent the dark months of a polar winter prisoned in a little house just beneath the eightieth parallel of latitude on Danes Island, off the shores of the northern archipelago of Spitsbergen. Our square, stout little house was built on an ice-encrusted knoll, the timbers of the floor resting on protruding breccia strewn at the base of a steep cliff. The shoreward ends of the timber had been bedded by hewing into the ice, and the ends facing the sea were supported on piles of stone to level off the floor. The wedge-like sides and front foundation wall were built of loose rock, calked with reindeer moss. To make this solid cellar proof against the wind, the rude masonry was later on plastered with ice and banked with snow.

This snug little house stood opposite to the relics of a camp once occupied by Andrée. In this camp were intimate reminders of the gallant Swede, reminders vibrant with the last moments of this determined, earnest man. But it was a camp haunted only by memories, for no material or actual part of the travelers remained. If the camp held an element of death, it was only that of the last contact with men before disaster, hundreds of miles away. But on every point of the horizon were headlands and mountains and glaciers familiar in the annals of polar suffering and discovery. Here came William Barents and John Cornelius Ryp in 1596— Barents, the ice pilot and discoverer, destined to perish in Nova Zembla, far to the south.

And here, too, past the Pyramids and the great Cape of Hakluyt, sailed the indomitable Heemskerck and the able Hendrik Hudson, also to perish in frozen seas. But the names of those who sailed north to die fill a scroll of ample

length. In 1620, the track of the Dutch discoverers was followed by a blaze of fortune that, for a time, transformed
the wastes of the north into a place of turmoil. The waters
were thick with the black flukes of leviathan. The wide
lanes between the pan ice spouted continual jets of vapor.
Fifteen thousand seamen came to those northern shores in
the short summer months. Close to the little house on Danes
Island, on an adjacent level plain, stand relics of the abandoned city of Smeerenburg, the most remarkable settlement
of all time. It once held shops and bakeries, and lodgings,
inns and drinking booths, and brothels, for the whale fleet
was followed by women and the whalemen held carnival
when they drove their barbs into the huge, fat fishes spouting near the shore. The smoke of the trying-kettles rose upward in thick columns, standing in the summer calm, the
trembling black plumes on an unearthly hearse.

This ancient killing (and how tremendous is the killing of a mighty whale!) went on amid the rendering of
thousands of tons of fat and the carousing of reckless men
and women, smeared with blood and blubber and profli-
gate with life and treasure. It was a time of fabulous fortune spouting golden streams of gore and oil taken from
the cold blue sea. Two hundred and sixty Dutch ships
visited the Spitsbergen whaling-ground in the few months
of a summer season, first fighting and besetting the English
ships of the Muscovy Company, for, wherever free treasure
was to be had, fighting and license held sway. All of this
ancient killing and rendering of fat and roistering of flesh
went on shamelessly beneath the unwinking sky of continual day. There was no dark intermission of night to
cover them. Thousands left their bones to bleach upon the
arctic shores. Countless rude coffins of oak, often fashioned
from the staves of casks, lay in shallow graves amid the
stones, the ground too hard for deeper burial. The whales

were killed off and all this terrific life departed, this summer life of a brief score of years, centuries ago. Never did
human beings survive the night; the few who wintered
perished.

Then came an interval of a hundred years and still
more adventurous prows forced past the site of Smeerenburg and the headland of Hakluyt. The *Racehorse* and the
Carcass, commanded by Phipps, with young Horatio Nelson, a midshipman, in the steerage of the *Racehorse,* sailed
by the gruesome souvenir of graves. These were followed
by Buchan and John Franklin and Parry, by sailors who
dragged heavy boats over hummocks, rupturing themselves
in the hopeless battle with the ice, breaking hearts by inhuman labor on the polar field. These, too, left their
corpses on those shores to join the great colony of perpetual
bones, for in those regions there is no decay. Then followed Nordenskiöld, Malmgren, Fabvre, Leigh Smith,
Wellman, Nobile, Amundsen, continuing the struggle
northward, leaving their trail of death and hopes behind.

Three sailors left in this bleak surrounding were simple
men. One was the veteran of many winters in the polar seas
and one was only a sailor, a far voyager who believed the
things he saw and knew and who had heard many things
he could not understand. The first, Paul Bjoervig, bearded,
bent with years, was sturdy and uncomplaining. The second, Morten Olaisen, was more voluble and uncertain, for
to him the creeping on of the Arctic night came with grim
precision, each darkening hour casting deeper shadows
across his mind. I was a youth, but with a fair record of
sailing, long miles of sea spun out in the wake of my experience. I was the navigator, the officer, and in charge. Upon
me devolved the command, the responsibility, in the
changing world slowly sinking from light and life.

For a time we busied ourselves by tasks, setting our house in shape amid the increasing powderings of snow—piling driftwood and lighting huge bonfires on the dim line of the beach, taking cheer from the crackling flames, noting the shooting of blue-green tongues of light, catching the alternating waves of heat and cold that circled about the flames of driftwood in a world of endings. Always the fires left us more cold. Once, as the blaze burned low, a ghastly knob protruded from the ashes, a grinning skull burned black, the eye sockets filled with glowing coals of wood. This was our last fire. Morten muttered something about smoke in his eyes; then, too, the deepening snow buried the driftwood. Our conversation became less buoyant; small things took on sinister importance in our evasive contemplation of the long black months ahead.

And then we began to talk of the dead.

"Did you see it?"

"What?"

"The coffin," Paul whispered, bending over his pipe, slowly puffing, while Morten worked at the kitchen stove. Pungent smoke filled the small kitchen.

"No. I piled the wood. The rocks and wood is gray. It's getting dark. You can't see so well. No, you can't see."

"It rolled over."

"It rolled over—hot—red-hot."

"The dogs ran."

"Yes, they ran."

"I went back. It's gone."

Fragments reached me. I was determined to be cheerful. Further fall of snow prevented fires; the subject was dropped.

The silence came very close as November shaded into a monochrome of gray, blackening toward the night of inky gloom. The birds left the cliff, and the snow, constantly

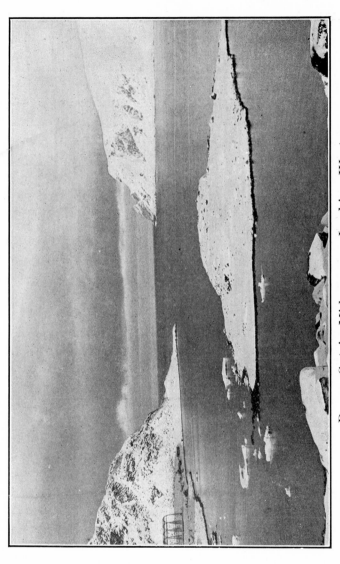

Danes Gat in Midsummer, Looking West

(The little house can be seen at the foot of the cliff to the right of the Wellman hangar.)

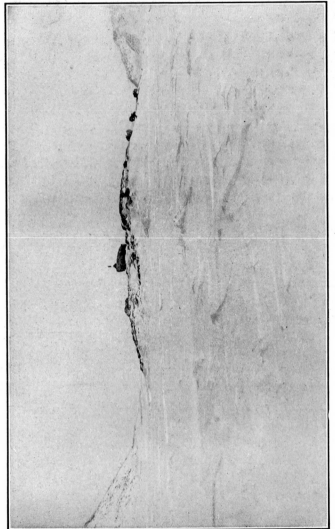

Deadman's Isle

falling, gave an illusion of upward motion; one could feel the friction of impalpable flakes scratching the ether. It was the silence of interstellar space, of complete insulation in the midst of an enormous cemetery draped in white.

So much had happened in that world of close, deceiving snow. So much was bound to happen again. Silence hung over us like a threat. Often I would wake from deep slumber startled by a dream in which I found myself far aloft, high over the black side of Smedburg's Mountain, with its cap of ice, looking down into the valley to the shore where stood the house, a nub of white almost buried. Once I noted its strange resemblance to a small headstone; a shudder came over me, I seemed to see the mound heave up as if from the struggle of three men buried alive. Everything for many hundreds, and for a thousand miles, was absolutely dead. I would have these dreams during periods of moonlight, for by December the curtain of polar night had drawn its fold across the midday skies.

Once the dream came when the moon was gone. I jumped up in the cold and stole to the small double window and saw a strange light without. Cautiously opening the outer door, having thrown on a heavy robe, I saw a vault of sky covered with waving plumes of fire—the aurora. I ran back to my bunk and prayed, shivering for an hour until sleep came.

That night the only black thing in a world of ghostly white was the moving shadow cast by a curious stone on Deadman's Isle, the great Sarcophagus Stone, standing above the snow where the Isle lifts from the plain of the frozen sea, like the mound of a mighty grave. And it was a grave, a gruesome grave holding the bones of a company of ancient sailors under the snow, graves revealed in ghastly bareness in the lazy summer when the ground is clear and

294 TOLD AT THE EXPLORERS CLUB

lidless coffins show their skulls and skeletons bleaching in the sun.

If you could look to the north over the festering tidal crack, groaning in the calms with unearthly mutterings, noises that sometimes sound like uncouth words, great mumbling words and moans given back again by the distant glacier fronts and cliffs, if you could look across the smooth white sheet of Dane's Gat to the mound of Deadman's Isle and see the Sarcophagus Stone lifting above the place, the fantastic light of polar winter playing its pranks with the things that are, you would sometimes also see wreaths of mist above the ice. You, too, would see things moving where nothing should move. Graves are thick on Deadman's Isle—and also along the shore where stood the house sheltering three sailors.

Once in the night, night by clocks rather than by any change in the complexion of the sky, a shiver ran through the solid little house, the timbers creaked for a moment and all was silent again. For many days before, the growing gloom carried with it an increasing sense of melancholy, a gradual burdening of the spirit as the mounting depth of snow lifted to a level with the eaves of the house, buried completely but for a hollow scooped out by the scouring wind, a providential trench that bared the narrow windows. It was then that old Paul Bjoervig began to talk of his dead comrade, Bentzen, Brent Bentzen who lay dead in the snow hut in Franz Josef Land while Paul slept alongside the corpse of his companion, in fulfillment of a mutual promise that the one to survive, in the event of death, would not cast out his shipmate to the prowling bears.

Bjoervig was constantly talking *with* Bentzen, talking with him in his sleep, and denying the conversation when awake.

Morten Olaisen became a man of monosyllables. His

brows lowered with a haunting frown as his eyes sought the
face of Paul, always smoking, smoking and grave. The
wind whined over the top of Smedburg's Mountain, crashing down the valley in harsh gusts, screeching across the
ice-crusted tar paper on the roof of our house, whirling the
metal Jack-in-the-wind that topped the chimney. These
winds seemed to suck the heat from the fire, to drain off the
vitality of the little house, as if some force without was determined to extinguish all alien life clinging amid the
snow.

"Was you awake—last night, sir?" Morten ventured the
question after a day of silence.

"You mean the house?"

"Under the house." Morten nodded to the bare floor.
Paul, pipe in mouth, looked in from the kitchen door, his
face serious, his eyes troubled.

"Only the snow bearing down—timbers adjusting." I
had plenty of explanations.

"But the voice. Paul heard it, too. It spoke."

"The voice?"

The house seemed so much colder than before. The
weak, asthmatic fire coughed, its consumptive splutter
burning up precious coal, with no return in heat. Then,
too, the oil lamp seemed so dim, and the wind—it was
blowing a gale from the northeast—backed into the valley,
recurving down on the little house in violent counter-
blasts.

"Perhaps it was the dogs. You know they howl. It might
have been the echo coming down the chimney. You hear
lots of things in the calm. It was calm last night. The wind
began at four, according to the anemometer." I pulled on
my finskoes and, slipping into a gabardine, left the house,
picking a rifle from the rack and murmuring something
about "bears." Anything to get outside of the house—away.

I stepped into skis and slid to the lee side of a large hummock a quarter mile away. Two dogs followed. I was glad. Of course it was not a voice, it was merely a sound, a human-sounding sound. I had thought it the voice of a woman. But it was *not* a voice, certainly not a woman's voice.

.   .   .   .   .

For days nothing was said about this happening—if it was a happening. The sky had cleared and the aurora smothered us under a covering of flashing beauty, painfully vivid, like leaping blood gushing over a milk-white breast. It was an overpowering brilliance that caught us, looking upward into the magnificence and mystery of the polar night. Was the truth so utterly gorgeous? Why? I wondered, why? With eyes wide open, our puny minds were blind.

For a time we could not sleep. We hung awake, tired, with staring eyes and agitated minds. We crept into bunks and tossed through sullen hours devoid of rest. Every moment seemed laden with significance. We were listening, always listening for the voice. At last we hardly dared address each other, for even our own voices took on a chill of fear. And then we heard the *thump*.

It came suddenly. We had almost forgotten that they were awaiting its summons. The chill of the room suddenly increased. Dogs howled—that unearthly howl, lifted from the canine throat in long-drawn, agonizing moans. The men lifted their covers and looked at me accusingly. Something was moving beneath the floor of our house. Below, everything was sealed against the inrush of wind and cold. Many feet of snow banked the walls. There was but one entrance, the square trap in the middle of the floor.

By an almost superhuman effort I left my bunk and braced myself in the cold, the dim lamp throwing my shadow on the wall. I stood over the trap, the cold sweat trickling from my forehead. Behind me Paul and Morten peered with breath suspended.

I lifted the trap. It seemed to lift itself, to yield without weight. My whole balance was disturbed for the effort I had nerved myself to exert.

"Look!"

Both men in the bunks shrieked at once. The open trap gave out a musty draft; it was impenetrable to sight. A fog swam before my eyes, my breath halted, my legs shook. Someone besides us was in the room. Oh, how cold it became—how unnaturally cold! We shook violently. I pushed down the suspended trap and the men huddled in their bunks.

A white form came up out of the trap and dissolved when the door was back in place. It was only a mist—the colder air of the cellar condensing in the warmth of the room, for the room was certainly warmer than the dank hole below. But does cold air rise against warmer air? And the thump?—

We were again in our bunks. That morning we said nothing. Already we had talked too much—too lightly, perhaps—of the relics of men scattered about us under the snow. The continual night made us secretive, morose. We could not sleep; then, of a sudden, we could not stay awake.

Everything was asleep about us; everything dead. A resistless gravity pulled down our eyelids, smothered our thoughts. When we slept, we were warm, we were secure and, in the depth of delightful dreams, we heard ravishing music and bell-like laughter. Limpid water cascaded over sunlit falls and we again knew the beauty of flowers.

But these slumbers were also interspersed with the low grumbling of men talking in their sleep, and the fire went out and the lamp burned its wick to a brittle carbon. The outside chill penetrated the room and the increasing snow

mounted each day in a shroud of dull white already many
fathoms deep above the house-top. Even Deadman's Isle
was levelled in the thickening pall and the high Sarcophagus Stone became a mere bulge on the surrounding
plain. The black sides of Smedburg's Mountain, too steep
to afford a hold for snow, towered in stark grandeur, a
giant sounding-board, against which the wailing of hungry
dogs set up a constant din.

The chronometer had run its indicater down to "wind,"
the anemometer clock died down and the scratch of the pen
on the cylinder and the metallic click of the ratchet were
silent. Everything seemed prepared for our burial. The
dark was thick with the hoarfrost of men who still breathe
and, in a moment, voices were apparent in the gloom. I lay
still, as if dead. My feet were cold, devoid of feeling. Then
low words, guttural and slow, told me my companions were
still alive.

"I saw it." A voice, thick and indistinct. "Below the
house."

"The grave is under my bunk. I have just been down
there with *her*."

"Did she touch him?"

"Yes. He's dead now."

"He's dead."

I heard no more. I drifted into oblivion. Was this also
a dream?

The dogs, flattened close against the house door,
moaned with pitiful insistence. An avalanche descended
upon the house, shocking it to its creaking frames, and a
sluicing rain, a terrific downpour of warm black water,
swept through the valley, washing deep canyons in the
piled-up snow. The room was heavy with damp. The warm,
sweet odor of fresh rain lifted me from my bunk like a
green stalk striking upward. I tottered on clay-like feet,

the dead nerves tingling with the shooting pains of a million needles. The impossible had happened—rain in the Arctic night!

I stumbled toward the corner of the room. My numb fingers sought the shelf of the medicine chest; a bottle of whisky was stowed behind the bandages, an almost forgotten bottle. I lifted this and drank. For a while there was no taste, nothing but a bitter, nauseating trickle down my dry throat and along my spine. Then my heart seemed to awaken, my brain began to throb, I stumbled to the door and the wet dogs burst in from the storm, and great draughts of moist air filled the house. The skinny dogs jumped on me, howling incessantly. This, with the thunder of an internal tornado in my head, steadied me. The northern shores of Spitsbergen were being laved by the freak intrusion of a violent southern storm. Unholy clouds of fog rose upward from the melting ice, mists and humors upset the frozen equilibrium of the night.

I found matches and a can of oil; I lit the smudgy lamp and searched for hard tack and canned beef. My head was light as I reeled about and dragged half a sack of coal to the fire, lighting it with precious scraps of newspaper and kindling wood. I walked about and talked like a fool. The dogs were snapping at the half-frozen beef, panting and snuffing and nuzzling the cans. I kept away from the two silent forms lumped up under the blankets in their bunks. Then the half-empty bottle standing on the table looked at me accusingly. I pulled back the blanket from Paul's head and forced a thick tumbler of whisky between the reluctant teeth, spilling the stuff on the old man's matted beard. The sailor grunted. I went to Morten, forced his jaws apart and poured down a fiery shot. For an hour I fed them, drinking myself whenever the clutch of cold seized me. The room reeked of liquor; the fire roared; the dogs, giving off wet vapor, were clustered at the base of the red-hot stove, sometimes thumping their tails on the floor and barking in short, ecstatic grunts.

That night the wind veered into the north. The cold came back and the country lay beneath a frosting of translucent ice. We sat before a stew of reindeer meat, bending our heads, our eyes dimmed, our minds humble.

In a few weeks the twilight told of the returning sun. A month later three thin, yellow-faced men, with long, light-colored beards, stood on the summit of Smedburg's Mountain, gazing to the south at noon. The upper limb of the sun lifted for a moment above saw-toothed crags of ice. A purple, wind-sped cloud rode across the brilliant arc of day. Without comment we slid back down into the dimming valley of our experience and entered the small house filled with memories.

When our relief ship burst into view past the Cape de Geer in the early weeks of June, summer and daylight had long returned and the world of birds and song replaced the blackness of night.

The surgeon, in charge of commissariat, was seeking stowage for additional stores. He reported finding the remarkable skeleton of a female resting below the trap. The coffin boards, better than usual in those rude graves, lay in a heap below the bunk of Paul.

ALL IN THE DAY'S WORK

George F. Shearwood

After active service through the World War on the western front and in East Africa, Captain Shearwood, when the armistice was declared, became the administrative officer in charge of the Karamoja district of northern Uganda, with its native population of sixty thousand primitive black folk. It was while on this post that he experienced the eventful twenty-four hours here described.

ALL IN THE DAY'S WORK

By George F. Shearwood

T HE LENGTH OF SIX SPEARS, LOKOLOI! THE ROAD MUST be six spears wide and by sundown your clan must have cleared to the river."

I was in charge of an African tribe. As the tropical sun rose rapidly in the east, I gave that order to a headman of the tribe, the Karamoja, and strolled slowly back to camp and breakfast, followed by my orderly.

Another day had begun. It promised to be just one more day in the routine of attempting to administer this remote section of northern Uganda. Far to the south and on the border of my territory the sun was gilding the majestic mass of Mount Elgon, the world's largest extinct volcano. Out to the east lay Rudolph, the lake of brackish waters. Behind me, to the north, grew the dense bush that spread far into the Sudan, while to the northeast rugged mountains marked the southern fringe of Abyssinia.

That section of the panorama I liked least, for it was there that most of the troubles of this country were brewed. Out of those mountains came outlaws, ivory poachers, slave raiders—wild bandits whose depredations were the bane of all the tribes that lived near the border.

However, this morning I looked forward to an ordinary, uneventful day. I planned to watch Lokoloi's people clearing the road in the direction of my headquarters, Loyoro, three days' march to the east. Then a leisurely *safari* on to the next rest camp, where I intended to stay the night. I had no premonition of the crowded day that fate—and Africa—had marked out for me.

I sat down to breakfast, one of my boys waving a fan to keep flies off the food in transit between the plate and my mouth.

Before the meal was over, Corporal Nasaneri, the most intelligent non-commissioned officer of my small force of native soldiers, approached, escorting a "levy." The levy, so-called because he was attached to my personal retinue and was distinguished from his people by a small red pennant at his spear-head, bore a message from the next village.

The chief of that section, Lokonomoi, wished me to know that the murderer of a girl had been caught and that the headmen were gathering for a meeting of the Atuk. "Would the *effendi* desire to attend?" he asked. I had been in the district but a short time and, as I had not yet seen this tribal court dispense justice, I sent word to delay the trial until I arrived.

Though the white man's rule holds sway in Karamoja, no attempt had yet been made to interfere with the native tribunal where crimes committed within the tribe were concerned.

Fortunately, the Atuk was meeting in the village to which I planned to move, so I called the *syce* to harness my riding mule and ordered the boys to pack and follow with the porters.

·   ·   ·   ·   ·

At the river toward which the road builders were working, I found a roaring torrent, for this was the end of the rainy season and the usually dry river-bed was in full flood. Here began the day's adventures.

I started to ford the stream. The mule floundered and staggered in the rushing waters and the sandy, insecure bed. Unexpectedly, he leaped forward and I found myself sitting up to my neck in water, the saddle still beneath me. The mule was scrambling up the further bank. Thanks to the careless *syce,* the animal had managed to jump clean out of the saddle.

My sudden bath probably tickled the small group of *askaris* and levies, but it didn't feel a bit funny to me. I was soaked to the skin and my porters were too far behind to supply dry clothing.

Only one thing to do—go on and hope the wetting would not result in fever. Four years in the wildest parts of Central Africa had taught me to take care of my health. Besides, if I got fever, I'd have to cure myself, for the nearest doctor was distant ten or twelve days' tedious march.

Oozing water and abusing the *syce* with every Swahili swear-word I knew, I resumed my journey.

By the time I rode up to the waiting circle of tribal elders at my destination, my shirt and shorts had dried, but water still seeped out of my boots. I was not too good-tempered, and the prospect of sitting in the grass hut of the Atuk, while some thirty very dirty savages squatted solemnly in a semi-circle before me—and the flies did their worst—had lost its early appeal.

However, in such a situation, before the critical eyes of many warriors, most of whom I was meeting for the first time, such discomfort must be overlooked. I led the way into the hut. These men, powerful in their own sections of the tribe, would be curious to sum up the new white chief.

The dramatic trial began. In reality, I had nothing to do with it and sensed that the whole spectacle was a test for me. I knew the tribal punishment for murder. Solomon in all his wisdom never bettered the Karamojan's simple code. If the man was found guilty, the father of the girl would put him to death. Doubtless I would have to watch it done

—watch it, too, without betraying by a flicker of an eyelid that the scene was nauseating.

Kulu, the prisoner, was led in. A hide thong around his neck, the ends of it in the hands of his victim's brother, prevented any break for liberty.

His accusers told their stories. He had coveted the girl and, finding her one evening bringing in her father's sheep and goats, had attempted to force unwelcome attentions on her. Maddened by her resistance, he slit her throat with the knife-edged bracelet every Karamoja warrior wears, and fled. When the animals returned without their keeper, the girl's family searched and found her body. Kulu's craving for her being known to them, his disappearance marked him as her slayer, and every warrior in the section was quickly on his trail. They caught him hiding in the rocky crevices of the great escarpment which frowns down upon the Turkana country.

The evidence was clear enough. The prisoner was allowed to speak in his own defense. With that sense of fatalism so strongly marked in the African savage, he surveyed the immobile faces of his judges. He turned and for a moment his eyes looked straight into mine. In them was the blankness of despair. He shrugged his shoulders. He had no answer.

Then the spokesman of the court arose and standing before me said:

"The *effendi* has heard the talk. This dog's life is forfeit by the law of our land. Does the *effendi* agree?"

It was a polite little piece of play. I knew that and told him gravely that the verdict of the court was indeed just.

The father of the girl appeared, a spear, already stripped of its guard, in his hand.

Tugging at the thong around Kulu's neck, he pulled the condemned warrior out into the glaring sunshine, while

the rest of us sat, still as the death to which this man was
going.

A muffled exclamation, a scuffle, the thud of a falling
body just beyond the thin grass wall of the hut, and the law
of the Karamoja, unchanged since the beginning of time,
once more had taken retribution.

The next move, I sensed, was up to me. The half-circle
of elders still squatted silently before me, waiting my departure or my words. Though death was a familiar sight to
me, I did not relish the idea of walking out into the blind-
ing sun and facing the crumpled heap that had once been
Kulu. So, for all the hot, fetid odor of the hut and the ever-
increasing hordes of flies, I decided to stay awhile and improve my acquaintance with the men before me.

. . . . .

The Karamoja owned vast herds of cattle. Meat, milk
and blood formed their food and drink. The clans measured their importance and power by the size of their herds.
Cattle, sheep and goats were the sole means of barter. With
them men acquired their wives. The animals were the
tribe's only possession and the needs of those animals controlled the daily lives of their masters. Lately rinderpest
and pleuro-pneumonia had afflicted the beasts through hundreds of miles of the eastern Nile country. In an attempt to
save all I could, I had sent out orders that all the cattle
must be moved to the hilltops, even if it meant the temporary desertion of villages in the one or two cases where
clans actually were settled. (Most of the tribe, always need-
ing new pastures, were perforce nomadic.)

I turned to Lokonomoi, the venerable paramount chief,
and asked: "O Lokonomoi, how fares it with the cattle of
your people? Have my commands that cattle be taken into
the hills to avoid the sickness been obeyed?"

Lokonomoi, six feet of magnificent ebony nakedness,

topped off with a grizzled thatch of wool, arose. Some of the younger men glanced nervously around and I saw that Lokonomoi himself appeared ill at ease.

"*Effendi,*" he said, "all of us here present obeyed thy orders. Our flocks are in the hills, even though this part of our country seldom is afflicted with the sickness. The *effendi* is our father and we obey him."

"All of you who are present, I heard you say, O Loko-nomoi. Are there then some chiefs missing from the Atuk?" I asked.

"*Effendi,*" replied the old man slowly. "I am an old man and have the wisdom of the old. I know that the *effendi* is our friend, but there are some who, because of their youth, disregard the *effendi's* orders. The people of Nudo, who live in the thick bush yonder, have not obeyed. Nudo and his elders returned when they learned the *effendi* would be here. Nudo and his people, *effendi,* are of my clan, but they are wild and headstrong, and I am an old man."

Thirty curious pairs of eyes peered steadily at me. Here was a challenge, indeed. Well I knew that, if Nudo and his people were not made to obey, the word would flash through the whole tribe that the white man need not be obeyed. That would mean that I had failed and, through my failure, the white race I represented would be discredited and all the work that had been done would be wasted. This I knew. Action was needed!

"Nudo and I will meet this day," I said, as I rose. "You will guide me to his village and everyone in this hut will come with us. Nudo must learn that my orders are for the good of his people and must be obeyed."

Getting out into the open air, I found that the body of Kulu had been removed. The porters had caught up, my tent was pitched and lunch was ready. It was good to get out of those soggy boots and hose.

This Nudo business was going to be ticklish and more than a little dangerous, for force was no use in such a case. In any event, my *askaris* would be of little use to back up my orders. They were too few. Lokonomoi might be counted on, but how about the younger men? Just how, underneath their outward show of loyalty and deference, did they regard the white man who sought to rule them? They were glad of the aid my trained native soldiers could render when the wild men from the north raided their land. They were simple, peaceable enough on the surface and easy to handle, but they were savages, who lived by the law of the survival of the fittest. The spear and battle were their proving-grounds of courage. The strongest men were the rulers.

.   .   .   .   .

The heat of the afternoon was intense as we set out for Nudo's village. The road was nothing but a narrow path through the spear-like elephant grass, which reached high above my head. As we moved on, the country became thicker. This, I knew, was the home of the most unruly elements of the Karamoja. Here outlaws fled to preach resistance to the white man's law—and, for that matter, resistance to any law. In these fastnesses of primeval forest, no man, white or black, could rule with any certainty of success beyond the reach of his arm.

How should I deal with Nudo? Well, the problem would have to be solved on the spot.

Unexpectedly, after about three hours' hard march, we turned a bend in the trail and came to a large clearing. In the center rose a rough stockade, which circled the huts of Nudo's village.

Grouped about the open entrance stood eight or nine

warriors, spears and shields in their hands. The center figure, burlier than the rest, was Nudo.

They stood as though awaiting my arrival, though no word had been sent of my intended visit. This was no surprise to me. Though the Karamoja do not use drums, yet messages pass with the swiftness of light through the forests and across the plains. The mysterious "grapevine" system of communication for which all Africa is famous, apparently requires no drums. It is the more uncanny and, at first, more terrifying, for its silence!

When I reached a spot some twenty yards from Nudo, I halted and motioned my three *askaris,* Lokonomoi and the other headmen to wait at a distance.

Nudo and his warriors advanced till they formed a half-circle around me. Well, if it had to be a spear in the back, so be it. Out of the corner of my eye, I saw Corporal Nasaneri quietly loading his rifle in the distance. Clearly, my intelligent corporal expected trouble, but his rifle would be too late to save me if Nudo meant to use a spear.

"Hail, O Nudo," I greeted him. "I did not see thee at the Atuk in the village of Lokonomoi today. How came it that thou didst not share the burden of justice with thy brothers?"

For a moment the surly headman was silent. Then he replied, "We fear that the Habash will attack our village, O *effendi,* and spend our days making it more secure."

Habash (literally, "strangers") was used to designate raiders, usually Abyssinians.

"The Habash seeks cattle and your daughters, O Nudo," I said. "Why should they attack your village when the cattle and the women are gone to the hills?"

Here came the test.

"The cattle and our women are here, O *effendi,*" slowly answered Nudo. At least, he did not lie.

"The cattle of Karamoja are sick and in my wisdom I strove to save them by sending them to the hills until the foul air of the valleys clears. Nudo," I said gravely, "thou hadst that order and knowest that I am the friend of thy people. What hast thou to say for delaying thy departure? Is this outlaw talk?"

"The sickness has not come to our cattle. Why, then, should we move from our village?" returned the headman.

The group of men, many of whom were well known as the least law-abiding of the tribe, closed in with sinister slowness around Nudo and myself. Fingers tightened around the shafts of spears.

"Nudo," I said, "the sickness may come to your cattle. I desire to take no risk that any shall die. I have given the order. It is late now, but, when the sun rises in the morning, thou and thy people and their cattle must be on the way to the hills yonder." I pointed to the ridge in the west toward which the sun was sinking.

"We will not go," angrily defied the headman.

"Nudo," I said again, "I can put thee in jail at Loyoro and leave some soldiers here to see that my orders are obeyed. But I do not want to do that. Thou wilt do as these other chiefs have done," (indicating the party in the background). "Take thy cattle to the hills and, as soon as all danger has passed, thou canst return. *Basi,* it is enough," I finished and turned slowly as though to leave.

As I did so, from the corner of my eye I saw a young and villainous-looking warrior at Nudo's side deliberately raising his spear.

Wheeling, I took a few quick paces toward the man and hit with all my strength. The blow caught him squarely on the chin and he dropped like a log.

"I need no spear and spill no blood," I called almost instantaneously with the action and looked straight at Nudo, who, with his followers, was staring at the suddenly stricken spearman on the ground. The swiftness of the whole thing momentarily paralyzed the warriors. Action was respected above all else by these savages. He who took the initiative was the man they would obey.

My *askaris* and the other chiefs were running toward us, but I waved them back and said very quietly to Nudo:

"The white man needs no weapon against fools, O Nudo. Take heed and see that my orders are obeyed."

Nudo looked up from his fallen warrior, now squatting and rubbing his jaw, and said, with a note of respect in his voice, "The *effendi's* orders will be obeyed."

Without a word I turned and walked back to the edge of the clearing, trying to disguise the fact that my right hand felt as though all the bones were broken, and suddenly conscious that I was very weary.

That I had emerged from the ordeal with my object achieved and having obviously won the respect of that group of malcontents was more an accident than anything else, I decided, as I led the way to camp and dinner. It was the closest call with sudden death I had ever known, not excepting that hand-to-hand fighting in the Ypres salient in 1914. I rather blessed those days, for they had taught me to keep my head in an emergency such as this.

.   .   .   .   .

It was night by the time we reached Lokonomoi's village and I was glad of the bath the boys had prepared.

After dinner I sat by the campfire. The village had quieted down for the night, but I was too tired and overwrought to sleep. A little distance from me, a sentry paced slowly back and forth, the flickering flames lighting him each time he passed. Africa, with its challenges, lay quiet, with a silence that always threatened dreadful sound—far more savage, more mysterious than by day, for, with all its sullen quietness, there was no hint of peace. One sensed that all around, unseen yet seeing, moving yet apparently still, the plain and bush teemed with life—life, in a kingdom where speed and strength held sway, as truly as among the waking humans of the day.

Presently I roused from my reverie to notice that the sentry was staring intently into the night beyond the corner of the hut. I hailed him. He came at the double, halted and saluted.

"*Effendi*," he reported, "there is fire out there in the night. I think Nudo's village burns."

I jumped from my chair and walked out into the open. Sure enough, there was fire. The black, moonless sky was aglow far away over the trees in the direction of the unpleasant ordeal of that afternoon.

"Wake the camp and call Lokonomoi," I directed Tomasi, the sentry, and hurried to my hut, yelling for my boys. The blaze meant one of two things. Either Nudo had had another change of heart and gone berserk-mad and was destroying his village, or else the Habash, the dreaded Abyssinians, had swooped down through the night, pillaging, ravaging and destroying. The first possibility was beyond reason.

Tired though I was, here was just another occasion when fatigue must be forgotten. The white man's labors in a savage land know no hours nor days.

If this were the work of the Habash, for once I was near enough to have a real chance to catch them. I had tried many times before, but the news had always reached me too late.

Corporal Nasaneri, freshly aroused from sleep, came running up.

"Get the men on parade at once. *Safari maramoja.* Hurry!" I ordered.

"Ndio, effendi." The old Sudanese soldier impassively saluted and turned to assemble his *askaris* and the porters with the machine-gun.

Lokonomoi arrived with his two sons. "Lokonomoi," I said, pointing to the distant fire, "what do you think of that? Is it not the work of your enemies, the Habash?"

The old man looked and said: *"Ndio, effendi.* Nudo, who did not obey the *effendi's* orders, now is sorry, for without a doubt his village is given to the flames. What does the *effendi* do?"

"We find the Habash, O Lokonomoi," I said. "Bring all your warriors, for there will be work for them tonight."

Getting into my equipment, I gave orders to my boys to follow at a safe distance. Soon my dozen native troops were ready and we started off toward Lokonomoi's village. Quietly, my men marshalled the old chief's warriors, almost a hundred in number.

As we entered the path we had followed earlier in the day, I sent two levies ahead, with orders to report back as soon as they found what had happened. Just behind me walked Lokonomoi, spears and shield in hand and wearing the ostrich-feather head-dress of the fighting man. I issued instructions that his warriors were not to get into action with the *Habash*—presuming we caught up with them— until I gave the order. I didn't want that howling horde of spearmen spoiling the lesson I hoped to teach the raiders. Their turn could come when I was through.

The march to Nudo's village, which had required three hours in the heat of the day and under less urgent circumstances, took considerably less now. Spurred by the desire to catch the raiders, I forgot weariness and urged the men along.

When we were still half a mile from the village, one of

Karamoja Chieftain Ready for Battle

the levies came loping back, accompanied by a youth from the stricken village. I heard the story as we hastened on.

The youth described how, soon after dusk, as the men were putting the huge grass gates of the stockade in place, guns had cracked from the edge of the clearing. Before any attempt at defense was possible, the gate had been rushed by a band of Abyssinians. Swords and guns made short work of the utterly unprepared warriors. The women's fires were kicked into the huts and in a few moments the dry grass and wood made a roaring inferno of the village. As the fire spread, the cattle were driven out and the wild men of the north searched among the cowering females, tearing the young women and girls from their mothers. With the swiftness of all evil, the thing was done and protesting cattle and wailing girls were being driven off to Abyssinia and slavery.

The story was an old one in this border land, but lacked nothing in drama because of familiarity.

. . . . .

The scene, as we eventually rounded the bend in the trail, was one of desolation. Flames still leaped high in the night air, licking the edge of the trees beyond the clearing. Cries of the wounded mingled with the crackling of burning wood. Two or three figures rose and came running toward us, their naked limbs silhouetted grotesquely against the fiery background.

Where was Nudo? I asked the survivors. They led me to a mangled heap at the still smouldering gateway. Nudo lay there among others of his warriors, a spear in his hand and a sword thrust through his throat. Poor savage! I could not help reflecting that he was the victim of his own folly. Had my orders been obeyed, the raiders would have found nothing but an empty village to sack.

While inspecting the moaning wounded, the old women and babes, I inquired the road the Habash had taken.

There was nothing to do here, so I left two of Lokonomoi's older men in charge and led my party forward.

As we skirted the camp, one young boy came edging toward me and said he knew a path that was shorter than the one the enemy had taken. He explained that it would enable us to reach the pass leading down the escarpment into the Great Rift Valley before the enemy, whose route was longer and whose progress, hampered by captives and the cattle, would of necessity be slower.

This was a stroke of luck and we moved off without further delay. The route was the narrowest of game tracks, tortuous and winding. The darkness of the forest made the moonless night still blacker. It was necessary to keep the party close together, almost to make each man hold to the back of the one before him, in order to insure that the party would not become hopelessly divided at some twist in the trail.

Slowly and painfully we plodded forward, stumbling in the broken undergrowth, torn and cut by the unseen thorn-bush which reached out at us from all sides. Every now and then a sudden rustle proclaimed that we had disturbed some wild creature.

Away in the distance, the howl of a laughing hyena split the silence, as though mocking us for fools. There is no sound on earth quite as eerie and maniacal as the howl of that laughing jackass!

Hour after hour we fought on through the bush, trying to reach the brink of the rocky escarpment before the dawn.

My watch said four a.m. when our youthful guide warned us that we were near the edge of the bush. We must move with care. The trees and underbrush were thinning out, so I halted to rest and reorganize my heavily laden *askaris*. The machine-gun was assembled and slung on a pole, so that it could be brought into action without delay. I was relying on that machine-gun.

We resumed our march cautiously, with several levies ahead to give instant warning if the enemy were encountered. Soon we reached the edge of the escarpment, an almost perpendicular wall of rock. Our guide led us northward along its brink, seeking the pass. The hour of dawn was rapidly approaching.

Presently the guide halted on the brow of a small hill and, pointing down, said that the pass lay just below. The levies returned, reporting nothing. I sent Lokonomoi and some others down to examine the ground for signs of recently passing cattle, while my *askaris* lined the hilltop and the machine-gun crew took up their position behind some scrub. Lokonomoi, creeping back to me with the excitement of battle in his old eyes, reported that he had found no signs of cattle. I sent him back to his warriors, hidden at the base of the hill. When I gave the signal, they could sweep forward and slay to their heart's content.

Hardly had we settled down to await the dawn, when the protesting moo of a cow reached our straining ears. Tense and ready, we waited. Then out of the night came the sound of moving hoofs. We had won the race to the pass!

The next few moments were anxious ones. It wanted only a little time to dawn. Already the sky was lightening and the ghostly grey of approaching day made it possible to distinguish objects close at hand.

Down in the clearing I spotted something moving. An *askari* stirred and the moving object stopped. It was a sheep, strayed from the captured cattle. Alarmed by the *askari's* movement, the animal swung around and scampered back to the bush. Bad luck! Its return would warn the enemy advance-guard that danger lurked ahead. It would put them on the alert.

So it proved. As the light grew momentarily stronger, I saw that many figures of humans and animals had emerged and were halted on the edge of the bush.

Two men, armed with guns, started to steal forward. Suddenly one of them halted, waved and fired his gun. He had discovered Lokonomoi's men. As the gunshot jarred the stillness and echoed down into the valley, thirty or more of the Habash came tearing up. Yelling, they charged at the Karamoja, firing as they ran.

Forgetting my orders, Lokonomoi and his warriors were up and racing to meet their hated foes.

I snapped an order to my machine-gunners. The gun was swung around and instantly its staccato bark broke out, greeting the coming day with a rhythmic rattle of death. The first burst of fire cut a wide swath in the ranks of the raiders and panic gripped them. The survivors broke and ran, followed by the spitting bullets as the gunners tried to catch them before they disappeared in the shadows of the bush.

The Karamoja had halted when the machine-gun fire began, astonished and not a little afraid. This was new magic to them. They forgot the enemy as they stared up at the still working gun.

Then suddenly Lokonomoi, old but clear of eye, screamed a warning and, turning, I found about twenty of the raiders creeping up on us from behind. As I turned, they scrambled to their feet, only a few yards away. The leader, a huge, dead-black fellow, whose wool stood straight up on his head, came lunging at me with a sword. One shot from my revolver, fired at point-blank range, dropped him, the sword falling at my feet.

Now the rest of them and the *askaris* were mixed in a

struggling, kicking, stabbing jumble around me. Corporal Nasaneri's rifle butt cracked the skull of one man as he shot a spear wildly just above my shoulder. My revolver finished another as he stabbed at the corporal's back.

Then, with a wild whoop, Lokonomoi and his vengeful warriors were in the fray, sweeping the remnants of the Habash down into the clearing below. There the enemy turned, at bay.

Courage no one who knows them will deny the wild men of the Abyssinian fastnesses, but they were outnumbered and had no chance. The Karamoja, mindful of many another foray and the loss of lives, women, cattle and homes, killed on exultantly, till at last the sun, peeping over the horizon, found the battle over. The Habash had paid in full.

I turned to face the welcome sun, now streaking the sky with its glory, bringing life once more to Africa. It was the dawn of another day. The one just ended, which had started out so peacefully only twenty-four hours before, now seemed a nightmare a year long. Yet it had been merely a routine day in the life of one whose job it was to help bear the white man's burden in a savage land.

The corporal was standing before me, waiting for orders. The routine must go on.

"All right," I said, "the men can dismiss, Nasaneri. *Simama hapa leo*. We stay here today."

THE ROYAL ROAD TO HUMDRUM

Vilhjalmur Stefansson

"Stefansson will stand for all time as the Great Interpreter of the North," is the apt characterization of Dr. Isaiah Bowman, Director of the American Geographical Society.

Born in Manitoba, he began his work as an explorer with two journeys to Iceland in 1904 and 1905. Between 1906 and 1918, he made three extensive expeditions along the northern coast of Alaska and Canada, among the Canadian arctic islands and over the unknown polar sea, adding islands, rivers, lakes and mountains to the map of those regions and bringing back much scientific information.

Eleven years among the Eskimos, some of whom had never seen a white man before, gave him an intimate knowledge of their language and ways of living.

He is a former president and a medallist of The Explorers Club and gold medallist of the leading geographical societies of the United States, Great Britain, France and Germany. For his field work and writings he received in 1921 an official vote of thanks from the Canadian government—the only time in Canadian history that this honor has been given to an explorer. An alumnus of the University of Iowa, he holds a graduate degree from Harvard and doctor's degrees from the universities of Michigan, Iowa, North Dakota and Iceland.

In addition to scientific reports, he has written *My Life with the Eskimo; The Friendly Arctic; Hunters of the Great North; The Adventure of Wrangel Island; The Northward Course of Empire,* and a gem of Voltairian satire, *The Standardization of Error.*

THE ROYAL ROAD TO HUMDRUM

By Vilhjalmur Stefansson

My favorite quotation is Stefansson's dictum: "Adventures are a mark of incompetence."—Roy Chapman Andrews, *Saturday Evening Post,* August 22, 1931.

IN A BOOK OF ADVENTURES I LIKE THE CHANCE TO DEFEND by anecdote and narrative a saying that has been quoted frequently with disapproval, although I managed to discover a favorable vote on it to place at the head of this article.

There is a bit of exposition and argument in the quotation itself, if it is taken somewhat *in extenso* from page 43 of "My Life With the Eskimo" (New York, 1913):

"An adventure is a sign of incompetence. . . . If everything is well managed, if there are no miscalculations or mistakes, then the things that happen are only the things you expected to happen, for which you are ready and with which you can therefore deal."

In that book a narrative which supports this thesis is found on pages 165-167. Condensed and adapted, it runs:

"Through incompetence, I came near having a serious adventure; that I did not actually have it was due to the incompetence of a polar bear.

I was hunting caribou eastward along the sea front of the Melville Mountains that lie parallel to the coast (Dolphin and Union Straits) a few miles inland. . . . I had seen no caribou

323

all day nor the day before and our meat was low; therefore I stopped whenever I came to the top of a commanding hill to study the country with my binoculars. . . . Ptarmigan there were but they are uneconomical for a party of four that is to go a year on nine hundred and sixty rounds of ammunition; even the foxes were too small for our notice, but a wolf that came within two hundred yards seldom got by, for a fat one weighs a hundred pounds.

This day the wolves did not come near, and the first hopeful sign was a yellow spot on the sea ice about three miles off. It was difficult to determine whether or not it was merely yellow ice. I put in a half hour watching this thing that was a bit yellower than ice should be. Now and then I looked elsewhere, for a caribou or grizzly may at any time come out from behind a hill, a polar bear from behind a cake of ice, or a seal out of his hole. On perhaps the sixth or seventh sweep of the entire horizon with the field-glasses, I missed the yellow spot. It had moved away and must therefore have been a polar bear that had been lying down; after sleeping too long in one position, he had stood up and lain down again behind an ice hummock.

In a moment I was running as hard as I could in the direction of the bear, for there was no telling when he would start traveling or how fast he would go. I had taken careful note of the topography of the land with relation to the rough sea ice, for it is as difficult to keep a straight line toward an invisible object among pressure ridges as it is in a forest. I kept glancing back at the mountains as I ran and tried to guide myself towards the bear by their configuration.

When at last I got to the neighborhood of where I thought the animal would be, I climbed an especially high pressure ridge and spent a longer time than usual sweeping the surroundings with the glasses and studying individual ice cakes and ridges, with the hope of recognizing some of those I had seen from the mountains. But everything looked different on near approach, and I failed to locate myself definitely. I decided to go a quarter of a mile or so farther before beginning to circle for the bear's tracks. My rifle was buckled in its case slung across my back, and I was slowly and cautiously clambering down the far side of a pressure ridge, when I heard behind

Antonio Salemme, sculptor

Vilhjalmur Stefansson

me a noise like the spitting of a cat or the hiss of an angry goose. I looked back and saw, about twenty feet away and almost above me, a polar bear.

Had he come the remaining twenty feet as quietly and quickly as a bear can, the literary value of the incident would have been lost forever. From his eye and attitude there was no doubting his intentions; the hiss was merely his way of saying, "Watch me do it!" Or possibly the motive was chivalry and the hiss a way of saying *"Garde!"* Whichever it was, it was the fatal mistake in a game well played to that point. No animal on earth can afford to give warning to a man with a rifle. And why should he? Has a hunter ever played fair with one of them?

Afterwards the snow told plainly the short—and, for one of the participants, tragic—story. I had overestimated the bear's distance from shore and had passed the spot where he lay. On scenting me, he had come up the wind to my trail and had then followed it. The reason I had not seen his approach was that it had not occurred to me to look back. I was so used to hunting bears that the possibility of one of them assuming my role and hunting me had been left out of consideration. A good hunter, like a good detective, should leave nothing out of consideration."

A thing I have too frequently left out of consideration in my travels has been my high-school education, whereupon I have had distressing and thrilling physical adventures. By considering my education, I have sometimes had intellectual adventures that were equally thrilling but less disagreeable.

One of the fundamentals in the training and belief of explorers has been the theory that, when lost or unable to find shelter in a blizzard or in very cold weather, you must on no account go to sleep; if you did, you would never wake again. There is still vividly in mind the thrill I had when I first applied to this belief what I had learned in the eighth grade about physiology and in high school about physics.

I show the problem and background of this adventure

by quoting the most famous of American polar explorers before Peary, the physician and popular hero, Elisha Kent Kane. In describing a winter march in extremely cold weather, he says ("Arctic Explorations: The Second Grinnell Expedition." Phila. 1857. Vol. I, pp. 194-197):

"Bonsall and Morton, two of our stoutest men, came to me, begging permission to sleep. 'They were not cold, the wind did not enter them now; a little sleep was all they wanted.' Presently Hans was found nearly stiff under a drift; and Thomas, bolt upright, had his eyes closed and could hardly articulate. At last, John Blake threw himself on the snow and refused to rise. They did not complain of feeling cold; but it was in vain that I wrestled, boxed, ran, argued, jeered or reprimanded. . . . It required desperate efforts to work our way, literally desperate, for our strength failed us anew. . . . Our halts multiplied and we fell half-sleeping on the snow. I could not prevent it. Strange to say, it refreshed us."

Refreshed as he was and impressed as he was by the startling discrepancy between belief and experience, Dr. Kane was not jolted out of his folk-belief that going to sleep in cold weather is dangerous. To him evidently this experience was a strange and unaccountable break in the orderly process of what he thought was natural law.

The belief in the danger of going to sleep out of doors in cold weather flourishes even today and even in the schools, side by side with opposite teachings.

In the physiology class you learn that the body is kept warm by the combustion of food that has become fuel in the blood stream. You can get more warmth by burning more fuel. It takes fuel also to move the body around from place to place. The motion itself does make you warmer but only at the expense of disproportionate fuel consumption. While you are still, most of the fuel is being used for warmth, but when you are moving, although you use still more for warmth, you use in addition something extra to produce motion. This means that, with a certain amount of food in your belly or a certain amount of fat distributed through your tissues, you can keep warm longer if you move less. Accordingly, when in danger of freezing, you should move only when, in your judgment, it is absolutely necessary either to avoid some outside risk or to increase temporarily the body warmth.

In the human body there is not only less use of fuel during idleness than action but also less during sleep than wakefulness. Apparently, then, wanting to live long without meals in cold surroundings, you should be as idle as possible and you should sleep as much as possible.

In the physics class you learn that the body is a heat engine and can do only a certain amount of work on a certain amount of fuel. Your teacher adds that fuel used for one purpose cannot be available for another.

In physics you learn, too, that air is a comparatively good non-conductor of heat, which means in everyday speech that it keeps away the cold. Air useful for this purpose in human clothing is found inside hollow hairs or imprisoned between hairs or in cavities. Water, on the other hand, is a good conductor. If you move around too much you perspire. The perspiration gets into your clothing, fills the air chambers and displaces the air, making the garment a good conductor and preventing it from keeping out the cold. One of the most important things, then, if you are lost out in the cold is to guard against perspiring. One way of doing that is to move around as little as possible.

A matter of such common knowledge that it is seldom if ever mentioned in the schools is that you do not sleep soundly unless you are comfortably warm. There are few in the United States, even in Florida, who have not been awakened in the night by too great a chill coming in through a window. They have either closed the window or found an extra blanket.

But the same man who knows from experience that a chill wakes you up in a bedroom believes also that a chill would put you to sleep under other conditions, this reversal of the familiar natural law taking place only when you are lost somewhere, preferably in a snowstorm and best of all in the Arctic.

I had not as yet read Dr. Kane as quoted above when my first turn came to stage an encounter between schooling and inherited folk-belief. The occasion was a starlit night with a temperature probably around fifty below zero. I was coming home from a long hunt. As I walked along with fifty or a hundred pounds of caribou meat on my back, I became gradually sleepier—and quite reasonably, for I had been on my feet for something like twenty-four hours. So I stopped, lay down on the snow with one of my arms for a pillow and went to sleep.

I don't suppose it can have been more than five or ten minutes till I began to have the old familiar feeling of being in bed on a chilly night with too few blankets. That feeling woke me up. I was as refreshed as I discovered twenty years later that Kane had been fifty years before.

. . . . . .

This being a volume of adventures, I have tried above to produce a thrill and to make myself a bit more of an adventurer by holding out on the reader. I fear I may have known at the time of our story the Mackenzie Eskimo rule for what to do when lost in a blizzard. According to them, you sit down on something with your back to the wind and go to sleep if you can. During the storm you move about as seldom as possible, only to get your blood into circulation when you feel cramped or to warm up if you are getting unendurably cold.

VILHJALMUR STEFANSSON 329

The first Eskimo I knew to be lost in a storm was an old woman who was poorly dressed in comparison either with the rest of the Eskimos or with us explorers. That blizzard lasted three days and she had been sitting it out only about a half-mile from the house. She came home smiling and cheerful when the weather cleared and explained that she wasn't even so very hungry because she had slept most of the time.

Another winter two sailors ran away from a whaling ship at Herschel Island. They were better dressed than the old woman, but they believed, if they went to sleep, they would freeze to death. Their bodies were found by a search party a few days later. Following their belief, they had kept moving and, when going to sleep became imminent, they had tried to keep awake by moving about so violently that they had perspired and their clothing had become wet. Under that condition of extreme exhaustion and with garments which no longer protected them from the cold, they had been able to substantiate at the cost of their lives the theory in which they had so firmly believed. They had gone to sleep and never waked again.

. . . . .

It was the soda counter rather than the high school which furnished the background for another of my early polar thrills. My mother had cautioned me when I was growing up in North Dakota that on a cold winter's day I must not eat snow but was always to come into the house for a drink if I got thirsty. Then I got to know people who had traveled in Switzerland and who had learned from their mountaineer guides that under no condition must you eat snow when you are scaling one of the tourist peaks. Eventually, on my first journey to the Arctic I met a Hudson's Bay Company trader on the average every two hundred miles for the 2,000-mile stretch of the Mackenzie system and I think nearly every one of them cautioned me —the accent usually Scotch and the words usually to the effect that some time I would find myself in bitterly cold winter weather where there was no possibility of liquid water; under those conditions I must not eat snow. And they fortified the warning by tales of men they had known who had eaten snow and taken violent cramps, dying or nearly dying if they were alone, or becoming burdens on their companions otherwise.

One arctic day a few months later, when I got thirsty, I began wondering what would be the difference between eating snow and eating ice cream. I experimented gingerly, for, after all, these folk-beliefs are not always wholly without rational foundation. A little snow did not hurt and so I ate more. I continued the practice through ten winters and all the members of our various expeditions have done the same. We begin eating snow in the morning to forestall, rather than quench, thirst and we eat it all day. It never has hurt one of us.

However, most things can be done in a way that is injurious. The reason why there has been some injury in polar exploration from eating snow is found is a combination of a strong belief with a weak will power. If you believe that eating snow will hurt you, you refrain until the thirst becomes so intense that your will breaks down. Then, if you try to eat the snow fast enough to quench thirst, you will also be eating it fast enough to freeze your lips, tongue, and even your gullet. The whole secret is to have the amount of snow you put in your mouth at any one time so small that the chill of it shall be easily neutralized by the warmth of your mouth.

You can safely swallow snow as snow if the temperature of it when swallowed is only a little below freezing. If you try to swallow it in great quantities while its temperature is still sixty or seventy degrees below freezing you will produce almost the effect of applying liquid air.

That brings us to another of our small adventures with folk-belief. According to revered precept, the thing to do when you freeze your nose is to rub snow on it. But you learn in your physics course that, if you bring together two bodies of different temperatures, the warm one becomes colder and the cold one warmer. Assume now that the skin on a nose which is beginning to freeze is at a temperature of a degree below freezing. The snow on the ground is always at the same temperature as the air, and you are not likely to freeze your nose unless the air is at least fifty below freezing (twenty below zero). If now you apply to a body (a nose) already slightly frozen another body (a mittenful of snow) which is fifty degrees colder, there is going to be that transfer of heat about which we learned in school. The snow will become a little warmer and the nose will become a whole lot colder.

According to the physics course, you ought to bring a warmer body near the cold one if you want the cold one to grow warmer. But the only warm thing you are always sure to have with you at the time of a frostbite is the rest of your body. So you naturally apply your hand to your face. The hand is not necessarily the warmest part of your body, but it is peculiarly well situated for applying to the face and usually it is quite warm enough.

On a cold day, with a moderate head-wind, we freeze our faces dozens and scores of times, but we thaw them out just as often, and we never allow the frost to become more than skin-deep, in which case it is no more serious than a sunburn. Neither is it more painful.

.   .   .   .   .

A case where a folk-belief really had me going was about the well known depressing effect of the long arctic night.

Why should a long night be depressing when a short one isn't? The first winter, I was so firmly convinced it would be that I don't remember ever posing to myself the contradiction between that belief and the well known hilarity of city nights, with their midnight revelry against which the clergy inveigh. I actually felt the midwinter polar depression, even with the Eskimos about me behaving as if Billy Sunday ought to come and scold them for it.

That winter I rejoiced at length in my diary when the sun returned, but now believe this to have been due to auto-suggestion. Anyhow, I have never been depressed by any of the nine following arctic winters. More convincing, I have noticed that the conservative and uncritical members of our expeditions have been depressed the first season by the sun's absence, while the younger and more intellectual have been able to convince themselves in advance that the gloom, if it came, would be only the result of auto-suggestion.

The thrill of conquering arctic blizzards did not come to me in any particular blizzard. I had at first been a good deal worried by several of them, and then it occurred to me one day to ask myself what was it that made an arctic blizzard so much more terrible than the ones I grew up among in North Dakota. The answer came in a flash and, with elation of a newish kind, for here it was not high-school training but a university course in logic that had slain the dragon. If there was no difference in strength of wind or degree of cold between polar and temperate-zone blizzards, then the different effect on me had to be due to something in me. All I had to do was to recapture my commonplace attitude toward blizzards. I did, and they never worried me thereafter.

A whole series of intellectual adventures came when I discovered that you could overcome many of the arctic terrors by simply changing their names. The dreaded Barren Ground becomes reasonably innocuous if you think of the grass and flowers and then name the treeless country "prairie." The Long Arctic Night is deprived of half its gloom if you call it the Time of Short Days. That is more descriptive, too, for out of doors you have daylight enough to read a newspaper around noon at very midwinter—for instance, on the Ross Sea, where most of the famous ant-arctic expeditions have had their base, and at Smith Sound, where Peary used to winter.

An adventure in part physical, though it concerned also a tussle between the biological sciences and folk-belief, is foreshadowed by the reading of the typical polar book. The case is put in a nutshell by Roald Amundsen on p. 211 of his "My Life as a Polar Explorer" (*Mitt Liv Som Polar Forsker*), Oslo, 1927:

"A more indefensible misrepresentation of conditions in the North has never been advanced than the claim that a good hunter can live there by hunting. Stefansson has never done it, although he says he has. Moreover I am willing to stake my reputation as a polar explorer, and to wager everything I own, that, if Stefansson were to try it, he would be dead within eight days, counted from the start, if only he makes the experiment on the polar ice which is steadily drifting about on the open sea."

The view here so clearly stated by Amundsen had not yet been specifically contravened, so far as I know, by any book in print before 1914, when three of us (Storker Storkerson, Ole Andreason and myself) made the experiment of living by hunting under just the conditions laid down by Amundsen—on polar ice that was steadily drifting about on the open sea at distances varying between scores and hundreds of miles from land.

The thrilling side of our adventure was the intellectual

—that we were staking our lives on the rightness of what we had learned in school. According to physics and physical geography, no sea water could be colder than twenty-seven Fahr., and waters of that temperature were known to be crowded with animal life in other parts of the world. Why not equally crowded in the polar seas, too, especially as the great fisheries of both the northern and the southern hemispheres are found exactly in the coldest water? The ice on top of a sea could not deprive the life in the water of the necessary oxygen for at any temperature it is broken into drifting cakes by the stresses of tides, winds and currents, so that it does not come so near hermetically sealing the water as does the heavy unmoving and shore-fast ice of lakes like Winnipeg or Great Slave, which are known to be excellent fishing grounds toward spring.

Just as the same man will tell you that a chill wakes you up in a bedroom and puts you to sleep out of doors, so the same book will tell you in general that all the conditions of the Arctic Sea are favorable to animal life, and then in particular that little or no animal life exists there. We decided to be logical, to conclude that two opposed statements could not both be right and to bet our lives that animals would be found in places known to be suitable for them.

The reasoning which led to the decision was simple. We had examined all the arguments and had come to the conclusion that they were the kind that would appeal to a philosopher but would probably not appeal to a fish. To begin with, we did not believe that the fish knew the philosophers had drawn a line in the ocean beyond which they must not swim, and secondarily we believed that, if the fish knew enough to turn back at the right place, there were nevertheless ocean currents which would carry with them all over the polar sea millions of tons of those sea animals and plants which do not swim but float wherever the water takes them. We would live on these directly or indirectly—most probably indirectly, on the swimming seals that follow and eat the drifting shrimps.

There was, however, a certain nervous tension about traveling north from the known arctic lands with provisions for less than two months and a plan to be gone a year. For, as said, not every folk-belief is wrong and there are cases where high-school knowledge fails through the omission of something true or the inclusion of something untrue. It was not merely the scientists who clung to folk-belief despite their contradicting knowledge; nor merely the explorers like Amundsen, who believed that animals sufficient for a hunter's life would not be found beyond a certain limit. The whalers, who had been seeking the bow head in the western Arctic since 1889, and the Eskimos, whose forefathers had been there for generations, held the same view.

The thrill, both physical and scientific, came after several weeks of travel on the "polar ice which is steadily drifting about on the open sea," when we were two hundred miles from land and our food gone. For it appeared, then, that we three and our six dogs were about to lose our lives through a condition as little expected by us as it had been by Amundsen. He was wrong in believing the seals would not be there, but we were really equally wrong, for it seemed we were not going to be able to live on them because we would not be able to get them. We killed them all right, but they sank.

The explanation proved simple—there had been something missing from our high-school training. The ocean is salty by Scripture and by the schools. The salt makes things float readily by the physics textbooks, but by an omission in the geographies it had not been pointed out to us that the reason why most oceans are fairly uniform in saltiness is that the winds keep churning them up. If you have half a glass of brine and pour fresh water into it gently enough the fresh water will float unsalted on top of the brine.

In summer on the polar sea it rains and the sun is warm between the showers. The rain and the thaw-waters flow gently off the ice. They are as fresh as if distilled and float on top of the brine sometimes for a depth of ten or fifteen feet. If the seal we killed was at all far from us, he sank from our sight; because of the gap in our high-school training, we were unaware that he would stop sinking ten or fifteen feet down, where the salt and fresh waters met. Against that situation we could use a harpoon with a long handle, we could convert our sledge into a boat by wrapping a tarpaulin around it, we could paddle out where the seal had sunk and harpoon the carcass as it lay floating and clearly visible to anybody who was straight above him.

Not understanding these things, we had out there on the ice a day or two of semi-panic, if not exactly despair. Then one of the killed seals, instead of sinking, floated and we thought it must have been because he was fatter or for some other reason more buoyant. That may have been so, but we realize now that more probably the motion of the ice cakes or a direct breeze had churned up the sea in that particular locality, mixing the salt with the fresh.

. . . . .

There is much to be said, then, for polar adventures. The hardest are usually easiest; the most dangerous, safest. Doing in the Arctic what the public believes impossible frequently becomes the safest possible routine after you have gone through a bit of mental gymnastics, such as changing your mind where you are obviously wrong, or filling up, by reasoning or experience, a gap or two in your education.

TRACING THE COLUMBIA TO ITS SOURCE

J. Monroe Thorington

Following in the footsteps of his father, a distinguished ophthalmologist of Philadelphia, Dr. Thorington is a practising physician in that city and associate ophthalmologist at the Presbyterian Hospital.

But he is also a mountain climber of the first rank, having to his credit more than twenty-five first ascents in the Canadian Rockies, as well as the discovery of many new routes: Waputik Icefield (1923, 1926, 1930), Freshfield Group (1922, 1926, 1930), Columbia Icefield (1923), Athabaska Pass (1924, 1928), Lyell Icefield (1926, 1930), Athabaska source (1931) and exploration in the Purcell Range in 1928, 1930 and 1931. He has taken glacier measurements (Freshfield since 1922 and Lyell since 1926) and constructed the first relief maps of the Howse Pass and Athabaska Pass areas.

His 1930 expedition, which he here describes in part, was the first to determine and map the source of the Columbia River.

Dr. Thorington is a member of the American Alpine Club and the alpine clubs of London, France, Switzerland and Canada. He is editor of the *Bulletin of the Geographical Society of Philadelphia,* author of *The Glittering Mountains of Canada* and, in conjunction with Howard Palmer, a fellow member of The Explorers Club, co-author of *A Climber's Guide 'o the Rocky Mountains of Canada.*

TRACING THE COLUMBIA TO ITS SOURCE

By J. Monroe Thorington

Opinion of hazard in exploration has clearly changed during recent years. The modern explorer knows that hardship is a mistake if it can be avoided; opprobrium, rather than glory, attaches itself to a tale of starvation. Adventure subsists amply on a well planned objective attained in the most direct manner possible. Frequently the intricacies of devising and the interpretation of results present more thrills than all the work in the field.

Often the subjective sensations within the explorer far transcend anything that can be communicated in subsequent description. I shall expect you to understand the unusual spectacle of a mountaineering party searching for the source of a river, but I am by no means so certain of my ability to convey feelings and reactions. The essence of exploration, it seems to me, lies in the personal experience which no one who has not partaken of it can ever entirely realize. Even one's companions will vary in their receptivity. A guide of mine once remarked, "Snaring mice can be just as exciting as hunting elephants if you get the point of view"—wisdom that was born of observation in the Altai and many far parts of the earth.

. . . . . .

In the year 1837 my grandfather, then a young man, was in St. Louis. During the two years ensuing he engaged in the fur trade, met Kit Carson on the Plains and hunted and trapped on the Missouri and Columbia rivers. So my interest in this northwestern stream can be described as almost hereditary. Having looked down from many points on the Continental Watershed, formed by the Rockies, into the deep and misty canyons of the western slope, desire long ago stimulated my wish to see the furthermost source of the Columbia River.

This was intensified by a climbing expedition in the Purcell Range in 1928, when from the snowfields immediately south of Earl Grey Pass we looked into cirques where there were waterfalls and frozen lakes, opening on a deep, forested valley with clusters of peaks beyond. We could not tell on which side of the main watershed it might be, for dense stands of timber and distance masked the direction of stream-flow; but somewhere, off to the south, we knew must be the source of the great river.

The Purcell Range links with the Selkirks in filling the "island" of uplift within the loops of the Columbia and Kootenay rivers. The Purcell Trench separates the two mountain groups and is occupied by the opposite flowing Beaver and Duncan rivers and by Kootenay Lake. The broad, terraced Rocky Mountain Trench lies grooved between the Rockies and the Purcells; and here again one finds two rivers flowing in opposite directions, the Columbia and the Kootenay. But once this was not so, for in ancient geologic time, when glaciers extended into the Columbia loop, the upper Columbia was a southward-flowing stream and emptied into the Kootenay. Bush River may then have been the source of the Kootenay, and all of the lateral tributaries to the Columbia between Spillimacheen River and Columbia Lake have old deltas that trail to the south, evidence of the former direction of its drainage.

When David Thompson, geographer of the North-West

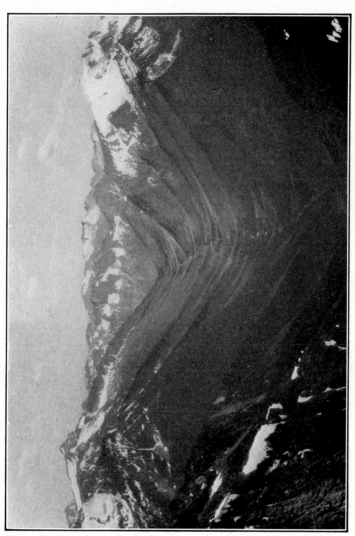

The Purcell Range, South of Earl Grey Pass

Hamill and Toby Groups from Saffron Peak,
Purcell Watershed

Company, crossed the Rocky Mountains by Howse Pass and reached Lake Windermere in the summer of 1807, the news of Trafalgar had just arrived, and he named a conspicuous peak to the west Mount Nelson. Thus it came about that the name of a British admiral was given to a mountain at the headwaters of the Columbia, before the source of that river was known. Thompson, to whom credit is usually given for the discovery, considered that the river rose in Columbia Lake and in his own words one reads, "At the foot of the above steep measured mountains is the scource of the Columbia River; it is a lake of nine miles in length by 1¼ miles in width, its direction nearly due south and north; it receives no water from the east, nor from Mount Nelson on the west, but appeared wholly supplied by springs in the lake; it appeared always to have the same level, and from its north end it sends out a brook which forms a second lake [Windermere], from which I measured the mountains."

Now Thompson makes an unaccountable error in this statement, because, some two miles above the emergence of the main river, Dutch Creek, a sizable stream, enters Columbia Lake from the west. Lewis R. Freeman makes a clear exposition of the actual state of affairs when he writes:

"One is usually told that the source of the Columbia is in Canal Flats, a hundred and fifty miles above Golden and immediately south of a wonderfully mountain-begirt lake that bears the same name as the river. This is true in a sense, although, strictly speaking, the real source of the river—the one rising at the point the greatest distance from its mouth—would be the longest of the many mountain creeks which converge upon Columbia Lake from the encompassing amphitheatre of the Rockies and Selkirks. This is probably Dutch Creek, which rises in the perpetual snows of the Selkirks and sends down a roaring torrent of grey-green glacier water into the western side of Columbia Lake."

The Hawke ranch, on the convexity of Dutch Creek, where the pack trail swings up from Fairmont, has a setting equal to any foreign alpland. Chickens and turkeys preening and parading in the barnyard are roused to indignant squawkings by the erratic circles of a collie pup. Cows are placidly munching the hillside grass and horses stand dozing by the fence. A whitewashed house of squared logs is gay in its clinging border of sweet peas, larkspur and currant bushes drooping with the weight of clustered berries. A terrace of new-mown fields edges almost imperceptibly into the hazy purple that hangs above the Columbia River valley, foreground to the ruddy foothills of the Rockies. In July, 1930, this was our starting-point.

. . . .

What things of mischief, what children of deviltry are pack-horses new to the trail! With a clanging of bells and a clicking of hobbles they bunch into the corral before a wild-riding wrangler. Strikings and snarlings, the packs that must be readjusted many times during the first days, the kicking and fighting for place in the line! Trail through light stands of birch and poplar, with grouse whirring in heavy flight, stretches along the margin of terrace, where the triangular cups of white and lavender mariposa nod sedately and the creek below makes riffling whitecaps and moves the stones of its bed in rhythmic thudding. From wooded copses and boggy hollows soft-eyed, long-horned cattle disappear with mysterious silence as we ride by. Topping a hillock of sand and sage-roses, we look above the pine-tops to an azure lake, with cloud shadows of lapis and violet wavering across its surface. The ground beneath our feet becomes scarlet with bear-berries, merging into a carpet of white flowers as the forest is reached. Cotton-

wood, cedar and Douglas fir lift rough and furrowed trunks
until the highest twigs seem near the sky; some are rent and
scarred black with lightning, and fronds of blue-gray moss
hang down toward the low undergrowth of fern and bunch-
berry.

Again an opening at a steep curve of the stream, with
sheer gravel banks worn and weathered into fantastic stone-
capped pillars and turrets. Well trodden paths from the
water cross our fainter trail; the scrubby bush is waving
cottony tassels of yellow-white hair and on a high meadow,
amid fallen logs, goats are grazing unconcernedly, while
an old billy stands guard below.

A fire-swept area is a depressing sight to one who is in-
expert with an axe. The grey, weather-bleached stems of
jackpine stand at grotesque angles, with brown, withered
tips bent and swaying. Massed magenta in islands of fire-
weed intensifies the green of its leaves against desolate
ashen background. The trail is obstructed by windfalls,
heaped up in crazy pattern as if a petulant giant-child had
cast away jackstraws. Here is slow-motion ready for the
taking: sweating men ahead, with the recurring chop and
snap of dry branches as the broken pieces are pushed aside;
the rasping of wood against canvas as the pack-train moves
on a few more yards under the blazing afternoon sun. Then
the cool of primeval forest again and the horses running in
the open trail, with boxes bumping and creaking, the
hitches awry and ropes trailing.

Dutch Creek has become narrower, the waters re-
strained between rocky walls and sometimes bridged by
long, straight tree-trunks. The stream has lost the quiet of
its maturity in the broader valley behind us and is here a
roaring infant, casting up spray from whirlpools and eddies.
At last we are down on its very edge and halt the horses
beside an old cabin, its logs bearded with moss and the

roof collapsing. A porcupine scuttles away and climbs to a tree-limb, where he is stoned by the packer, who is thinking only of his saddle. When the baggage is unloaded, the horses, slapped on their rear-ends, trot off to roll in the dust of the trail and force their way though a thicket of willows to the water. Soon the fire is smoking and crackling, mingling its pungent odors with those of balsam boughs piled up for our beds. Later on, when city-bound muscles are hardened, we will put our sleeping-bags on the bare ground, but now the arranging of branches to the exact degree of springiness is an important ceremony. Always beside us the stream, here a dashing cascade that, as day draws to its close, grows quieter, its impetuous rush turned to soft and even harmony.

In the morning, as the pots and pans were being cleaned and put away, a tiny weasel with white vest came bravely to investigate discarded tins, darting from one to another in evident approval of their contents. We rode out in a line of horses across slides of alder into the angle below Mount Coppercrown, where a lateral stream is crossed in the forest amidst a tangle of tall ferns and mossy logs. Here the valley changed its westerly course and we turned sharply southward toward a far horizon of snow peaks, apparently our destination. The hard-baked silt of the trail was crisscrossed with deer tracks and, in a clearing, we were witnesses of another tragedy in survival, the hooves and crushed skull of a young buck in velvet, the soft earth pitted with the footprints of an enormous grizzly.

We had gained altitude and the open slides were covered with arctic willow and alder, obscuring the trail. The horses, pushing their way through and nibbling the branches as they passed, were almost hidden, only the heads and shoulders of the riders emerging above the green. There were many little rivulets to cross and the blazes on

the trees were old and coming to an end, the deep cuts
puckered into cups by calloused overgrowth and filled with
dry, amber resin. In all directions there were fainter trails
of winter trap-lines diverging, with no imprint on the
ground but with light blazes far apart and high on the trees
above the snow level. Even these were old and the marten-
sets, notched in larger trunks, were decaying and the guarding slabs had fallen away. Once we passed the ruin of a
deadfall trap, the bleached and broken skull of a lynx
lying near by. Progress became slow from the numerous
trees that must be cut in clearing the way, and the horses
were bothered by flies. It was late when we camped on the
far side of a fork in the creek. The pack-train had crossed
a slide before reaching the water and a few minutes later
a gigantic grizzly bear raised head and shoulders above the
alders, looked at us and then ambled slowly back along
the way we had come.

    ·   ·   ·   ·   ·

On the third day it became increasingly evident that
the horses could not be taken much further. The dense
growth of trees forced us to the bottom of the valley, into
traps of boggy silt and sunken logs. The creek had subdivided into a myriad of streamlets, running swiftly in deep
and straight-sided channels of glacial sediment. The ter-
mination of the valley was visible as a deep pocket, with
ramps and echelons of jackpine rising one above the other,
thinning in higher planes and giving way to scattered
larches. From this last camp we must go on foot.

In the early morning the bushes were white with frost,
but we found an old bear-trail in the edge of the woods, a
path that took us across a saddle in the mountain's shoulder
and down again through the trees in a bend of the stream.
Here again we found a fork and chose always the branch
coming from the south, following it up the margin of a

narrow, rocky canyon, where the constricted stream foamed
and sprayed. The wet underbrush soaked us thoroughly,
but at last we came to timber-line, where the larch trees
gave way to a carpet of white heather and crimson painter's
brush and marmots sunned themselves on the rocks.

From a broad cirque waterfalls and bubbling brooks
come spraying down from melting snow. In the far corner
a glacier, larger only a short while ago, forms a tiny icy
arch over its marginal boulders, through which the river
Columbia emerges from its source. It swirls through the
stones in its hurry to reach the green grass, gathering to
itself other countless lacy threads of sparkling water. In
places it passes almost out of sight in channels between
the windblown tufts of anemones, then dashes into pebbled
spaces with only the lush leaves of yellow avalanche lilies
for a margin. There is a tingling of the spine when one
stands where a river begins.

We climbed ice-polished rocks and crossed the glacier
to a depression on its western rim; this was the divide, the
Purcell watershed, with West Kootenay beyond. The valley
below could be only that of Carney Creek, the main branch
of Fry River, which enters Kootenay Lake, the unknown
valley that we had seen two years before. Southward for the
first time since leaving the Coppercrown stream we again
saw snow-draped peaks; on the foreground slopes stood
eight black-tailed deer in line, two of them with enormous
antlers. Slowly they filed down the ice, scarcely two hundred feet away, when, startled by our unexpected appearance, they began to race in the soft snow, their splendid,
bounding leaps soon carrying them out of sight.

We walk to a col at the south side of the glacier and
gaze into a basin of meadows, lakes and streamlets, the beginning of Findlay Creek, which is tributary to Kootenay
River. Almost opposite to us a gorgeous peak, Mount

Findlay, is clothed in a sweep of glacier that ends in an ice-tongue near a grove of larch. A little summit scarcely four hundred feet above is the apex of the triple divide between the Columbia and Kootenay rivers and Kootenay Lake. Its position places the source of the Columbia some twenty-five miles west and four miles south of Canal Flats at the upper end of Columbia Lake, the total length of Dutch Creek to its mouth being not less than forty miles. We decide to attempt the ascent of Mount Findlay and descend a rocky couloir to the grassy slopes of the basin. Along the heaped-up chaos of moraine our path leads to the margin of the glacier, where the rope is put on. From the edge of the snowfield the course rises through an icy corridor, winding past gaping crevasses to gain the southern rim. The snow becomes steeper, but at last we reach the solid granite blocks that make up the summit.

Again the valley of Carney Creek is deep below us, its terminal branches extending subdivisions for a surprising distance north and south. A snow peak rises in the west and behind it a misty gorge, which we know contains Kootenay Lake. Not many miles to the southwest a group of pinnacles forms a massif near the source of St. Mary River, one dark and outstanding, cleft like scissor blades, the others crowning a plateau of snow and ice. South, and immediately before us, another branch of Findlay Creek contains a lakelet, partly frozen over and with icebergs bobbing and gleaming in its blue open water. A ring of larch trees thinly circles the shore line. Behind it, hanging glaciers depend precipitously from two sharp rock peaks. At last when, in the evening, we reached the bear-trail leading toward the tents, a passing shower left scarves and banners of moisture swung across the heights, catching last flaming colors from the sun as we walked into the friendly twilight of the pines.

This is all I shall tell you. True, we spent other hours and days tramping across fields of snow, working paths through broken glaciers, clinging to angles of granite below the last spires. The topography is all clear now; we even made a map, as if cartography were necessary to justify our intrusion. In its very solution something is lost; never again can this objective be something so desired. Some day, when the last contour is drawn, men may lock up all the books of travel and discovery that have been written. Then the earth will be new again and they can start once more with Ortelius for a guide.

Here then is only the problem and its conclusion, little of the action, for this story rests on the newer dictum of Sir Francis Younghusband that the picture and the poem are as legitimate a part of geography as the map. All the poignancy of this experience lies in its aftermath, when we stood on a Montreal hillside later on, beside a plain column surmounted by a sextant that marks the resting place of Canada's greatest geographer.

Ragged hunters in a line of bark canoes entering the upper lake; my grandfather crossing the watershed beyond the Missouri; David Thompson, sentinel of the sunset, on Mount Royal; and for myself, as a perspective, the years between. So for me this adventure consists not in discovery itself—the being and the doing, so vital at the time, are past —but in an intangible, kaleidoscopic picture that I see when my eyes are closed: of peaks, dark and serrate against the glow of fathomless morning; of sparkling ice and antlered deer arching their effortless leaps toward a thread of silvery stream—the new-born Columbia River, babbling joyously across the meadows as it starts its journey to the Western Sea.

CROSSING THE LABRADOR BARRENS

Dillon Wallace

Dillon Wallace has endeared himself to thousands of boys—and to numberless grown-ups as well—by his long line of books of adventure, chiefly placed in the Labrador he knows so well.

He made three expeditions into that little-known region, in 1903-1904, 1905 and 1913, on the second of which he had the close call with death that forms the climax of his present story.

He has also done research work in Mexico and has written about it with his characteristic talent for narration and description.

Among his many books are *The Lure of the Labrador Wild; The Long Labrador Trail; Ungava Bob; Beyond the Mexican Sierras; Saddle and Camp in the Rockies.*

CROSSING THE LABRADOR BARRENS

By Dillon Wallace

O N THE TWENTY-SIXTH DAY OF JUNE, 1905, MY SECOND
Labrador expedition set out from its base at Northwest
River and entered the wilderness. The personnel of the
expedition included Clifford H. Easton, botanist, George
M. Richards, geologist and topographer, and Leigh
Stanton, general assistant, with Peter Stevens, an Ojibway
Indian, serving as hunter, packer and cook. I directed the
work and kept the records and the meteorological and
other observations. Duncan MacLean, a native Labrador
man, was engaged to assist us with the packing for a short
distance into the country, but on July twenty-third he was
released to return to Northwest River with dispatches and
a small amount of collected material.

It was my plan to divide our party on the central
plateau, one section returning to our base at Northwest
River with such specimens as might by that time have been
collected, together with records made to the point of sepa-
ration, while the other section would proceed northward
to Ungava Bay. With this in view, and also as a precau-
tionary measure, caches of pemmican and other provisions
were made at suitable intervals along the inland trail.

On reaching Lake Mishikamau, September third, I
placed Richards in charge of the collected material and
detailed him to return to the base with Stanton to assist
him. As assurance that they might not go astray and in

order that no failure in relocating the provision caches might occur, Pete was attached to the return party as guide.

Though Easton was but twenty-two years of age at the time and had had no previous experience in exploration or wilderness travel, I selected him as my only companion in my northern work because of his ready adaptation to conditions. He had developed into an excellent canoe-man, was always ready and willing to bear his share of the burden without complaint and never shrank from necessary action, though it might involve peril.

Our first objective, after leaving Lake Mishikamau, was the George River post of the Hudson's Bay Company, situated some twenty miles above Ungava Bay. We were to locate the source of the George River, somewhere on the plateau, and trace its whole length. This required that Easton and I should traverse a distance of upwards of five hundred miles, a considerable portion of it through the Barrens. Though we had seen no human life since our departure from our base, we had hopes of making contact with Indian hunters on the northern slope.

For this journey our provision supply consisted of seventy-eight pounds of pemmican in six-pound tins, designed as reserve or emergency ration, twenty pounds of flour and other cereals, seven pounds of salt pork, half a pound of desiccated vegetables, one pound of coffee, a quantity of tea, half a pound of salt, one ounce of crystallose and a supply of matches and tobacco. These were meager supplies for so long and uncertain a journey, on the eve of the sub-arctic winter. But game and fish had been plentiful and we were confident that we could kill sufficient food to fill our needs. For this purpose we carried one .33 Winchester rifle, one double-barreled shotgun and a .22 caliber pistol with ten-inch barrel—the rifle for large game,

the shotgun for ducks and geese and the pistol for ptarmigan shooting.

.   .   .   .   .

On September fourth Richards and his party turned
back toward Northwest River, while Easton and I, in an
eighteen-foot canoe, set our faces to the northward. Three
days later we reached the northerly end of Lake Mishikamau and, after a series of portages, with intervening
lakes, on September fifteenth fell upon a small stream flowing in a northeasterly direction, which proved to be one
of the headwater streams of the George River.

Here we were delayed for several hours by snow. The
temperature dropped to 22 degrees and, in our rather light
clothing and with no other covering than a five-pound
woolen blanket at night, we looked forward with some
concern to the early closing in of winter. The stream soon
expanded into a large, swift-flowing river, in which rapids
with white water were frequent. High winds prevailed and
at times interfered, though our progress was not unsatis-
factory.

After reaching Lake Mishikamau and continuing northward, we found game plentiful and fared well without
drawing on our reserve rations. Between Mishikamau and
the next lake we crossed, caribou had recently passed in
thousands and the rear of the great migratory herd was not
far away, as was evidenced by the frequent howling of
wolves. In the morning we often found wolf tracks in the
sand around our tent, where the beasts had prowled at
night while we slept. Though this condition continued the
entire length of the George River, we saw only a single
wolf. We made no kill of caribou at this time, as it
would have necessitated delay in preparing the meat for
preservation, the weather not yet being cold enough to insure its keeping. Geese and ducks were shot without turn-

ing our canoe from its course. Ptarmigans were seen in flocks along the river bank and secured with small effort, as needed, with the pistol.

On a lowery afternoon, three days after entering the George River, we were paddling through an expansion when I descried some Indians on a hill that rose from a small island a quarter-mile below us. They were waving their arms as a signal to us to join them and, with pleasurable anticipation, we directed our canoe toward the island. Twelve weeks had elapsed since we had left Northwest River and this was our first contact with the Indians.

There were five Indians in the party. Gathered on the shore, they directed us to a suitable landing-place. All were armed with rifles. Two canoes lay on the rocks behind the Indians. It was a hunting party, on the lookout for caribou.

They met us with friendly greeting and were apparently quite as glad to see us as we were to see them. They informed us that we were the first white men ever to enter their hunting-grounds. In this they were mistaken, for seventy years earlier John McLean, a Hudson's Bay Company factor, had reached this point with the assistance of Indians, but even tradition among the Indians had not retained his achievement and he had left behind him no workable map useful to those who might follow him. No white men had been there since, and we were the only ones to pass through the country without the assistance of Indian guides.

After the custom of the wilderness, Easton and I proceeded to "boil the kettle" for tea. The Indians laughed joyously when Easton produced the kettle from the dunnage in our canoe. In a jiffy a fire was lighted and a kettleful of water was on to boil. When the tea was made, the five drank cup after cup, like starved creatures, until the kettle was emptied. Toma, the chief, told me they had had

neither tea nor tobacco for a long time and were hungry
for both. I at once presented each with a plug of tobacco
and to the group two pipes which I had in reserve. It was
gratifying to witness their eagerness as they filled and
lighted the pipes, passing them from mouth to mouth with
the greatest enjoyment. When we were about to throw
away the tea-grounds and rinse out the kettle, Toma
stopped us, carefully gathered up the grounds and placed
them in a buckskin pouch for further service.

The tea and tobacco established a most cordial and
friendly relationship between the Indians and ourselves.
We were invited to visit them in their lodges and to camp
with them. With an Indian canoe at each side of ours, we
set forth down the river. A three-mile paddle brought us
to the camp. It was situated on an elevated point, commanding a view of the river for several miles in either
direction, so that continual watch might be kept for bands
of caribou.

The entire population men, women, children and dogs,
greeted us as we landed. The reception was tumultuous
and cordial. The men were tall, lean, sinewy and graceful.
They were bareheaded, their stiff, straight, black hair,
reaching to the shoulders, held in place by means of a red
band passing around the forehead and fastened in the
back. Some wore canvas jackets, others buckskin, with vari-
colored leggings and buckskin moccasins. In general, the
women were as fat as the men were lean, reminding one of
Jack Sprat and his wife. They wore their hair in a twisted
bunch over each ear; over each bunch was a small pocket of
decorated buckskin, some of them beaded.

There were two lodges of deerskin. One was conical in
form, heated by a single central fire. The other was an
oblong wigwam, also of deerskin stretched on poles; it was
heated by three fires distributed at intervals from front to

rear, with openings above through which the smoke might escape.

Our belongings were carried to a suitable camp-site selected by Chief Toma. While we pitched our tent, the Indians brought boughs for our bed and wood for our fire. When we were comfortably settled and our fire lighted, Toma and ten of the men paid us a formal visit, crowding themselves into our little seven-by-nine balloon-silk wedge tent with Easton and me, while the remainder of the population congregated outside.

At my suggestion the Indians brought forth the largest kettle they possessed, filled it with water and placed it over the fire. When it boiled, I made tea and requested Toma to supervise its distribution. No one was slighted and the ecstatic enjoyment of all was evident. The tea leaves remaining in the kettle were carefully preserved by the Indians for a future brewing. After the tea we passed out plugs of tobacco, Toma again directing the distribution. So eagerly and gratefully did the Indians drink the tea and smoke the tobacco that Easton and I were moved to present them with as much of each as we could well spare from our stores. In appreciation of this the Indians brought us gifts of jerked venison, slabs of smoked fat and caribou tongues.

These Indians were living wholly on the product of their hunt—meat, fish and such berries as they might find. Vegetables were unknown to them and they were unaccustomed to flour or other cereals. They were armed with breech-loading .44-40 carbines and muzzle-loading trade guns. The spear was often in use in caribou hunting and the bow and arrow in hunting ptarmigan and other birds.

Our visit was made the occasion of a holiday. No hunting party went out the morning after our arrival. We were treated as guests, with the greatest consideration. We asked for nothing and in consequence received much. We shared with them our tea and tobacco, the things they most desired, and their gratitude was profound. We were traveling like Indians and hunting our living in the same manner, and this, I believe, aroused their respect. At any rate, they treated us as they would have treated friendly Indians from a distant region. We wandered about the camp at will and some of the men guided us to the summit of a near-by hill, where we had a wide view of the surrounding country. Our property, meanwhile, was left exposed and unprotected but, when we returned, not one thing had been taken or disturbed. This in spite of the fact that traders on the coast charged that the Indians were instinctively thieves and would filch at every opportunity.

When we prepared to depart at midday, Toma and some of the older Indians warned us seriously against any attempt to run the rapids of the lower river. Farther down, they said, the river was joined by another large river and then became a "big, big river." For two days' journey beyond the junction, it was good. After that it was so bad that the Indians never ventured to use it. This was tradition handed down from former generations. None of those living had ever ventured on the lower river. They invited us to spend the winter with them; in midwinter a party would go overland to Fort Chimo with furs to trade and we might go with them.

We were firm, however, in our determination to proceed down the George River and solve its problems. When we had broken camp and were ready to depart, the men carried our duffle to the water's edge and loaded our canoe, while the women stood in line along the trail, each of them presenting us with a gift of smoked fat, smoked caribou tongues, marrow fat in bladders or jerked venison. This is a custom with them when friends are leaving on a long journey. It is believed that a gift by a woman to those departing will bring good luck to the giver.

.   .   .   .   .

The current was strong, with occasional rapids. That afternoon and the following morning shot us forward some forty miles, to an expansion approximately twelve miles in length and two miles wide. Many bays and arms proved extremely confusing. The lower end was masked by islands and innumerable rocky bars, partially submerged, which extended far out into the water. A strong southwest wind sent whitecaps rolling down the lake and canoeing was hazardous. We put into a sheltered bay and I climbed a near-by hill to view our surroundings. A signal from Easton brought me back, to find two caribou swimming across the bay. It was desirable to make a cache of provisions here, to cover a possible retreat. I set the sights of my rifle at 350 yards and, as the first animal gained its feet and its body rose above the water, I fired and the caribou fell. A second shot killed the other one.

We dressed the meat and, as conditions were unfavorable for traveling, built racks and proceeded at once to dry the lean meat over a slow fire, reserving some of the better cuts to be used fresh. The fat we rendered into tallow. During the succeeding days several caribou were seen, so that we felt comfortably certain of securing game in future with little effort, should we require it.

Though there was no improvement in the weather, we made a cache of the partially dried venison, assured that the weather was now cold enough to preserve it, and, our canoe well laden with meat, set forth in a strong head-wind and driving snow.

Several rapids were run, though it was extremely dangerous, for we could scarcely see a dozen yards ahead. At midday the snow ceased, but the wind increased in velocity, until finally progress against it became impossible and we were forced to pitch camp.

There was a sharp drop in temperature and the shore was already lined with ice. All that day and the next we were held prisoners in camp. I occupied the interval in making dip candles of caribou tallow, utilizing twisted salmon twine for wicks.

On the morning of September twenty-ninth, though a strong wind added to the hazard of the rapids, we launched our canoe. The temperature had fallen to zero. Spray froze on our clothing. Ice began at once to accumulate on the sides of the canoe and our paddles became heavy with it. We ran two rapids without incident. Then came a long rapid. As we neared its end, heavy white water piled up around us. Below this the river expanded with no more than a strong current. Our course appeared clear, when without warning our canoe, deeply laden and heavy now with ice, struck a submerged rock a little back of the bow. The stern swung around and in an instant we were over and rolling down through the rocky rapid.

When I came to the surface, I was in steady water below the rapid. Twenty feet away I discerned Easton, clinging to the overturned canoe. I swam to him. The shock had been terrific and, when we spoke, our voices were strained and unnatural. We had been grossly careless, with the assurance that comes from close association with the elements, in failing to lash our outfit to the canoe. Now all was lost save one bag containing pemmican, one other small bag, our tent and our small folding tent stove. These had been jammed tightly under the center thwart and were still there.

We made a futile effort to right the canoe, so that the equipment under the thwart might not loosen and fall out. The tracking line was fast to the stern thwart and, with the free end of this in his teeth, Easton swam toward a little rocky island just below the rapid, while I swam with the canoe and steadied the things under the thwart. We worked in the icy water nearly half an hour before we finally succeeded in getting the bags, tent and tent stove on the smooth-polished rock that formed the island. Then the canoe was hauled up and drained. We were nearly helpless with cold. If we were to survive, fire must be had at once. Not a twig grew on the rock. On the east bank of the river, three hundred yards away, was a flat on which a mass of driftwood had lodged against some gnarled, stunted spruce trees. This was our nearest fuel. Our paddles were gone, but we launched the canoe and, paddling with our hands, quartered to the mainland, the current assisting us.

We drew the bow of the canoe up and I made an effort to reach into my pocket for my waterproof matchbox. But the hand, already nipped with frost, refused to respond and I was compelled, with much maneuvering, to loosen my belt before I could reach the matchbox.

More than half a foot of snow covered the ground. I cleared a small space and gathered some small, dry twigs. For tinder I gathered a handful of dry, hairy lichen, which hung from the limbs of the spruce trees. My matchbox was nearly filled with wax-taper matches and three oldfashioned sulphur matches. I tried to strike a wax taper. The head had absorbed moisture, the bottom of the box was wet and the match buttered on the bottom. My frost-bitten fingers were numb and as stiff as sticks and it called for no little effort to grasp a match. I tried another and another, with no better result than with the first.

Easton leaned against a tree, biting at the top of his box with his teeth, his fingers too numb to grasp it and unscrew it. His face was like wax and his eyes had assumed a vacant stare. The immediate restoration of circulation was imperative. I shouted to him to run and tried to run myself. Easton fell on his face in the snow and remained there. He had lost consciousness. My own legs refused to carry me and I fell prone on the snow. With much effort I regained my feet but again fell when I tried to run.

Our only hope lay in the remaining matches. One after another, the softened heads of the wax-taper matches rolled off, until the last one had been tried and failed.

The three sulphur matches remained, but I had small faith in them. With much care I manipulated one of them between my fingers and drew it across the bottom of the box. It lighted, but my grip on it was not firm enough and it fell from my fingers into the snow and was extinguished. I took another of the two that remained and, with the greatest care and no haste, fixed it between my stiff fingers. I scratched it across the bottom of the box and it lighted. I held it firmly, guarding it against drafts of wind, until the sulphur had burned off and the wood ignited. I applied the flame to the handful of lichen and the lichen broke into a blaze. Dropping to my knees, I laid it carefully on the earth, from which I had scraped the snow, and applied small twigs. As these ignited, I added larger sticks, which I could reach from where I knelt, for there was plenty of dry driftwood lying about. As the fire grew, I rose to my feet and, dragging larger wood, piled it on the flame. Tongues of fire mounted and the burning wood crackled and sent forth waves of heat. We had lost nearly everything we had, but life is sweet, no matter how uncertain, and I laughed with the joy of living.

I drew Easton to the heat. He revived quickly. When the blood began to circulate in our numbed bodies and the pain passed from our finger-tips, we removed our outer clothing and hung our garments near the fire to dry.

.   .   .   .

The sun was low in the west before we felt able to set out in search of possible salvage. Within half a mile of the scene of our disaster, we recovered from eddies along the shore Easton's and my own waterproof duffle bags, my instrument and record bag and our two paddles. Nothing else was to be found.

In each of our duffle bags were a five-pound blanket, changes of underclothing and small personal effects. Wrapped in each blanket was a quantity of matches. Though the contents of the bags were damp, the matches, with a little drying, proved to be uninjured. My instrument bag had not fared so well. Some of the instruments were ruined and others were beyond present usefulness, though my records were in readable condition.

We paddled the canoe to the island on which we had first landed and recovered the bags, tent and tent stove. In one of the bags we found eight six-pound cans of pemmican and in the other our tea and about six pounds of the candles I had made from caribou tallow. Everything else was lost beyond recovery—provisions, guns, axes, cooking utensils, the pipe for our stove and other necessary articles of equipment. We had not so much as a cup remaining and no other tools than our jackknives and my sheath-knife. Easton had lost his sheath-knife in the rapid.

It was agreed that henceforth each man's daily ration should be limited to one pound of pemmican and four ounces of tallow. The top was cut from a pemmican can and a piece of copper wire, which I found in my duffle, attached as a bail. This served as the only utensil we had. Tea was made in it, and we drank from it in turns. When a raisin was discovered by one of us in his pemmican ration, the lucky one shared it with the other.

Our limited ration was sustaining and served well enough. We quickly adapted ourselves to the restraints of necessity. Without firearms or fishing tackle, we could neither hunt nor fish. The late season and growing cold did not permit us time to attempt the building of snares or traps, by which we might have secured game.

In the barren regions through which we passed, firewood was often scarce, consisting of driftwood carried down in the previous spring floods and lodged along the river bank. It was often difficult to utilize it without an axe. We plunged through many rapids each day and their roar was constantly in our ears. The Indians had not exaggerated the bad character of the river; we could well understand why they avoided it. We encountered falls and chutes, and rapids so mighty that no canoe could have lived through them. Around these we perforce carried. But withal we suffered no great hardships and on October sixteenth reached tidewater and the trading post of the Hudson's Bay Company near the mouth of the river.

AN ADVENTURE ON THE GREEN RIVER

Carroll H. Wegemann

Born in Wisconsin and educated at the state university, Carroll H. Wegemann joined a prospecting party in the forests of Ontario, spent a year at the Isle of Pines and then became instructor in geology at the University of Illinois.

For ten years, 1907-1917, he worked on the U. S. Geological Survey, specializing in the geology of coal and oil in the Great Plains and the Rocky Mountains.

Since that time he has held the position of chief geologist with several oil companies operating in the United States and Mexico.

This account of what happened to him on the Green River in 1925 shows that even a chief geologist has to take his chances.

AN ADVENTURE ON THE GREEN RIVER

By Carroll H. Wegemann

IT WAS IN THE SPRING OF 1925 THAT GLEN RUBY AND I alighted from a train at Green River City, Utah, on the west bank of Green River, which, rising in the mountains of Wyoming, flows southward into Utah and joins the Colorado River just above Cataract Canyon. Green River City is about ninety miles north of the junction of the two rivers, while the little inland town of Moab is some sixty miles east of it, on the Colorado River. Between the two towns lies a barren, waterless desert, across which the two rivers have cut deep canyons.

Oil development had been undertaken below Moab on the Colorado River, and Glen and I were desirous of making a trip by boat down the Green River to its junction with the Colorado and thence up the latter stream to the town of Moab, in order to study the geology of the canyons. The trip had been made repeatedly and, so far as the rivers were concerned, was not dangerous. There was only one bad rapid and that need not be run. The risks of the trip lay in the difficulties of traversing the desert, should an accident occur. In the canyons there are no continuous bottom-lands. Sand bars are formed on the inside of the river curves and in many places are of considerable extent, but they invariably end against canyon walls, so that, were one to attempt travel along the river on foot, he would be compelled to swim the stream every half-mile. Should he endeavor to climb the canyon walls and proceed along their brink, his course would be interrupted by the side canyons. Should he leave the river entirely and strike out across the desert, he would be traveling for days over a country without water. In brief, the trip which we contemplated was simple if all went well, but it might be extremely difficult, should an accident occur.

We were taking with us a Mormon guide whom, for convenience, I will call Bill. We had acquired a heavy, flat-bottom river skiff and a small Evinrude outboard motor. The day of our departure was sunny and warm, as are most days in the desert. The morning was spent in buying supplies and making a few minor repairs on the old boat. The outboard motor had been overhauled in the local garage. We did not take a tent; for bedding we depended on the old-time cowboy bed rolls. One important item of our cargo was twenty-five gallons of gasoline, put up in five-gallon cans. We were anxious above all things to have an adequate supply of gasoline for the little motor on the one hundred and fifty miles of travel which lay before us.

We were leaving on a Tuesday and the boys were optimistic about the time required for the entire trip. I left word with a friend of mine who was making headquarters in Moab that, if we did not reach that town by the following Saturday night, he was to start down the Colorado River from Moab in a motor boat. I assured him that, whatever happened, he would find us at the junction of the Colorado and Green Rivers. This arrangement seemed at the time a useless precaution, but I was glad enough afterwards that I had made it.

We waved goodbye to our friends a little before noon and traversed some eight miles of the river before landing at a deserted cabin for lunch. This cabin was the last on the river. Two miles below it, the river entered the canyons.

That afternoon we traveled between sheer cliffs of sandstone, three or four hundred feet high, emerging from the shadows now and then where the canyon walls receded and there were flat sand bars, covered with cottonwoods, on one side or the other. Just before dark we made camp under an overhanging ledge of rock on the right bank. The night was cold and we slept well.

．　．　．　．　．

We were up at daylight and, after a hurried breakfast, loaded the boat and set off. The motor was not working well, so, after two hours, we landed on a flat rock and proceeded to take the motor down. The local "garage" in Green River City had apparently not been familiar with Evinrude motors, as we found that several of the parts had been put back "wrong end to." Considerable damage had already been done, but we hoped for the best as we readjusted the little engine.

As we proceeded that day, the canyons grew deeper and the widenings of the valley less frequent. In the late afternoon a cold wind swept down the river and a rainstorm threatened. As we had no tent, I remarked that we might be in for a rather unpleasant night. Bill replied that somewhere below us on the river there was a cabin, built some years before by a young engineer, who had rafted the material down from Green River City. The cabin had long been deserted, but was now occupied by an outlaw who was Bill's personal friend. Bill assured us we would be welcome for the night.

In about an hour we came to a large bottom-land on the right bank, covered with cottonwoods and fringed with willows, where stood the outlaw's cabin. The landing was just around the point. As we pulled into it, I noted an old dugout which stood on the very bank of the river, so close that the next flood might sweep it into the stream. It appeared to be very old, but I gave it only a passing glance as we headed for the cabin, which stood some distance back among the trees. Being discreet, we requested Bill to walk in advance of the party, as an indication that our intentions were peaceful.

As it happened, the outlaw was not at home. A pair of chaps and a quirt hung on the wall and some greasy pans were on the stove. The condition of the food indicated that the occupant of the cabin had been gone at least two days. We swept the cabin and, starting a fire, cooked a good supper. By that time the sky had cleared and the threat of a storm had passed. In spite of our efforts, the inside of the cabin was not an inviting place, so we spread our bed rolls outside under the cottonwoods. After supper Bill gave us in detail the history of his friend.

Bill assured us that the outlaw had never killed anybody but had only sold whiskey to someone who had killed somebody. He had been imprisoned in Moab with his partner and the two had broken jail and escaped in a boat into the canyons. When the sheriff and his posse followed, the two had hidden in the rocks of the canyon wall and opened fire on their pursuers. The sheriff, his discretion getting the better of his valor, decided to let well enough alone and returned, leaving the two outlaws to their own devices. One of them had found his way to the lonely cabin on the Green River and was running a moonshine still and stealing cattle for a living.

.   .   .   .   .

It was the next day, as I remember it, that we came to the first signs of the cliff dwellers, not far from the great horseshoe bend in the Green River. The two curves of the stream run so close to each other that they are separated by a wall of rock only a few hundred feet wide, but it takes an hour to go around the bend. It was, I believe, just below

The Start-off
(The author in the center)

The Rescue
(Glen Ruby in the bow)

this bend that we saw a round stone watch-tower, some ten feet in height, built on a prominent point on the left bank of the river. There is a broad, tree-covered bottom-land surrounding this point, where the ancient cliff dwellers raised their corn. Under the overhanging ledges of rock below the watch-tower are little stone bins, which were used for storing the corn and in which one may still find a few corncobs.

That afternoon we came to a bottom-land on the left bank, back of which rose a cliff of sandstone several hundred feet high. The cliff overhung the bottom-land in such a way that, except in a driving rain, one would be completely protected from storm in the hackberry trees at its foot. High up the slope of the cliff I could see a round stone corn bin, built on a jutting point of rock. Across the river was a broad bottom-land, backed by another cliff, and along the face of this cliff was perched a row of dwellings, clinging like swallow-nests to the almost perpendicular sandstone. On closer observation one realized that these cliff dwellings were built along a tiny ledge of rock, but that the approach to them had been swept away by a rock slide, which had destroyed part of the ledge since the days when the dwellings were inhabited.

It was late afternoon and our motor had given out. We made camp among the hackberry trees, and I said to my two companions, who were mechanically inclined, that I didn't care how long they took to fix the motor, among such surroundings. The smooth, swift-flowing river, the wild cliffs and those remnants of an ancient civilization of at least a thousand years ago formed a picture never to be forgotten; nor shall I ever forget the quiet camp in the shelter of the hackberry trees and the dinner that we enjoyed that night after the heat of the day.

The small motor had finally punctured one of its cylinders. With infinite care Glen Ruby repaired it with the bowls of two spoons which he riveted together, one on the outside and one on the inside of the cylinder, filling the hole with solder. We pronounced it a most artistic piece of work and one which should carry us safely to our destination.

The following morning, before setting out, Glen and I cut a young cottonwood and placed the trunk against the cliff, below the little corn bin which I have mentioned. We climbed up the tree and from the top were able to throw a rope over a projecting piece of rock on the cliff above. By means of this rope we reached some ancient niches cut in the face of the sandstone and climbed to the jutting point of rock on which the little corn bin was built. This bin was circular and would hold perhaps two bushels of corn. The stones were laid in mud and the cover was a large, flat slab of sandstone. The cover was still in place and within were ancient corncobs. On the mud of the wall one could see the imprints of the hands which built the bin no one knows how many hundreds of years ago. The people living in the fastnesses of the canyons must have been harassed by powerful enemies, to have taken such precautions for the storage of a few bushels of corn.

We longed to reach the cliff dwellings on the opposite side of the river, but their position was such that it was out of the question to do so.

.   .   .   .   .   .

It was on a Saturday morning that the real adventure of our trip occurred. The motor, after having undergone Glen's artistic repairs, would run after a fashion, but we decided that it was safer to keep it in reserve for such time as we should start up the Colorado against the current. We had oars and would make the rest of the trip downstream with their aid.

Our provisions were giving out and the boys suggested

that, as there were plenty of deer in the bottom-lands, we might do well to do a little hunting. We had come to a large bottom-land on the left bank of the river and pulled the boat up on a mud flat, below a cut bank about eight feet high. I remained in the boat, while my two companions took the rifle and climbed to the brush-covered flat above. The wind was blowing strongly and, as they reached the top of the bank, they called back something which I did not understand. As I sat waiting in the boat, I suddenly heard a crackling sound above me and, looking up, saw that the boys had lighted a grass fire, apparently for the purpose of burning out the game. I made a few mental observations on their carelessness in lighting the fire just above me and, getting out on the mud flat, proceeded to haul the heavy boat downstream until it was out of danger.

I then climbed to the top of the bank to see what the boys were doing, but, realizing that I was standing in the brush and might easily be taken for game myself, I walked over a few rods to a rocky ledge back of the narrow flat. My two friends were some distance away, at the other end of the bottom-land. The fire was blowing in their direction, as they waited for any game which might be concealed in the brush to break cover.

The wind in the deep canyons was constantly shifting. A sudden gust in the opposite direction started some smouldering grass into flame and drove the fire back in the direction of the boat which I had just left. Realizing the danger, I started for the boat but was compelled to go around the fire, which was spreading rapidly. Just as I reached the river bank, a spark blown by the wind ignited the gasoline. In an instant the entire boat was ablaze. Everything we had, with the exception of the rifle, was on that boat. I rushed forward just as Bill came plunging over the bank and into the quicksand and water beside the boat.

"Look out for the gasoline. The cans may explode," I yelled.

"To hell with the gasoline, we must save the boat," he answered.

As he spoke, he ducked under water to avoid a blast of flame driven by the wind and then began to throw water on the fire with his hands. His action shamed me and I plunged in on the other side of the boat. Between us we put out the fire in the bow and then, by rocking the boat, were able to sink it but not until seven feet of one side had been entirely burned to the water's edge. A charred bed roll, baked eggs and bits of boxes began floating off downstream. We rescued them and brought them to the bank. We saved everything that the fire had left, but this was comparatively little—a piece of charred bacon, the dry center of a sack of flour, the lens from my camera, some bailing wire and some small nails from the burned boxes. We carried everything to a place under the overhanging ladge of rock and, since our matches were gone, started a camp-fire from some smouldering coals.

Then we took stock of the situation. Glen thought we could walk out in three or four days, but, having heard stories of how other adventurers had come out of that country, I was not anxious to attempt the trip. I had had considerable experience years before in the handling of birch-bark canoes in the Wisconsin and Canadian forests and was under the impression that the shell of the burned boat could be repaired.

We unwrapped what was left of the bed roll and found on the inside a strip of canvas some seven or eight feet long and about thirty inches wide. It was large enough to cover the side of the boat which had been burned away. With the help of bailing wire, we made a gunwale of willow boughs and lashed it in place. Over this gunwale we folded the canvas and, with bits of burned boxes, nailed the edges of the canvas along the bottom and up the sides of the boat, covering the entire opening. With a small can of engine grease rescued from the fire we waterproofed the canvas. The bottom of the boat had been burned thin; to avoid breaking through it, we covered it with a mass of springy willow boughs. Paddles were made by nailing charred boards from some of the boxes to shafts of willow.

This work took most of the afternoon, but, when it was finished, we were delighted to find that our craft did not leak and was sufficiently strong to bear our weight. As night came on, we enjoyed a supper of baked eggs and charred bacon. We collected enough willow branches to make a bed under the sandstone ledge. Some bits of a red blanket left in the bed roll I sewed together with the help of a nail and strips torn from a sheet. The smell of burned wool was rather pronounced, but the warmth of the blanket was most welcome during that cold desert night. We did not sleep any too well, getting up at intervals to replenish the fire.

. . . . .

Next morning we loaded the boat with all our worldly goods. In the Dutch oven we placed a few live coals, covering them carefully with ashes. Thus provided, we embarked upon the river. Bill had lost all track of our location and we had no idea how far we were from the junction of the Green and the Colorado. As it turned out, we were only six miles above the junction; before noon, to our joy, we reached the large-timbered flat which lies just west of the mouth of the Green River. It was Sunday, the day Frank was to start from Moab, should we not come out on time. Glen and I spent the afternoon walking down the right bank of the Colorado to the fourth cataract in Cataract

Canyon and thinking with admiration of the trip Major Powell made through these rapids.

The following morning we again loaded the boat, with the intention of working our way up the Colorado to a rapid a mile or so above the junction. We were just shoving off when Bill exclaimed, "Listen! I think I hear a motor."

In a few moments the boat from Moab came in sight around the bend and headed towards us. As it pulled alongside, Frank and his companion looked us over with amused amazement. The charred boat, our blackened clothing and the old Dutch oven in the bow, from which smoke was rising, must have been a sight to be remembered.

"Let me get the camera," was the first remark.

It did not take long to start on the return journey. The motor boat pulled the charred shell as far as the rapid which I have mentioned. This rapid is formed by a landslide which has partly dammed the course of the Colorado. Two of us endeavored to get the motor boat up with oars and motor power, but it proved to be impossible and we finally had to haul it up by a rope from the rocks on the bank. The old burned shell we left at the foot of the rapid.

Five men and their equipment in a boat built for four was almost too much. One man was kept bailing most of the time and, in the swifter water, the little outboard motor could scarcely make headway against the current.

At one point I noticed an old rifle standing against a rock at the foot of a cliff. We wondered about it and Bill surmised that it had probably belonged to two men whose boat had been wrecked in Cataract Canyon the year before. They had endeavored to walk out and, before they were found by a hunting party, became so weak from hunger that they left everything they had along the trail.

It took us that afternoon, all the next day and until two

o'clock on the following day to reach the oil camp on the river, eight miles below Moab.

When I returned to Denver, a genial friend remarked that, whenever Wegemann went on one of these wild trips, something always happened that could happen only to a tenderfoot.

And to this I must perforce assent.

BOUNCING FISH-BALLS—AND OTHER TALES

Carveth Wells

It is hard to believe that Carveth Wells, the Prince Charming of lecturers, was once a mere surveyor and college professor, but this is no more unbelievable and at the same time no less true than the many incredible and yet authentic tales he has been telling the world from book and platform ever since be abandoned the theodolite and level for the more entertaining occupation of spinning yarns as true as they are preposterous.

He has been immortalized by President Thwing's *bon mot* as "the man who can make the truth sound like a lie." If you don't believe this after reading here his report of some of his experiences in the Malay Peninsula, try the whole story in his *Six Years in the Malay Jungle*. And follow up this prescription with his latest volume, *Adventure*, to cure your scepticism for all time.

Even his difficult ascent of Mount Ruwenzori, up to his waist in snow on the Equator in midsummer, furnished an abundant crop of impossible monstrosities and paradoxical absurdities for his *In Coldest Africa*.

He also wrote an excellent *Field Engineer's Handbook*—but that was when he was young and not so foolish—nor such good company.

P. S. He has traveled almost everywhere else, including Lapland, the Chautauqua circuit and the N.B.C. studios.

BOUNCING FISH-BALLS—AND OTHER TALES

By Carveth Wells

ONCE UPON A TIME, NOT VERY LONG SINCE, I SPENT TWO stay-at-home years at the Imperial College of Science and Technology, South Kensington, giving the third- and fourth-year classes the benefit of my engineering experiences in Canada and starting a system of summer surveying camps for the students. But I never could reconcile myself to the meagerness of a teacher's pay, so one morning I went up to London, presented myself at the office of the Crown Agents for the Colonies and suggested that they needed a railroad engineer with American experience. Publicly they did not like the American experience, but privately, I know, they rejoiced that here was an engineer who knew something about rapid railroading.

A few days afterwards I was directed to call on Messrs. Gregory, Eyles & Waring, consulting engineers of the government. My interview with Mr. Waring I shall never forget. He was at that time very old, but was still responsible for practically all the appointments made by the Crown Agents. He was a noted civil engineer and loved to talk about his jungle exploits. He instructed me in such matters as the art of walking across a slippery coconut log and a bamboo bridge and, as seasoning to his counsel, added, "We send dozens of young fellows like you abroad and the governments are continually asking for more; you see, they don't last long." Then he questioned me a bit and gave me an account of his own experiences in Ceylon.

The upshot of the interview was that I got what I wanted. "You are appointed a surveyor," said Mr. Waring, "and will sail for the Malay Peninsula within two weeks. Take my advice and keep your head cool and your stomach warm. Good day."

. . . . .

Within six weeks of leaving London I found myself in the heart of Malaya. I lived there for six years continuously, in the service of the British government, surveying a railway that was going from the great seaport of Singapore to Bangkok. It is a land where there are no seasons—no winter, no summer, no dry season, no wet season—it is the same all the year round. It is covered with jungle and is the home of tigers, black leopards, elephants, rhinoceroses, huge snakes, five different animals that can fly, forty different kinds of monkeys and twenty thousand wild women. (They are quite interesting.)

While I stood on deck aboard ship as we neared Penang, red-and-yellow-banded snakes—big, eight-foot fellows—were playing in the water. Once a bird came out of the sky, dove into the sea, caught a snake, carried him up into the air and tore him to pieces. Crocodiles, as much as twenty or thirty feet long, might, I knew, at any moment come to the surface within a few miles of land. Then there was the harbor at low tide, with its mud flats oozing sulphureted hydrogen and the smell of rotten eggs; and over the mud crawled fish. And they climbed up the trees and looked at us!

When I reached my hotel, I undressed, entered the bathroom and spent about ten minutes trying to find the bath. I saw an earthenware jar four feet high and a little tin cup on a shelf. My friend in the next room, evidently in the same fix, had managed to get into the jar and was vainly endeavoring to get out again. Instinct, however, told me to stand outside the jar, dip the water out with the little cup and pour it over my head. This method is wise, because to lie in a cold bath might produce a chill, followed by death in the morning and burial in the afternoon. Things happen quickly in Malaya.

In the dining-room, I saw a lot of little round tables all over the place, with Chinese waiters running about everywhere. I sat down before the most delightful dinner. Just as I was beginning to eat my soup, I heard a noise like a smack—and there, right in front of my plate, I saw a lizard about four inches long. He scurried over the tablecloth, jumped to the floor, climbed up the wall and ran across the ceiling. When I looked up, I saw twenty or thirty little lizards running about upside down. Suddenly two of the lizards got hold of the same moth and then they began to struggle, forgot themselves, let go and came right down into the middle of the soup-plate. The next time one of those lizards fell down, I covered him with my handkerchief. As soon as he had stopped wriggling about underneath it, I picked it up and all that was left of the lizard was the tail. That kind of lizard, if you chase him, always breaks his tail off and, while you watch the tail run about, he gets away.

A little while after the first excitement, an insect came to the window of the dining-room and deliberately looked in to see if another insect like itself was inside. If there had been, I found out later, it would not have come in, for fear of being received as a bridegroom and eaten by the bride! But there happened to be just a few moths on the ceiling, so the insect came in. First it sat on the tablecloth in front of me and looked me up and down, as much as to say, "You are a very funny-looking object yourself." Then it began to say its prayers. In fact, it was a praying-mantis and had innumerable relatives in the peninsula.

As it came toward me, I called the waiter and asked, "Here, is that thing going to bite?" "No, sir," he replied. "Pick it up and have a look at it." To my surprise, I found that I could handle it without its minding a bit. I opened its arms and saw for what evil end it kept them so piously folded—it had a lot of sharp spikes stuck all the way along them. When I let it go, it flew to the ceiling, caught hold of a moth, hugged it tight in those serrated arms and cut it to pieces. And the moth's wings and legs dropped off and went into my plate. One more strangely garnished dish!

My orders to go into the jungle were served to me in a long blue envelope at breakfast. I started from Penang by train. It took the train about three days of running past tapioca and rubber plantations, rice fields and palm groves to get to the end of the railway. Eventually I started into the jungle from a village called Tembeling, in the state of Pahang.

I knew the superstitious nature of the Malay well enough not to be surprised when an old woman came up as I was leaving Tembeling and offered me a black cat. "Here's a cat for you," she said. I did not want the cat— it had a crooked tail. I did not know then that Malay cats always have crooked tails. "If you take it, you may come back," she said. So I took the cat.

. . . . .

We started away in Indian file. That is to say, I had my *mandur*, Hussein, in front of me; then I came; then the coolies, carrying my baggage. We always walked like that, to look out for snakes. I had heard that in India twenty thousand people a year were killed by snakes; so I hired somebody to walk in front of me and then, if anyone got bitten, he was the man. Finally we reached a river and found two boats waiting for us. The Malays built sun-shades over the boats and placed a mattress on the bottom of my boat, and off we went.

While I was out on the river, I heard a shot and, look-ing up, saw a little boy jump from a tree into the river. He swam like a dog. He had been shooting fish; he sat up in the tree, throwing bait into the water; when a fish came to the surface, he fired.

I landed and looked at his gun and found marked on the barrel these words, "The Tower of London, 1800." The bullets were as big as marbles. The boy was a funny youngster about nine years old, a typical little naked *Orang Ulu*. He had a shaved skull, except for an absurd little tuft of hair, about a foot long, which denoted that he had not yet been initiated in Islam. His name was Isa, or Jesus.

When Isa found I could speak Malay, he took me to his village and produced a bottle containing a fish. Then a friend of his, called Noh—that is, Noah—came along with another bottle that had a fish inside and they placed their bottles on a table. The fish were about two inches long, rather ugly and ordinary-looking. Isa and Noh immedi-ately began to discuss them and talk about their good points. Isa's fish was the hero of no less than forty fights and had several scars on its little body. Noh's fish was larger than Isa's, but did not look quite so intelligent! The two bottles were now placed side by side and, as soon as they touched, the little fish glowed with gorgeous colors and began biting at each other through the glass. By this time a crowd had gathered, shouting and betting. As soon as the bets had been made, a referee poured the water from one bottle into the other. The fish fought until you could scarcely see them for the scales that were floating about.

"*Itu Dia, sudah luka!* (That's it, he's wounded!)" yelled Isa.

"Dia lari! (He's running away!) " cried Noh.

"Mampus! (He has kicked the bucket!) " shrieked Isa, as Noh's fish sank to the bottom of the bottle, dead.

That story sounds "fishy," but fish-fighting is a national pastime in Malaya, just as fishing is an everyday occupation. That afternoon Noh took me with him when he went fishing in his father's rice field. It was almost harvest time and the rice was nearly as tall as the boy. Instead of one good-sized rod, he carried no less than twenty little rods, each about two feet long, which he stuck all over the field, leaving the hooks dangling in the water in which the rice was growing. When he had set all the rods, he went back to the first one, took off a fish about three inches long and put it in a basket. He went from rod to rod until he had caught about a hundred fish. He was ready to start home but, just to amuse himself, picked out one of the fish and rubbed it on the ground. The fish began to get fat, swallowed air in big gulps and, as its body swelled, grew round and tight like a ball. Then Noh whacked it on the ground. It bounced up into the air, fell back into the water, squirted the air out and swam away—a perfectly sound Malay puffing-fish. It was new to me then, but afterwards it became familiar enough. I have seen Malay boys with several fish blown up tight prick them with a knife to hear them pop, but those did not swim again.

. . . . .

I left Isa and Noh regretfully and returned to my boat. Soon we were so far upstream that we ran on the bottom of the river. The coolies then got out and built a lock. After that they sometimes built locks two or three times a day, to enable the boats to go on up the shallow stream. When we came to a waterfall, four or five feet high, perhaps, the coolies would make an immense rope out of jungle vines and drag the boats up over the fall. One of the most amusing sights that my eyes took in during our slow progress up the river was a lot of monkeys that came down out of a tree at about sunset and waded into the water to wash their teeth. Eventually we got so far upstream that we could not go on in the boats, so we abandoned them and entered the jungle.

It was darkly closed in with leaves overhead. When I was used to the gloom, I could see the trees well enough to know that they were not like those I knew. They had no lateral branches but shot up straight and smooth for about eighty feet. Most of them were covered with vines and creepers that not only climbed up and down, but passed from tree to tree in every direction, tying the jungle together into one immense tangle of vegetation, vegetation strange in itself and sheltering still stranger forms of life!

One day, when I was walking along an old elephant track, I came to a little bush about a foot high, covered with red flowers. I thought I would have a boutonnière, so I picked a flower. As soon as I touched the bush, its leaves closed up, its branches folded themselves and it lay down. I waited quietly and watched it as it slowly and cautiously came to life again. I blew at it and, although it was used to real wind, it recognized the artificial breeze and at once lay down flat. It was a mimosa, or sensitive plant. Later, I saw large areas of it lie down when a buffalo began to eat one edge.

Once, about the middle of the afternoon, I came to a rock that it took me three hours to walk around—just one rock, white marble, two hundred and fifty feet high, with vertical sides and a jungle-covered top. Up there in the jungle were living the little Malay goats that are one of the sportsman's rarest prizes. In the rock were immense caves. At half-past six, the sunset hour in Malaya, I saw coming out of the caves hundreds of flying-foxes, enormous fruit-eating bats, with heads shaped like those of foxes. They were going off into the jungle to feast through the night. During the day, they slept in the caves. On the ceilings of the caves were hundreds of swallows' nests of the kind exported to China, at the rate of three million a year, to be made into soup. In some places in the caves I saw the floor covered with guano to a depth of twenty feet. Through the gloom I could make out ghastly white centipedes and white cockroaches, and once a white snake.

On the way to my camp I made a number of new acquaintances. First there were some comic cousins of the praying-mantis. I happened to be resting by the side of the track and noticed on the bushes and on the ground, all around me, little things like twigs. They were moving. "Moving twigs—how interesting!" I thought. Then the twigs began to walk towards me and climb over my boots; so I picked them off and they, with the cleverness peculiar to the stick-insects of Malaya, pretended to be dead and looked more twig-like than ever.

As I continued my journey, my back began to feel uncomfortable. I took off my coat and, seeing that it was wet through with blood, I removed the rest of my clothes and found six leeches. The Malay jungle swarms with these blood-sucking, segmented worms. I used to test a leech's sense of smell by carrying it fifteen yards away and leaving it on the ground, while I returned to my seat. The leech would stand on end, waving himself about and scenting the air in every direction. Then, without the slightest hesitation, he would make a bee-line for me, climb up and get through the eyelet of my boot. Fortunately, leeches, like human beings, go to bed at night. I doubt whether, if they did not, there would be many animals in the jungle.

While on the trail we did battle with another unpleasant jointed thing. One day Hussein suddenly pressed his hand against the leg of his trousers and yelled *"Adohi!"* At this cry of pain another Malay, covering his hand with a cloth, felt up the boy's trousers and pulled out a centipede about six inches long. Fortunately for Hussein, the centipede had bitten first through his shirt and, though it caused him much suffering, did not kill him, in spite of being so very poisonous.

.   .   .   .   .

Finally we reached camp. There I discovered that the Malays had made a clearing in the jungle and built two little houses for me in the middle of the open space. The first thing I did was to go up the steps and examine the roof. There were the usual lizards, of course, but something darted out of the roof and caught a lizard. It was a snake. I found that the roof of my house was full of lizards and snakes, scorpions and rats, mice, centipedes, frogs, spiders, cockroaches and other things. It was simply because the roof was made of the leaf of the nipa palm, which cockroaches live upon. So the roaches went up to eat the roof; then the lizards went up to eat the roaches; then something else went up to eat the lizards; last of all the snakes went up to eat everything. So I did what every engineer in Malaya does —I pitched a tent inside my house.

Still I was beset by creatures that creep and fly. As I sat at my table, drawing a plan, something dropped on my head and things began crawling over my neck. I brushed them off and found that my fingers were covered with tiny white spiders. Above me a spider as big as a saucer was walking along. She had attached to her a kind of soup-plate in which she had been carrying her babies, but she had tripped over something and I got the soup. A little later, when I was resting in a long chair, I heard a noise like this: *Whoo, whoo, whoo, whoo, ha, ha, ha, ha!* I called one of my servants and asked, "What on earth made that noise?" "It was only a bird, sir," he answered. "But what a bird!" I thought when I saw it. It was about five feet long from one end to the other and had short legs and black-and-white feathers and a beak about a foot long, with a huge casque on top. It was blessed with the name of "hornbill."

In the course of time I grew familiar with the squawks of the Malayan tree-hornbill and could tell the sound of his great wings quite a mile away. The Malays called him "the bird that makes a noise like a train." He is certainly a feathered oddity. Though his beak is huge, his tongue is tiny; so he is compelled to feed by throwing his food from the tip of his beak into the air, sometimes as high as five or six feet, and letting it fall into his wide-open mouth and drop down his throat. In some respects his diet is curious. He thrives, for instance, on *nux vomica;* during the nesting season he feeds it in huge quantities to his wife, whom he has put inside a large, hollow tree and plastered in with mud, leaving a hole about five inches in diameter through which she can stick her beak. There she sits, molting, for two and a half months. Her wings and tail and all her feathers drop out. When her two or three little birds have hatched and have grown to be about as big as ducks, they help the mother bird out of the tree by breaking down the mud wall and they all come out fat and healthy, because they have been fed all the time by the male hornbill. Of course, he does not spend the whole day near his family and let everyone see where his nest is. He visits it every two or three days. Also it happens that, at this time of year, the lining of his crop becomes loose. So he goes off into the jungle, has a feast, comes back to the nest, brings up his crop lining, full of the fruit he has eaten, and hands it to his wife!

Rather upsetting, hornbill manners and customs, but luckily unknown to me at that moment of my salad days, when I was green in jungle lore and first listened fearfully to the raucous cries of the great bird. As it was, I was feeling too "jumpy" to berate my old Chinese cook, Salleh, when he came to me at sunset and said, "I am sorry, sir, but I can't sleep in the house you have built for me; you have put it so close to the jungle that I can hear things."

Salleh was something of a character. Although a Cantonese by birth, he had married a Malay girl and turned Mohammedan. He had the usual trouble of the Chinese in pronouncing his *r's* and now, when he wanted to say he was afraid we might be attacked by a *rimau,* or tiger, he called it *limau,* or lemon! He was going to leave me, and I had never slept in the jungle before! I remembered that I had a revolver. It was an Iver Johnson and it always shot straight up into the air, no matter what I did to it. But I tapped my belt and said, "If you are frightened, you may go to sleep with the coolies." So off he went and left me alone.

As soon as it was dark, I lighted my lamp and began to read. When I had just got myself pleasantly settled, a tree fell down. I jumped a bit, for the tree was so covered with vines and creepers that, as it fell, it carried about a dozen trees with it and for several seconds the noise was like thunder. After it had died away, I could hear nothing for half an hour except the yelling of monkeys. They must have been sleeping in the tree-tops and been suddenly thrown out of bed. The crash had so unsettled my nerves that I thought, "Heavens! what is going to happen next?"

I did not have very long to wait. It was absolutely dark and still outside. I heard a muffled *Ho, ho, ho!* My hair stuck straight up at the sound. Then I heard it again, *Ho, ho, ho!* So I got an electric flashlight and went all over the house, trying to find the noise. Next I heard it outside the house, so I crept down the steps and came to a big rock. The noise was coming out of the rock. Soon I found a large hole and there at the bottom of the hole sat a frog as big as a coconut, with his open mouth uttering those hair-raising croaks.

I was so relieved that I went back into the house in good spirits, got into bed, with the lamp on a table beside me, tucked the mosquito net all around the mattress and was soon lost in my story. Presently something began to squeak up in the roof, the leaves rustled about, an object fell on top of the tent and slithered down the canvas to the ground with a flop, and I saw a snake swallowing a rat. When everything was quiet once more, it was really time for me to turn in. Just to be on the safe side, I put underneath my head a box of matches and my revolver. I can still remember how bumpy the pillow felt. Then I blew out the light.

About two hours afterward I woke with a start. There was something in my bedroom. I strained my eyes through the darkness and tried in vain to find the matches. Then I lay perfectly still, perspiring violently. Suddenly, close by my bed, about two feet from the ground, I saw, glowing and gleaming, two great green eyes. "Heavens!" I thought, "it's a tiger!" I got hold of my revolver, which was wobbling like a jelly, aimed at the eyes, shot with a bang right through the mosquito net and set it on fire. By the light of the burning net, I discovered that I had shot at my cat, but had not hit her. She had been sitting on my suitcase beside the bed and I, knowing that my revolver always shot up into the air, had aimed specially low—and fired right through the suitcase, spoiling all my clothes. I was so angry that, as I got back into bed with a piece of string and tied up the hole in the mosquito net, I said to myself, "I won't get up again tonight, even for an elephant!"

The next morning, when Salleh, who had heard my revolver, came back, he asked, "What was the matter last night, sir?"

"Nothing!" I said. "Bring my breakfast!"

And he brought me a dish of chicken. We had chicken for breakfast, chicken for luncheon, chicken for dinner. I had chicken three times a day for six years.

Salleh was a marvelous cook. Within fifteen minutes he could catch, kill, cook and serve a chicken, including soup. Just for sport, I watched him do the whole business one day, although he little knew I was looking on.

I had surprised him by returning early to camp, before he had begun to prepare luncheon. When I yelled at him, "Boy, *siap makan-an* (Boy, get food ready)," he immediately replied, *"Baik, tuan, makan-an siap* (All right, sir, food is ready)."

A moment later I saw him, with some rice in his hand, squatting on the ground in the midst of about a hundred chickens. They were all quite tame, since they were used to being killed regularly three times a day. Salleh took hold of them and felt their breasts as they continued to feed out of his hand. Then there was a squawk. Salleh had cut off a chicken's head. While the fowl was still beating its wings, Salleh plunged it into hot water, which removed all its feathers. It was then drawn and quartered and, while it was frying, the giblets were boiling! Salleh next took a soup-plate, quickly peppered the bottom of it, put in a teaspoonful of Worcestershire sauce and about a dozen canned peas and then added some of the hot water in which the giblets had been boiling. While I drank the soup, he opened a tin of sardines and a bottle of olives and served the next course. Finally he brought in the fried chicken. It was exactly fifteen minutes since the chicken had been walking about. I almost felt it flap as I swallowed it.

．　　．　　．　　．　　．

One day, when I was utterly tired of chicken, I asked Hussein what the coolies ate. He answered, *"Daging, tuan,"* which means, "Meat, sir." Then he showed me fresh meat hanging on strings around their houses. "It's deer meat, sir," he said. "Do you want a deer?"

It sounded easy. So I walked about two miles into the jungle with him. He took his knife and began to chop down some bushes to make a little hut. When it was finished, we both crawled into it and covered ourselves with leaves. As I stuck my gun through the side of the hut, I saw Hussein take out of his belt two little sticks about a foot long. Next he picked a broad leaf, laid it on the ground and rattled upon it with the sticks, making a noise like the *brrr* of a drum. When he had repeated the call two or three times, he said, "Look, sir," and I saw coming out of the jungle a deer.

Again Hussein beat his leaf, *brrr*. This time the deer came right out into the open, looked for a large leaf, put his feet on it and rattled with his hoofs, making exactly the same sort of challenging noise. Hussein replied, and man and deer began an alternate drumming. Each time, the deer came a bit closer and, when at last I fired, I could not help hitting him. I ran out of the hut, picked him up and put him into my pocket. I fried him in a frying-pan that evening. He was a perfect little deer only seven inches high, with a body about the size of a small rabbit, legs as thick as a pencil and dainty cloven hoofs. Though he was without antlers, he had in his upper jaw two very sharp tusks over two inches long, curved almost into a semi-circle. Hussein told me that, when this deer is chased by a tiger or a leopard and finds himself hard pressed, he jumps into the air, hangs to the branch of a small tree by means of his little tusks and pretends to be a fruit. He is the *plandok*, or mouse deer, as popular in Malay folklore as the fox is in western fairy tales.

When I returned to camp at night with my deer in my

pocket, I found outside my house a little dear dressed in silk, a Malay girl, who was hugging her face and saying, *"Tuan, sahya punya banyak sakit gigi,"* which means, "Sir, I have a terrible toothache." I took her into the house, opened her mouth and saw, from her newly filed teeth, that she was a bride. Her teeth had been cut so deeply that the nerves were all exposed in front. So I got out my medicine chest—I had a big mahogany box full of drugs purchased at government expense—opened the drawer, found a bottle of toothache mixture and some cotton wool and stopped the pain. She was delighted and went away and told everyone about me.

A few days afterward there arrived outside my tent an elephant. I have seen "the biggest elephant in the world" several times, but none was more than half as big as this one. Sitting on his back was a monk, dressed in yellow. He slid down, came up to me and said, "Sir, we hear that you are a clever doctor. Will you come to our monastery and give some medicine to the chief monk?" "By Jove," I said to myself, "here is a chance to have a ride on the elephant."

So I went into my tent, packed a little bag with medicines and scrambled upon the back of the elephant—or rather, to be truthful, he put his knee out for me to step on, then he lifted me a bit, coiled his trunk under me and put me on his back. The first thing he did after we started off was to go of his own accord up to a tree and tear away a big branch of leaves with his trunk. Then all day, as we walked along, he whisked himself with the bunch of leaves to keep the flies off. He was more comfortable than I was, for he joggled me so that I felt as if I were aboard ship in a choppy sea. I had six meals that day, three down and three up.

When I came to the monastery, I rushed inside and there I saw on a bed an enormous man, holding his stomach and groaning. "The best thing for you is a dose of salts," I thought. So I opened my little bag and took out a bottle of effervescing salts. I put some in a glass of water and it began fizzing and bubbling. Then my patient said, "It's boiling," and refused to touch it. So I had to have three doses myself before he would take one. The next morning he handed me a dollar. Of course I did not want to be paid, but he was so anxious about the dollar that I took it just to please him. When I looked at it, I found it was a Spanish coin minted in 1776, in the reign of Charles III. When I asked him where he got it, he showed me an old box full of Spanish dollars. Then I remembered that the Malays had been pirates.

I am only one of many engineers who have had such experiences as I have set down in these pages, but I have discovered that it is more profitable to talk about engineering than to practise it. I have dwelt on the humorous side of my life in Malaya and have condensed the impressions of a half-dozen years. Things do not actually happen quite so quickly. If you find yourself questioning some of the statements I have made here, in any case do not doubt that fish can climb trees and lizards break their tails off, and that the hornbill brings up the lining of his crop.

WITH THE ABORIGINES OF NORTH AUSTRALIA
Sir Hubert Wilkins

This account of odd folkways among the aborigines of northern Australia is a reminder that, before he was knighted for his scientific exploration of the arctic sea by airplane, George Hubert Wilkins, as he was then, proved his mettle by conducting an arduous expedition afoot and by automobile through the northern wilds of his native land, as told in his *Undiscovered Australia*.

It was in 1913, while serving as second-in-command of Stefansson's Canadian Arctic Expedition, that he conceived the idea of exploring the unknown polar regions, north and south, from the air, especially with a view to discovering possible locations for meteorological stations. Two expeditions to the Antarctic and one as leader of the Wilkins Australia and Islands Expedition for the British Museum intervened before he could put the idea into execution.

There followed four gruelling years when, undiscouraged by indifference and derision and undeterred by many mishaps and the loss of three planes, he kept on with characteristic perseverance until he had achieved his purpose of scouting the polar sea north of Alaska for signs of solid earth. This done, he closed the chapter with the brilliant navigational feat of flying over the top of the world from Point Barrow to Spitsbergen. He has told the story in *Flying the Arctic*.

Turning now to the other Pole, Sir Hubert led two expeditions into the Antarctic, being the first to use an airplane in that region. His aerial surveying cleared up many geographical problems, discovering fourteen new islands and mapping over fifteen hundred miles of coastline.

His recent daring venture under the ice in a submarine from Spitsbergen toward the North Pole is still fresh in the public mind.

WITH THE ABORIGINES OF NORTH AUSTRALIA

By Sir Hubert Wilkins

T HE ABORIGINES OF AUSTRALIA ARE FAST DYING OUT AND it will not be many years before many of the tribes are extinct. In the area between East Alligator River and the Gulf Carpentaria and north of the 13th parallel the native population probably does not exceed four thousand. Each tribe considers that a particular area belongs to it, but you might find many people living in that area who do not belong to the tribe. Although it is difficult to obtain information as to which tribe a man belongs to, there is a distinct difference between the King River people and those of the Goyder River. The King River people are short-legged and long-bodied and average much shorter than the Goyder River people, who are tall, long-bodied and short-legged. I remarked on this fact to Olembek, my native helper, and he told me why the King River people were so short.

"Long years ago," he said, "all people lived in the part of the sky that lies directly overhead. One day rain came and it rained and it rained and there was a big flood. This flood flowed over everything and uprooted a big tree from the land where the people lived and this tree, which may be seen in the Milky Way, fell across the heavens.

"Many people clung to the tree, but the floods continued and the people were washed off and dropped to the earth.

"The people that fell on the Goyder River country were proper people, but the people that fell on the country to the east were formed like men, except that they were very tall and had no mouths. They are very thin and consume their food by placing it on their heads or by means of smell.

"The people that fell to the westward fell among rocks and some of them made such holes in the rocks as they fell that they now live in the rocks. They are invisible to the people of the Goyder River, but it is known that they are there, for they sometimes ask for food and, if the food is placed on the rock, it will disappear. Others were dumped up by the fall and have remained short ever since.

"The people that fell to the south are more or less normal in figure and speech, but they have a most distressing habit of tickling everyone. If you happen to meet one of them in the bush, he will tickle you and, if you cannot escape, you will laugh and laugh until you die from laughing.

"Some of the people that fell were very big people and they fell so hard that they went right into the ground and have had to live under the ground ever since. They have never been seen by the people of the Goyder River, but their big, strong teeth have been found."

. . . . .

Olembek was a married man; he had two wives and a son and daughter. One day he wished to cross from the mainland to an island about two miles distant. The only means of reaching the island was by swimming. Olembek supported the small daughter, about four years old. The boy, aged about eight, was considered able to swim the distance without help. The two women looked after themselves.

When they reached the shores of the island, the boy was

missing. No one had seen him disappear and the drowning was thought to have been brought about by evil spirits.

About a month after the accident, the first mourning ceremony was performed. I have no record of the details of this, but one night Olembek invited me to his camp. It was the night of the new moon, six months after the drowning of his boy, and the second ceremony was to be performed.

Olembek and his wives had spent the day making the ceremonial requisites. There were eleven string belts, each decorated with bunches of white feathers. A round pole about three feet six inches long was painted in curious design with red and white paint made from clay.

A spear-shaped figure was scooped out in the sand and two circles drawn within it. A rough stick about four feet long was placed at either end of the figure and eight of the feathered belts, tied together to form a string, were stretched from one post to the other.

About an hour before sunset Olembek took up a position between the two circles. He held in his hand two sticks with which to beat time. A musician, who played a long keyless wooden trumpet, sat outside the figure. A shell was placed at the end of the trumpet to give resonance to the sound. At frequent intervals Olembek chanted a mournful dirge and the musician trumpeted with long-drawn notes.

The mother of the boy sat beside her *mia-mia*. During each period of chanting she would spring to her feet and, taking a stooping posture, sway her body and hands to the rhythm of the chant. She lifted her feet to the time of the music and, with a smart, jerky motion, flicked the sand with her toes so that it was scattered over each leg alternately. This performance continued until the twilight faded.

Then other men joined in the performance and the wailing was continuous. The men went down on their heels and, shaking their bodies, gently raised themselves to an upright position. Then they suddenly collapsed and sank to the ground and other men standing about poured water over them. They were rubbed down from head to foot by many hands, while a wild and weirdly piercing song was sung. The singing, it was explained, was to call the spirit of the dead child.

The calling song continued with deeply felt sincerity for several minutes, more and more water was brought, and Olembek broke into a plaintive, crooning melody that ended with sounds of sobbing. This melody was repeated over and over again and, while it was too dark to see if there were tears in the eyes of the performer, there were surely tears in his voice.

He finally broke down, speechless.

A group of men made a fire and chanted several songs. A fire stick was brought from the fire and a pile of inflammable bark was placed beside the figure and lighted. The flames spread their light over an area that had been, until then, lighted only by the stars above. The feather-adorned strings were removed from the two sticks and the musician continued his trumpetings. The men returned and surrounded the figure, making a circle with the feathered belts. They danced and sang at intervals, while the two wives of Olembek and his little daughter, standing behind the trumpeter in the outer edge of the firelight, swayed their bodies and waved their hands to the rhythm of the music. The little girl wore a feathered string about her head.

The dancing continued throughout eight separate intricate figures, after which the ceremony was over. The strings were placed in a "dilly" bag that belonged to the mother of the boy, but the ceremonial stick was left standing. It had served its purpose and would be left there to rot and decay.

It was explained that I had witnessed a three-days' performance crowded into one, for Olembek, since the introduction of civilization, realized the value of time and he had his duties to perform on the morrow. In the ordinary way the singing, as they sat within the figure, would have continued for a day. The pantomime, performed by the men and illustrating the quivering growth of a young tree (for the boy's totem was a tree) and the cutting of it down, would have occupied another day, while a third would have been necessary to get in touch with the spirit of the boy by means of the plaintive song and the bathing performance.

· · · · ·

There was much to be learned from the men of Arnhem Land. It was noticed that many of them had a front tooth removed. One night I discovered the reason for this. Olembek came into camp and casually remarked that he had met the Big Spirit Moru in the woods. I inquired if Moru was a good or a bad spirit and Olembek told me that in years gone by Moru had control of all people and treated them very badly. One day, when engaged in a duel, a man had a front tooth broken by a spear and it was noticed that Moru, the Great Spirit, did not treat this man badly, so the other people had a front tooth removed. Moru is still met by the people even today; those who have a front tooth missing are treated to a drink of fresh, clear water, but those who have all their teeth are made to drink dirty water.

These people have many beliefs that are very real to them, but which are difficult for us to accept. After I had known one of the men for several months and had his confidence in other things, he assured me that it was his second time on earth and that he could distinctly remember events that had happened during his previous existence—in fact, there were many people then in the camp who had known him during that first life and could corroborate his statements. In that existence he had grown to young manhood, had married and had children. He had been accidentally killed while watching a duel between two other men and everyone had mourned his loss, especially his wife.

He did not want to die and in death he could sense the happenings on earth in a hazy sort of way and wanted very much to return to his wife and children. He found that this was possible only by becoming a child again and, while he had been born again, he nevertheless had the consciousness of being the same individual as before. Only a few months had elapsed between his first death and his reappearance as a child. As soon as he could talk, he informed his first wife and his old friends who he was and confirmed it by relating incidents that had happened and by describing in accurate detail places he had seen in the earlier existence. All the people then believed him and his wife looked after him and watched him grow up. He married her again as soon as possible, although there was now a difference of twenty-odd years between their ages.

His story was corroborated by several of the old men of his tribe and by his "sons," who are older than their "father." They claim that this man, now about thirty, has some resemblance to his previous form, but has not exactly the same physical appearance.

It was interesting to note that, in the pidgin English of the natives, white men were divided into three distinct classes. There are missionaries, white men and "proper" white men. Even missionaries are subdivided, for there are real missionaries, half-missionaries and English missionaries.

Real missionaries are usually old men; they know a lot

of prayers by heart and have different prayers every day. They tell the people something different at each meeting, without having to read from books. Sometimes their manner of speaking makes one feel "tight" inside and your eyes get full and you want to cry.

Half-missionaries read a great deal from books and say the same prayers day after day. They do not make one feel sad or uncomfortable when they talk, but people get very tired of listening to them and often fall asleep when they are talking.

English missionaries are different. They have a funny way of talking and are not always understood. They read a lot from books and that makes one tired, but their dress and actions are always interesting to watch and no one would go to sleep while watching them.

All missionaries distribute a lot of food and tobacco, but the missionary is not responsible for this, for he says that the flour and tobacco that he gives come from Jesus and that He has an inexhaustible supply. When food runs short at the mission station, it is because the missionary has been too lazy to take delivery from Jesus. Because of this, the people get angry when food is short.

Traders and others outside the mission stations must obtain their supplies of food from other sources and are not expected to distribute their food so freely; in fact, in their case, it is to be expected that something must be given in return, but it is not necessary to give the missionaries anything in return for food.

White men "humbug" all the time and make trouble "longa camp," but they are generous with their supplies of food and tobacco. Traders and "government men" (surveyors and such) are considered white men.

They could not place me at first, but they got over the difficulty by calling me a "proper" white man.

"You proper white man," they said. "You come and sit down longa camp. No humbug longa women. You eat food all same black people. You no more makem everybody work for tucker, no more makem everybody listen while you talk. You sit down quiet and listen and allatime eyes belong you look about and see everything. Everyone feels good when you are here and everyone wants to sit down with you and touch you."

This explained to me why it had often happened that the people about my camp came and sat beside me and put an arm through mine or one arm about me. They would sit for a while like that and then their place would be taken by another. I sometimes wondered if they were trying to find out if I was fat enough to eat, but I did not repel them, for I hoped to solve the problem without direct questioning.

Sometimes, when I would be sitting at my work, two arms would steal about my neck and a dusky face would be held close to mine, and very often, when I visited a new camp in which the people had heard of me and were not afraid, the men would gather round and hold my arms or legs or any part they could touch.

Among these people polygamy is practised extensively and wives are acquired as gifts from friends and in compliance with a complicated totemic system. As the young girls are generally given to the old men, few young men are able to obtain wives that are not quite old. This may be a conscious attempt to limit the population by preventing large families, for it is certain that the natives realize that the problem of food is becoming increasingly difficult. Not only do they control their marriage laws in a manner that restricts the birthrate, but they practise the custom of destroying many of the girl children.

The Two Natives Who Fought the Duel
(*The one with the hat won the woman.*)

What They Fight Over

If it should happen that a woman given in marriage to one man has great regard for another and the affection is returned, then the lover will make overtures to the lawful husband, who, if he is not particularly anxious to keep the woman, will agree to fight a duel and, if the lover proves the better man, the girl is his.

One of the men at my camp played the part of lover during my residence with these natives. An old man who had camped near by had three wives, one of them a most prepossessing lady.

The old man was not anxious to lose the woman, but agreed to fight a duel. The lover collected some of his friends and at an appointed time the duellists faced each other at a distance of about fifty yards. They were each armed with a *wommerah* and a handful of spears. The old man opened the duel and they threw spears, throw after throw. After each throw they each advanced a pace. They skillfully dodged or parried the spears and, when all the spears had been thrown without either being hit, although two of the interested spectators had been wounded, the younger man rushed at his opponent with his *wommerah* uplifted. The old man parried the blows for a while, but, after a short, sharp bout, he turned and ran, dodging between his friends or behind any convenient tree. With the vanquished on the run, the victor did not seem to want to inflict any serious harm on him but tapped him smartly with the *wommerah* whenever he got the chance. The chase was not long continued. After sharp taps the lover gave up the pursuit and marched back to his friends, who were gathered around the two onlookers who had been accidentally wounded.

The woman meanwhile had bolted for the main camp and there awaited the result. What her actual feelings were, I can only imagine, but the victor returned and claimed his bride and everyone seemed satisfied. Even the casualties with serious wounds, one in the foot and one in the arm, bore no grudge and submitted with stoical indifference to the painful operation of dressing the wounds.

One would judge from the behavior of the wounded men when under pain that the natives are without the finer feelings and sensitiveness that the white man displays, but, whatever may be the case with regard to physical suffering, in sentiment they differ very little from the more cultured races.

I have often watched the children playing on the beach when it has happened that one or other of the little ones got bowled over and slightly hurt. Its playmates would stop their play, pick up the little one, brush the sand from its knees and hands and wipe away its tears and sympathize with it. A young man will hasten to relieve his wife of a cumbersome burden when difficulties are met with on the trail and he will take and pacify or carry the baby on occasions. A man will often do a double share of work rather than waken his sleeping comrade.

I have seen lovesick black swains and coy young *lubras* sit for hours beneath a tree, holding hands and glancing at each other, or accepted suitors proudly stepping out in front of their brides with a bold defiance and haughty mien that I have also noticed in lighter-colored people newly betrothed or newly wed.

The dusky maidens and grass widows and others of the native women were not without their wiles and graces. After a few weeks' association with the aborigines, making your presence as unobtrusive as possible, you come to the conclusion that after all they differ very little from other humans in fundamental things.

ADVENTURE OFF THE ALASKAN COAST

Earl B. Wilson

Now prosaically established in business in New York City, Earl B. Wilson was in New Mexico in 1910 and 1911, surveying public lands for settlement and helping to fix the Texas-New Mexico boundary across the Staked Plains.

A couple of years later he was in General Land Office work in southern Alaska—and that was how he came to meet "The Runt."

TOLD AT THE EXPLORERS CLUB

ADVENTURE OFF THE ALASKAN COAST

By Earl B. Wilson

THOSE WHOSE WORK OR PLEASURE CARRIED THEM WEST-
ward from Seward, Alaska, in the neighborhood of twenty
years ago, no doubt have poignant memories of the good
ship *Dora*. During the four summer months the *Dora* plied
from Seward westward to Dutch Harbor or Unalaska in
the Aleutians, thence through the Bering Sea to Bristol Bay
and Nushagak, making one round-trip every four weeks.
The balance of the year she ran from Seward to Kodiak
and other nearer ports in the Pacific.

Originally a schooner, reported to have been in the sealing trade, she had been rebuilt for passengers and freight,
acquiring steam boilers capable of driving her about seven
knots. Probably her sailing speed before conversion had
been better than this, or at least as good; although still
equipped with sails, the increased weight of boilers and
passenger accommodations made running without steam
slow and ponderous. However, with a favorable wind, the
sails lent considerable aid to the undersized boilers.

The officers and crew of the *Dora* were of necessity men
in every sense of the word. The type of passengers carried
—fishermen, prospectors, trappers—and the weather encountered on a largely uncharted coast, taxed both the
physical courage and the seamanship of those handling the
ship. The history of this boat would record a romance of
the sea unbelievable to those familiar only with the com-

parative safety of ocean travel of the present day. Who would not thrill, for example, to the story of one trip to Kodiak that the *Dora* started out on, only to encounter storm and ice, disabling her machinery and carrying her almost to Japan? When it seemed help must soon be encountered, a storm from Siberia swept the unhappy boat back toward the United States, where, after an absence of months, she finally limped into Seattle. As this was before wireless was in general use, ship and all on board had long since been given up for lost. An epic of the sea! Wooden ships and iron men!

.   .   .   .   .

My first introduction to the *Dora* was in late June or early July, 1913, when I was accompanying J. Frank Warner, U. S. Supervisor of Surveys for Alaska, on a trip to the Alaska peninsula and the Aleutian Islands. We had arrived at Seward a day or two before the *Dora* returned from a trip to the westward. As soon as she tied up to the dock, we went down to see about our passage. As the passenger list exceeded the accommodations by at least two to one, some of the passengers were furnished a blanket and pillow and left to look after themselves.

Our first night out I tried sleeping on a wall bench, on which there was a thin cushion. This was narrow and the cushion had a most unpleasant, musty odor. After a short while I decided that the deck, between the tables, would be an improvement, so the balance of that night I spent there. The following day I noticed that my fellow passengers, practically all of whom were old-timers, slept almost anywhere except on deck. Inquiry brought out the fact that at night there was too much of what one might call wild life wandering around the deck to make it anything but a last resort. Two men had levelled off a pile of mail sacks in one corner upon which they had slept. They offered to share this couch with me, but I could see they weren't particularly enthusiastic in their offer, as it would mean rather crowded quarters.

Several passengers had slept on tables on which meals were served during the day and recommended these highly. I joined this group for the balance of the trip and, except for one rough night when I was rudely awakened by being rolled onto the chairs and then to the deck, enjoyed my rest.

About the first of each September the *Dora* would make her last trip of the season to the Bering Sea. On one of these last trips, I believe it was 1913, several stops were made between Dutch Harbor and Kodiak, including Chignik and Sand Point, salmon and cod fishing-stations, respectively. Among the passengers picked up was a group of fishermen bound for the States after a most profitable summer. The limited passenger accommodations were almost filled and the latest additions to the list were forced to be satisfied with bunks in the fo'castle. (I believe this was the last step before the table stage. No passengers were ever refused.)

The first night after this group came aboard, a poker game was started in the fo'castle, where, under the dim lights of smoking kerosene lanterns, one of the weirdest games took place that it has ever been my lot to witness.

One of the fishermen was a figure so grotesque that in the half-light of that dingy fo'castle he looked like a gnome from ancient folklore. His face showed an utter lack of any of the better human instincts. Brutality, viciousness and dishonesty were uppermost. A thick neck, set on massive shoulders; a deep chest; long, powerful arms. A man, one would judge, as he sat at the improvised table made of boards set on boxes, at least six feet in height and weighing around two hundred pounds. There is nothing as yet in this description unusual for that country and at that time. What placed him apart and earned him the nickname of "The Runt" was not apparent until he slid from the box on which he was sitting. He did not stand up, as an ordinary man would, but literally slid down onto the shortest, most bowed pair of legs I have ever seen. It was nothing short of marvellous that those legs held up that massive body at all, though naturally his gait was swaying and uncertain.

I had not been watching the game long, when I saw that everything did not appear to be on the level. After being convinced of this, I decided that here was one place that it might be well to be out of when the storm broke, as it was bound to do sooner or later, especially as bottles were circulating freely.

The weather was quite rough and the *Dora* could easily have qualified as one of "Teddy's own." I had just climbed up out of the fo'castle and paused to look down, when the ship gave an unusually heavy lurch, displacing a box on which some of the table boards rested and throwing off their boxes or stools several of the men, including "The Runt." When a certain amount of order had been restored, each began to claim that part of his stack of money (no chips were used) was missing. In fact the table stakes were entirely gone. Talk about a bunch of Kilkenny cats! I never again expect to see a fight start so quickly or by such common consent; it just seemed to enter the minds of all of them at the same instant.

The quarters were decidedly cramped for real action and the few disinterested witnesses, including a couple of the crew, came up from the fo'castle as though shot out. They were speedily followed by some of the combatants and it was only then that I saw that knives, whiskey bottles and everything else available were in use.

I had no interest in events other than to witness a good fight, but the appearance of knives materially dampened my interest, nor did I feel sufficient responsibility toward my fellow man to attempt to save him from his own misdeeds. I was well content to let him settle with his evil impulses and eviller *compadres* without my help. That is why I am none too clear as to the final events, as it was dark and I was not near enough to be able to distinguish individuals.

Members of the crew came charging up the deck with any available weapon and joined in the *mêlée*. I saw one figure go up the rigging so fast that he appeared to be hoisted by block and tackle. I afterwards learned this was "The Runt," who was set upon by a friend with a knife and, after two or three minor cuts, took to the rigging like a monkey and lived up to his reputation of being the fastest man in Alaska in going up a rope hand over hand.

Order was finally restored and, strange to say, the casualties were limited to a few cuts and bruises. It would appear that this was sufficient action for one trip of a small boat, but such was not to be the case.

At this point a more detailed description of the after part of the *Dora* is necessary. As I have previously stated, she was a converted schooner, the passenger-carrying part being in reality another deck built above the original one, which addition, however, stopped approximately ten or fifteen feet from the stern. This resulted in the boat having a sort of Romeo-and-Juliet-balcony effect at the stern.

A door opened from this balcony into a passage leading to the mess-room (it couldn't by any stretch of the imagination be called a dining-salon) flanked on either side by three staterooms. A staircase led from this passageway down to two more staterooms, occupied, if I remember rightly, by the steward and the purser. From the foot of this staircase a ladder descended to the vilest-smelling and evillestlooking cubbyhole imaginable by the rudder post and over the propeller. Here the colored cook passed his leisure (?) hours. Beside the bunk and a chair, the only article of furniture was a small table built against the bulkhead, on which he kept a dilapidated talking-machine.

All one evening, after leaving Kodiak for Seward, the end of the trip, the cook persisted in grinding out two or three popular airs over and over again on this phonograph. The repetition was wearing on one's nerves, but that was not the worst of it. The cook sang the words to the records and his voice had only one quality, namely, volume.

About the time we were ready to go to bed, we had had enough. So the steward called down in none too gentle tones for him to shut up. What the steward thereupon learned about himself, his ancestors, his ship and everything connected with him came as somewhat of a surprise. Right there I foresaw that our meals would probably be sketchier than ever until we reached Seward. I was correct.

The steward took off his coat, rolled up his sleeves, spit out his chew and descended. We followed to the foot of the staircase. From there we had a bird's-eye view. Yes, it was a good fight while it lasted. When the steward had finished, he picked the cook up from the deck and deposited him on his bunk. We had a good night's sleep and the incident was quite forgotten by everyone except the cook.

The galley was on the upper deck, above the mess hall and just aft the captain's cabin and the bridge.

The next morning after breakfast, I was walking up and down the deck, when a yell from near the galley attracted my attention. I saw coming down the deck the nearest approach to a madman I have ever seen. It was the cook, meat cleaver in hand, running along the deck toward the stern. He had on the same undershirt and trousers he had worn the night before. The shirt was dirty and stiff with blood which had flowed from his nose after the fight. His mouth and one eye were swollen. One of the crew stepped from behind a life-boat as the cook went by, catching him across the back of the head with some sort of pole or club. The cook literally dove to the deck, while his heels aspired to the elevation being vacated by his head. He lay where he landed.

Irons were brought and clamped on. He was then taken down to his bunk and deposited there. It was only a short run to Seward, probably not more than a day or so, but I doubt if anybody even took the trouble to look at him until we arrived there.

This was probably a more eventful trip for the *Dora* than the average, as I made four or five others without duplicating it. I do not know what finally became of this valiant little boat but, because of her inadequate power, it would be surprising if she finished her career in any other way than on the rocks of the rugged and uncharted coast of western Alaska.

ASSAGAIS AND NOTEBOOKS
George Witten

Leaving home at the age of ten to travel with "hobos" around the United States, then working his way on tramp steamers to South Africa, where he enlisted at fourteen in the British Army for the Boer War, it is rather surprising to find Major Witten now settled down as a more or less sedate and sedentary man of affairs in the heart of New York.

After his discharge at seventeen, he did mapping in Zululand, hunted and trapped thereabouts for two years, went through a military school and two years of college and then became a newspaper reporter and later a lecturer for the New York Board of Education.

He enlisted in the first Canadian contingent in August, 1914, and served through the entire war, after which he returned to New York.

Besides hundreds of magazine articles and short stories, he has written three books: *Outlaw Trails; Mutiny; Thieves Without Honor.*

ASSAGAIS AND NOTEBOOKS

By George Witten

At the time, I was quite a youngster, still in my 'teens. I had joined the Natal Mounted Police and had been sent with an escort to protect a surveying party whose mission was mapping Zululand. We were all mounted and had our equipment and instruments on pack-ponies.

My work was simple enough and rather pleasant. Part of the time I handled the chain; but most of the time I, with Tommy Mitchell, kept the outfit supplied with fresh meat by shooting blesbok and smaller game, of which there was an abundance. There were few dangerous animals in the section. The lions had migrated further north and it was only occasionally that we found a lone track or heard the forlorn roar of some old fellow who could not bring himself to take to new hunting-grounds. There were numerous leopards, but the leopard is a cowardly brute and we paid little attention to them. Our greatest concern was over the mambers. These were not numerous, though they were bad enough when you ran onto them and were always ready to fight.

We made our camps in sheltered spots on the banks of streams. Once a week a covered ox-wagon brought fresh supplies and mail. Altogether, it was rather an ideal assignment. The mapping went merrily along. We worked a reasonable number of hours each day and played poker and brag at night.

Then came news that Slangapiza and Umkaiya, two Zulu chiefs, had declared war against each other. We were working in their territory and, while the fight was among themselves and not against the white man, it meant that the mapping could be carried on only with difficulty and a certain amount of danger.

The first thing that happened was that most of our Kaffirs disappeared from camp. Many of them belonged to one or the other of the warring tribes. Others, who were neutral, did not want to be caught between the two factions in a fight.

Orders came by mounted messenger for the entire expedition to come into the post at Krantzkop, across the Natal Border. Packing our dunnage without the aid of Kaffirs, we made a night march to the police post. Here we received orders to go out and help suppress the uprising.

The tribes of Slangapiza and Umkaiya lived side by side along the Tugela. Most of the time they got along well enough; but every year or so they had to find something to fight, so expended their surplus energy on each other. Each of them commanded about five thousand fighting men. We had ten troopers and two sergeants on the post at the time and we were confronted with the job of stopping ten thousand crazy Zulus, armed with assagais, knobkerries and shields, from chopping each other to pieces. I began to think that I would never die of old age.

The senior sergeant seemed a little worried about me and what I might do when the crucial moment came. There was some talk of leaving me behind at the post. I had never seen a real "faction" fight among Zulus and didn't want to miss it, so begged to be taken along. The sergeant gave in, for our numbers were few enough and, after all, a uniform, even if worn by a youngster, always has a powerful psychological effect on any aborigine!

"No matter what happens," warned the sergeant, "don't draw a gun! If you do, we'll all be killed! This fight has got to be settled with pencils and notebooks."

He seemed to be addressing his remarks especially to me, for, though he had us all lined up, he never took his eyes off me once. Here was a new one on me. Twelve men had to go out armed with pencils and paper and bring reason to ten thousand crazy Kaffirs, who couldn't read or write and wouldn't have recognized their names in a full-page spread of a tabloid paper. I guess I looked puzzled. Most of the other men had had experience in "faction" fights and seemed uninterested in the sergeant's remarks.

"Ride up to any *enduna* (petty chief) you see," continued the sergeant, "write down his name in your notebook and tell him to take his men and go home. He'll know that, if he doesn't and lives through the fight, he'll be arrested later and sent to jail and have his cattle confiscated."

This meant disgrace and ruin for an *enduna;* also they had a dread of being sent to work in the mines, which most native prisoners were made to do.

"Suppose you don't know his name?" I asked, in my ignorance.

"You don't have to know his name, just write in your book and be sure he sees you write. That will be enough for him."

I saw the other men grinning and bit my lips shut.

. . . . .

We rode off for their favorite battling-ground and got there just in time to see the two armies meet, but too late to stop the first onslaught. The Zulu's method of fighting is to throw his assagai into the midst of the enemy and then fight his way to it with his knobkerry and cowhide shield. The fellow who throws and retrieves his own assagai the greatest number of times is the greatest warrior.

As we rode down the side of the mountain, the two painted, shiny-black armies came running along the valley, one up and one down, their bare feet hitting the ground with a rhythmic cadence, like the beating of many tom-toms in measured time. They came to within about thirty yards of each other and halted a moment, while their chiefs each bellowed a challenge; then they let drive with their assagais and rushed forward. The first shock of the assault sounded like the explosion of a mine; then came a continuous roar, like the rumble of distant thunder, as the knobkerries bashed against heads and shields. Piercing screams filled the air, some from dying and wounded men and some from fanatical warriors still issuing their challenges after the fight had commenced.

In a few minutes the black, struggling mass was enveloped in a cloud of dust, above which flew assagais and from within which came ten thousand weird noises. My heart almost stood still. Vaguely I wondered what good a pencil and paper were going to be in stopping this glorified cat-and-dog fight.

The sergeant halted us near the edge of the *mêlée* and there we waited on our horses till the rumbling of thunder and strange noises died down and the two armies drew back out of the cloud of dust to re-form and charge again. Then our work commenced. We rode between them and spread out. Wherever we saw an *enduna*—we could tell them by the black halos around the tops of their heads—we rode up to him, let him see us write in the book and told him to take his men and go home.

The first *enduna* I approached, I rather made a mess of things. I picked out an old fellow who didn't look so savage. But in my excitement I forgot my pencil and paper.

"Hey, *enduna!*" I yelled, trying to keep the fear out of my voice, "*Humbargy!*"—which means "Go home!"

He looked up at me and grinned, then said, "*Icona!*" —which is the African equivalent for "Nothing doing!" And a strapping young warrior, sharpening his assagai against a rock, let out a war-whoop and sprang into the air toward me with arms extended, brandishing his weapons. My hand almost reached my pistol; then I remembered the sergeant's warning and instructions and commenced to write rapidly in my book.

What did I write? Nothing. My hand trembled, so I just made scrawls all over the page. But it worked. The old *enduna* came up to a salute and pleaded with me not to report him to the Great White Queen. Then he called his men together and led them sorrowfully down the valley.

This gave me courage and in a few minutes I had routed a dozen or more *endunas* with their followers. By this time other leaders had managed to avoid our small numbers and another charge was effected. Again we waited until they drew back to reorganize, then rode in to wield our pencils and notebooks and win another bloodless victory.

Counting up the dead and wounded on both sides, somewhere near a hundred, we decided that the fight was a draw and there would probably be peace in the valley for another year.

The sergeant came to me as we rode back to the post and complimented me on my coolness. I didn't tell him that I was scared stiff all through the fight and mighty glad when it was over. But a pencil and paper is a great peace-producing equipment—when backed up by a Great White Queen.

THE END